CAMBRIDGE STUDIES IN LATIN AMERICAN
AND IBERIAN LITERATURE 4

At face value: autobiographical writing in
Spanish America

This study of Spanish American autobiography in the nineteenth
and twentieth centuries concentrates on literary, cultural and
historical issues. Spanish American autobiographies are fascinating hybrids, often wielding several discourses at once. They aspire
to documentary status while unabashedly exalting the self, and
dwell on personal experience while purporting to be exercises in
historiography, the founding texts of a national archive.

Professor Molloy examines a wide range of texts, from Sarmiento's *Recuerdos de provincia* to Victoria Ocampo's *Autobiografía*. She
analyzes their textual strategies, the generic affiliations they claim,
their relationship to the European canon, and their dialogue with
precursor texts, as well as their problematic use of memory and the
ideological implications of their repressive tactics. This method
enables her to identify perceptions of self and tensions between self
and other, thus shedding light on the fluctuating place of the
subject within a community.

CAMBRIDGE STUDIES IN LATIN AMERICAN AND IBERIAN LITERATURE

General Editor

ENRIQUE PUPO-WALKER
Centennial Professor of Spanish
Director, Center for Latin American and Iberian Studies,
Vanderbilt University

Editorial Board

In the same series:

CAMBRIDGE STUDIES IN LATIN AMERICAN
AND IBERIAN LITERATURE 4

At face value: autobiographical writing in
Spanish America

At face value
Autobiographical writing in Spanish America

SYLVIA MOLLOY

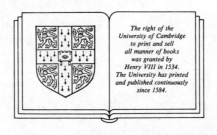

The right of the
University of Cambridge
to print and sell
all manner of books
was granted by
Henry VIII in 1534.
The University has printed
and published continuously
since 1584.

CAMBRIDGE UNIVERSITY PRESS

CAMBRIDGE
NEW YORK   PORT CHESTER
MELBOURNE   SYDNEY

Published by the Press Syndicate of the University of Cambridge
The Pitt Building, Trumpington Street, Cambridge CB2 1RP
40 West 20th Street, New York, NY 10011, USA
10 Stamford Road, Oakleigh, Melbourne 3166, Australia

First published 1991

Printed in Great Britain at the University Press, Cambridge

British Library cataloguing in publication data
Molloy, Sylvia
At face value: autobiographical writing in Spanish America –
(Cambridge studies in Latin American and Iberian literature; no. 4).
1. Prose in Spanish, autobiographical. Latin American writers. Critical studies
1. Title
868.08

Library of Congress cataloguing in publication data
Molloy, Sylvia.
At face value: autobiographical writing in Spanish America / Sylvia Molloy.
p.   cm. – (Cambridge studies in Latin America and Iberian literature: 4)
Includes bibliographical references.
ISBN 0–521–33195–1
1. Spanish American prose literature – 19th century – History and criticism.
2. Spanish American prose literature – 20th century – History and criticism.
3. Biography (as a literary form.)
4. Autobiography.   5. Self in literature.
1. Title.   11 Series.
PQ7082.P76M65   1991
860.9′492′098–dc20   90–1731   CIP

ISBN 0 521 33195 1 hardback

CE

Para Geiger

Contents

Acknowledgments

To trace the genesis of this book in an orderly way is an act of fiction that defies my talents. Looking back on the years I have spent thinking about Spanish American autobiography, talking about it with ever patient listeners, teaching it in my courses, and finally writing about it in this book, I can, above all, remember voices, fragments of conversations with colleagues, students, friends. A fleeting remark (Daniel Balderston, many years ago, saying that the only possible form of autobiography was one's own necrology); a joke (Severo Sarduy claiming that the autobiographical first person was still in the closet in Latin America); stray bits of information and comments, stored in my memory and by now mostly dissociated from whoever shared them with me, have doubtless found their way into this book and have led to profitable reflection.

My interest in Spanish American autobiography dates back to 1976 and arose from research done while I was on a Fellowship from the National Endowment for the Humanities. Subsequent research was aided by a grant from the Social Science Research Council, by several summer grants from Princeton University and, more recently, by a Senior Faculty Fellowship from Yale University and a Fellowship from the Guggenheim Foundation. My greatest appreciation goes to those institutions for their show of interest and their very effective support.

Amongst the many friends who have contributed to this book, I wish to thank Julio Ramos very specially for the patience and the lucidity with which he has read me and for our ongoing dialogue, which I greatly value. I must also thank María Luisa Bastos for her incisive comments after reading parts of my text, for her refreshing good sense and her unfailing friendship. Oscar Montero, always on the lookout for pertinent information concerning my subject, also read this text with intelligence and care. Ana Diz's useful remarks contributed positively to certain sections. Gladys Wurtemburg provided helpful editorial comments. I have also benefited inestimably from conversations with Doris Sommer on a topic that is of interest to us both. Enrique Pupo-Walker's support, as editor and friend, was important throughout.

I am grateful to my colleagues and friends at Yale, to Nicolas Shumway, Marta Peixoto and James Fernández, for their generous readings and very thoughtful suggestions, and to Roberto González Echevarría for stimulating conversations on this and other subjects. Last but not least, my thanks to the many graduate students at Princeton University, now my friends, with whom I have fruitfully discussed many of the issues this book addresses, particularly María Elena Rodríguez Castro and Antonio Vera León.

Portions of this book appeared in *Modern Language Notes*, *Revista Iberoamericana* and *Nueva Revista de Filología Hispánica*. I am grateful to the editors for permission to reprint them in revised or translated form.

To attempt to thank Emily Geiger for her patience, support and refreshingly quirky humor during the rather bleak period spent in the final writing of this book defies all my efforts. The dedication of this book to her is a mere token of my deepest affection and gratitude.

Introduction

Prosopopeia, it has been suggested, is the trope informing auto-biography. Self-writing would be that attempt, ever renewed and ever failing, to give voice to that which does not speak, to bring what is dead to life by endowing it with a (textual) mask.[1] The writing of an introduction, I would venture, is a more modest though no less demanding form of the same trope. Inasmuch as it is finished, one's text needs to be given a face, needs to be made to speak, with one's voice, one last time. An introduction is precisely that occasion, marking the last time that one speaks for the text, and also, disquiet-ingly, the first time that one begins to sense how distant that text has become. Like autobiographies, introductions too begin at the end.

But that is as far as I shall pursue the parallel. I am not tempted, as more than one critic when writing on the subject, to suggest that writing about autobiography is in itself a form of autobiography, nor to posit that the organization of this book mirrors a personal itinerary. If I choose to write about autobiography, and more concretely, about Spanish American autobiography, the choice is due to sheer critical inquisitiveness. I wish to take a look at texts that purport to do the impossible – to narrate the "story" of a first person that only exists in the present of its enunciation – and I wish to observe how that impossibility is rendered plausible in Spanish American texts. I do not tackle the paradoxical nature of auto-biography itself nor is it my goal to do so. Instead, I am interested in analyzing different forms of self-figuration so as to educe the textual strategies, generic attributions and, needless to say, perceptions of self that inform autobiographical texts written in Spanish America. In other words, while not ignoring the linguistic and philosophical quandary autobiographical writing necessarily poses, I have attempted to address issues that are basically cultural and historical in nature. I have tried not so much to find out what the "I" is trying to do when it writes "I" but, more modestly, what are the fabulations to which self-writing resorts within a given space, a given time, and a given language, and what do those fabulations tell us about the literature and culture to which they belong.

Autobiography in Spanish America has suffered from more than a measure of neglect on the part of readers and critics. This is not because, as has so frequently and thoughtlessly been asserted, autobiography is unusual, nor is it because Hispanic writers, for elusive "national" characteristics, are not prone to record their lives on paper. The perceived scarcity of life stories written in the first person is less a matter of quantity than a matter of attitude: autobiography is as much a way of reading as it is a way of writing. Thus, one might say that, whereas there are and have been a good many autobiographies written in Spanish America, they have not always been read autobiographically: filtered through the dominant discourse of the day, they have been hailed either as history or as fiction, and rarely considered as occupying a space of their own. This reticence is in itself significant. For the reader, in denying the autobiographical text the reception it merits, generically speaking, is only reflecting a disquiet that the text in itself harbors, at times well hidden from view, at others, more manifest. The anxiety of being translates itself into an anxiety of being in (for) literature.

The neglect or the misunderstanding that has greeted autobiographical writing in Spanish America make it, not surprisingly, an ideal field of study. As it is unfettered by strict classification, canonical validation or cliché-ridden criticism, it is free to reveal its ambiguities, its contradictions, the hybrid nature of its composition. It is then, in that state of flux, that the autobiographical text has the most to say about itself – provided, of course, one is willing to hear it out on its own, uneasy terms. In addition, from the ill-defined, marginal position to which it has been relegated, Spanish American autobiography has a great deal to say about what is not itself. It is an invaluable tool with which to probe into the other, more visible, sanctioned forms of Spanish American literature. As that which has been repressed, denied, forgotten, autobiography comes back to haunt and to illuminate in a new light what is already there.

I have chosen to restrict my study to the nineteenth and twentieth centuries, chiefly though not exclusively for generic reasons. First-person narratives, it is true, abound in Colonial literature. Chronicles of discovery and conquest, especially those involving some measure of self-awareness on the part of their authors – Cabeza de Vaca's *Naufragios* and Garcilaso de la Vega's *Comentarios reales* would be two such texts – might be seen as distant forms of the autobiographical mode. In the same way, self-reflexive documents such as Juana Inés de la Cruz's *Respuesta* to the Bishop of Puebla or confessional depositions before the tribunals of the Inquisition, given the defensive strategies they adopt and the vindication of self they propound, may also be considered, and indeed have been considered, autobiographies. While not denying the preoccupation with self at work in these texts, I contend that their primary concern is not autobiographical – even if the latter may be one of their unwitting achievements. Furthermore, the circumstances in which these texts were written preclude, or at least considerably modify, the textual self-confrontation – I am the matter of my book – that marks autobiographical writing. The fact that the abovementioned texts are conceived primarily for a privileged reader (the King of Spain, the Bishop of Puebla, an ecclesiastical tribunal) who has power over writer and text; the fact, too, that the narration of self is more a means to achieve a goal than the goal itself; the fact, finally, that there is rarely a crisis in this self-writing (or a self in crisis), make these texts, in my view, only tangentially autobiographical.

At the same time, I am loath to declare peremptorily that Spanish American autobiography "begins" in the early nineteenth century, and I would also hope to avoid (it remains to be seen with what success) the notion that autobiography is a form progressing from nineteenth-century hybrid clumsiness to twentieth-century aesthetic perfection. This evolutionary view of literature, which has Spanish America always "catching up" with its purported European models (when the whole point of Spanish American literature is to deviate from those models), seems particularly inadequate in this case.[2] If I choose to begin my own study of Spanish American autobiography in the early nineteenth century, it is because I am especially interested in the peculiar awareness of self and culture brought about by ideological crisis, and because I am curious about the way that crisis is reflected, better yet, incorporated, into the very fabric of Spanish American self-figuration. The crisis I speak of, brought on by the influence of the European Enlightenment and by the independence from Spain that was to mark its culmination in Spanish America, is, of course, a crisis of authority. It is no coincidence, I believe, that questions about the validity of self-

writing, or reflections on the goals of autobiography, should appear
at the moment a received order is slowly replaced by a produced
order; that it should appear, in addition, within the context of the
more general debates over national identities and national cultures,
debates in which relations to Spanish, and more generally European, canonical authority are forcibly renegotiated. If, in the case of
Colonial writers, self-writing was legitimated by an institutional
Other for whom one wrote (the Crown, the Church), in the case of
the post-Colonial autobiographer, those institutions no longer
accomplish their validating function. Indeed, the very notion of
institution, as it had been understood, comes under serious questioning. If one no longer writes oneself down for King or Church, for
whom, then, does one write? For Truth? For Posterity? For History
– the discipline that so many autobiographers will turn into their
validating source? To this crisis of authority corresponds a self in
crisis, writing in an interlocutory void. The predicament of the
Spanish American autobiographer, the very tentative figurations of
self that he or she engages in, the constant search for reader
recognition, give rise to a pattern of tantalizing ambiguities that
always allude to (but never openly ask) the same question: For
whom am I "I," or rather, for whom do I write "I." The vacillation
between public persona and private self, between honor and vanity,
between self and country, between lyrical evocation or factual
annotation of the past are but a few manifestations of the hesitancy
that marked (and even now may mark) Spanish American self-
writing.

While interested in the connections between self-figuration,
national identity, and cultural self-awareness, and in the repre-
sentational patterns that such connections, or contaminations, give
rise to, I do not wish to align this book with the many attempts,
within and without Spanish America, to elucidate, define – invent,
finally – a "national" Spanish American essence of which literature
would be an unmediated manifestation. Nor do I entirely share the
view that all Spanish American texts, however "private" in appearance, are really, and invariably, national allegories and should
specifically be read as such.[3] This view might not seem inappropriate
at first glance when considering Spanish American autobiographers
intent on merging self and nation into one memorable *corpus gloriosus*:
Sarmiento's calculatingly messianic *Recuerdos de provincia* in the
nineteenth century and, in the twentieth, Vasconcelos' nationalistic

histrionics in *Ulises criollo* may indeed be read (but need not be read) in this way. Such a view, however, supposes unchanging modes of textual production in Spanish America, ignores the fact that, as politics diversifies its discursive practices, so does literature – and, indeed, so does autobiography. The "I" speaks from more than one place. Reliance on either view – the text as national essence or as national allegory – cuts critical reflection short instead of encouraging it and channels the text into one exclusive reading. What seems more profitable, instead, is to allow the preoccupation with national identity (undeniably present in Spanish American self-writing) to reverberate in the text as an ever renewed scene of crisis necessary to the *rhetoric* of self-figuration; to see it as a critical space, fraught with the anxiety of origins and representation, within which the self stages its presence and achieves ephemeral unity.

Autobiography is always a re-presentation, that is, a retelling, since the life to which it supposedly refers is already a kind of narrative construct. Life is always, necessarily, a tale: we tell it to ourselves as subjects, through recollection; we hear it told or we read it when the life is not ours. So to say that autobiography is the most referential of genres – meaning, by reference, a somewhat simplistic referring back to "reality" and to concrete, verifiable facts – is, in a sense, to pose the question falsely. Autobiography does not rely on events but on an articulation of those events stored in memory and reproduced through rememoration and verbalization. "My name, more than naming me, reminds me of my name."[4] Language is the only way afforded me in order to "see" my existence. In a sense, I have already been "told" – told by the very story I am telling.

In considering the narrative mediation occurring in all autobiography, I am interested in some of its more textual aspects; that is, not only in the unwritten "text" (a pulsion, a shard, a trace) stored in memory that guides the autobiographer's inscription of self, but in the "cultural forms"[5] and fragments of actual texts that the autobiographer calls upon, when writing, as vehicles for what memory has saved. Spanish American autobiographers often resort to the European archive for textual fragments with which, consciously or unconsciously, they forge their images. In the process, those precursor texts are considerably altered, not just because they are treated without reverence but because the European cultural archive, evoked from the margins of Spanish America, *reads differently*. I devote considerable attention to the textual fabrication of self and to the scene of (mis)reading that serves so frequently as its emblem since it is in that scene that the autobiographer's difference becomes manifest. In this context, I find autobiographies whose authors are distanced from the European canon for reasons additional to the fact that they are Spanish American (for being a slave, like Juan Francisco Manzano, in the nineteenth century; for being a woman, like Victoria Ocampo, in the twentieth) especially rewarding. Marginalized by the institution (partially excluded, in the case of the woman, totally shut out, in the case of the slave), they resort to particularly ingenious ways of using texts to which they do not have total access, for the purpose of self-representation.

Spanish American autobiographies are not comfortable texts. The difficulty with which they assert themselves as viable forms, the derision with which they have been and may still be greeted (Sarmiento's *Recuerdos de provincia* ridiculed by Alberdi for its frivolity, Vasconcelos' confessional stance in *Ulises criollo* compared to the *boleros* of Agustín Lara) turn the autobiographer into an inordinately wary writer, conscious of his or her own vulnerability and of the reader's potential disapproval. Self-writing is a form of exposure that begs for understanding, even more, for forgiveness. *Que me perdonen la vida*: the Spanish idiom used by Victoria Ocampo to summarize her plea to her readers may be extended to many Spanish American autobiographers. Not only should the phrase be read literally – that the autobiographer's life be forgiven, that it be read sympathetically – but in its other, more drastic sense: that the autobiographer's life be spared, that his or her execution be stayed. The notion of transgression evoked by the phrase and the power it gives the reader whose forgiveness it solicits are not infrequent. There is often a sense that what one is doing might be wrong, not morally but tactically; a sense that, given the insecure status of the genre, one may be going about self-writing in the wrong way. Spanish American autobiographers are most efficient self-censors who, within their life stories, map out silences that point to the untellable – and often tell what they feel cannot be told autobiographically in other, less compromising texts.

One of the most expressive silences in Spanish American autobiographies of the nineteenth century concerns childhood. I dwell on this issue at some length since it reflects some of the interdictions weighing on autobiographical writing that, to a certain extent, live on today. The fact that the first years of an individual's life are given short shrift tells us a great deal about the spirit in which the autobiographer chooses to validate his story. Considering it a form of history – a biography, not of a heroic or exemplary other but of a heroic or exemplary self – he finds it hard to accommodate, within the limits of his document, a *petite histoire* whose sheer triviality might question the importance of his enterprise. Thus, when references to childhood appear, they are either viewed proleptically, as foreshadowing the achievements of the adult, or used for their documentary value. The boy Alberdi bouncing on General Belgrano's knee is not so much a charming detail as it is an ideological marker signifying the allegiance of the Alberdi family to the cause of Argentine independence. It is noteworthy that of all these nineteenth-century autobiographers and ardent admirers of Rousseau's *Confessions*, only one devoted to childhood an elegiac account in the spirit of the master. It is especially noteworthy that this account was written from a triply marginal position: it was written in exile, in a language that was not the subject's native tongue, and it was written by a woman, the Condesa de Merlin, whose pretensions to historical documentation were nil. However, the documentary imperative will never quite disappear from Spanish American self-writing; it will take on more varied and more subtle forms. My reading of Miguel Cané and Mariano Picón Salas views their texts – also childhood memoirs – as ideological statements and examples of group bonding. Vested in the seductive garb of the quaint and outmoded, sheltered from the intrusions of history and defying all change, childhood stories become, in this instance, ideological credos. It takes a special kind of "eccentric" writer – I choose to consider Norah Lange here, but Felisberto Hernández would do equally well – to liberate childhood from such ideological constraints.

For texts so concerned with the representation of self in the past, Spanish American autobiographies are reluctant to dwell on that which makes them possible. Memory is often accepted as a faithful replicating mechanism, its functioning seldom questioned, its deceptions rarely contemplated. Although this blind acceptance is more characteristic of the nineteenth century than it is of the twentieth, it provides a good point of departure for further inquiry into the workings of memory within these texts. I wish to identify the tactics of a mnemonic practice that – as all manners of recollection – is a form of fabulation. Unlike Janet's *fabulateur*, begging for a clue that would allow him to discern what had been from what he thought had been, I am not looking, however, to discern fact from invention. If I inquire into the practice of memory and the fabulation of self that results from it, I do so because I wish to examine the societal models of representation that, as surely as the patterns fostered by the scene of reading, guide the retrieval of the past in a manner satisfactory to the remembering self. The past evoked is molded by a self-image held in the present – the image the autobiographer has, the one he or she wishes to project or the one the public demands. Like Ña Cleme, the old beggar in Sarmiento's *Recuerdos de provincia* who, enjoying the notoriety brought upon her by rumors that she was a witch, "worked in her conversation" to bolster a prestigious image with which she had begun to identify, the autobiographer "works in memory" with a similar purpose in mind. While the self-image may not be as clear-cut as that of Ña Cleme, it is nonetheless there, as the impulse governing the autobiographical venture. An individual construct, no doubt, that image is also a social artifact, as revealing of a psyche as it is of a culture. Thus, for example, Sarmiento carves out his past in accordance with the image of the self-made intellectual and *pater familias* of a community, in *Mi defensa*; five years later, he carves out a somewhat different past in *Recuerdos de provincia* to agree with a different image, that of a worthy son, a link in a chain of prestigious intellectual forebears. The different images, at different times in life, and resulting in two distinct life-stories, tell us much about Sarmiento. But they also tell a great deal about how history – and what was then judged one of its forms, (auto)biography – was conceived in early nineteenth-century Spanish America: as a pantheon of heroic, exemplary figures. In the same way, Lucio Mansilla's autobiography, set out in the form of a leisurely stroll through the old city of Buenos Aires, tells us as much about his self-image – the perpetual and elusive *flâneur* – as it reveals a turn-of-the-century conception of literature that questions the notion of an organic whole and values the fragmentary.

A strong testimonial stance informs autobiographical writing in Spanish America. If not always perceiving themselves as historians – the perception seems to wane as generic difference becomes more specific in Spanish American literature – autobiographers will continue to see themselves as witnesses. The fact that this testimony is often endowed with the aura of terminal visions – the autobiographer bearing witness to that which is no more – not only aggrandizes the author's individual persona but reflects the communal dimension sought for the autobiographical venture. Spanish American self-writing is an exercise in memory doubled by a ritual of commemoration, in which individual relics (in Benjamin's sense of the term) are secularized and re-presented as shared events. Of particular importance, in this connection, are the *loci* of memory, the chosen sites for communal rites: the *casonas* or family homes, the sleepy provinces, strongholds of tradition, the cities that time has irrevocably changed, if not destroyed. Equally important is the emphasis on collective memory and the reliance on what might be called a mnemonic lineage. Family romances are reservoirs of memories: like Borges, thanking his mother "for your memory and that of your elders," the Spanish American autobiographer forays into the past through familial, most often maternal reminiscence.

While on the one hand this combination of the personal and the communal restricts the scrutiny of self so frequently associated with autobiography (a view, one should not forget, that applies to just *one* type of autobiography), on the other, it has the advantage of capturing a tension between self and other, of generating a reflection on the fluctuating place of the subject within its community, of allowing for other voices, besides that of the "I," to be heard in the text. Even those cases which seem to favor one of the poles of this oscillation between self and community to the apparent exclusion of the other – say, on the one hand, Mariano Picón Salas' first person plural in *Regreso de tres mundos*, so deliberately "representative" that it becomes an abstraction, and, on the other, the blatantly private "I" of Norah Lange's *Cuadernos de infancia* – even those cases allow, unsuspectingly perhaps, for that tension. So, although it might be tempting to see in Spanish American autobiographical texts a subject, enmeshed in different tactics of repression (what cannot be told) and self-validation (what must be told in a way acceptable to a nation, to a community) that has not yet come into its own (i.e. the story of the self "alone"), it would be ill-advised to conclude that progress towards introspection, from the constraints of the document to the freedom of fiction is a necessary goal for these texts. Given this history of the genre, the components that gradually, secretly, have come to integrate what one might term a Spanish American autobiographical tradition, such an evaluation would be unwarranted. If in the nineteenth century the emergence of the autobiographical subject was rendered difficult because there was no place for it, institutionally speaking, and if that tentative subject, in order to give itself texture, needed to resort to tactics of self-validation that included claims to historicity, to public utility, to group bonding, to testimonial service – claims, in short, that opened the self to a community – by the twentieth century, those tactics have been naturalized, have been incorporated into an auto-biographical rhetoric. No longer forcibly considered a historical necessity, strictly speaking, they nonetheless continue to inform the discourse of self-representation in Spanish America, have become an intrinsic part of the writing subject's perception of self.

I wish to add a few brief comments now, of a more practical nature, to explain my reason for choosing the texts I have chosen. From the use of the term "Spanish American" instead of the more usual "Latin American" the reader will by now have realized that I shall not speak of Brazilian autobiographies. The exclusion may seem surprising given the rich tradition of self-writing in Brazil. Precisely because of that fact, and because I am well aware of the limitations of my competence in the field, I have preferred to leave that portion of Latin American autobiography to more qualified colleagues and concentrate on the linguistic domain I know best. Another exclusion that may seem open to question is that of the more recent type of autobiographical text known as *testimonios*, the narratives of marginalized members of society who, either directly or through the mediation of informers, tell life stories that heretofore had remained untold. My exclusion in this case responds to two reasons. On the one hand, the very rich production of testimonial literature, the conditions that govern its production, the unwritten rules that give it shape, make it a genre unto itself. As such it should be considered. On the other hand, I have chosen to study texts written by writers, that is, autobiographers who, when sitting down to inscribe their selves on paper, are aware, in some form or another, of the bind of translating self into rhetorical construct; writers who, with a fair amount of literary awareness, resign themselves to the necessary mediation of textual representation. In the same way that I have excluded *testimonios*, I have excluded autobiographies of politicians and statesmen for whom the writerly side of the auto-biographical exercise did not appear problematic. One last remark concerns women's autobiographies, or rather my way of dealing with them in my study. Dissatisfied with the usual mode of classifying women's texts in Spanish America – grouping them into

ahistorical categories such as *literatura femenina* or *poesía femenina* with
no regard for chronology or literary currents – I have preferred to
consider them together with their male counterparts, the better to
judge the characteristics they share with them and the better, too,
to evaluate their difference.

I have only worked on a small portion of the autobiographical
writings published in Spanish America since the 1800s. Why these
texts and not others is a matter of personal preference – or rather,
the choice made by my critical fictions. I have, however, in the
Bibliography given a list of all the autobiographical texts that I have
been able to find in Spanish America in the period covered in this
book. Discovering the existence of these texts – through an obscure
entry in a history of literature, through random searches in university libraries, through intuition, through hearsay – was a difficult,
often trying task. Since I refer only tangentially to some of these
texts and to many not at all, I thought it fair to list all their titles in
the hopes of saving others much time and annoyance. The list, I am
sure, bears addition; I am aware that some countries are better
represented than others. I would imagine (and hope) that there are
many more autobiographical texts than those I have located, texts
that might challenge, even contradict, some of the arguments I have
set forth in the following pages. I look forward to what others might
have to say on autobiographical writing in Spanish America and to
the dialogue they will establish with this book.

PART I

The scene of reading

Each one of us lives in his own autobiography, each one believes in his own personality, that mixture of perceptions interspersed with quotations.

(Jorge Luis Borges, *Inquisiciones*)

Books are the memory of mankind, covering thousands of years. With a book in our hand, we remember Moses, Homer, Socrates, Plato, Caesar, Confucius. We know, word for word, action for action, what they said or what they did: we have therefore lived in all times, in all countries, we have known all men . . .

(Domingo Faustino Sarmiento, "El monitor de las escuelas primarias")

I

The reader with the book in his hand

Not surprisingly, Borges provides us with a beginning. In one of his later stories (those his critics hailed, with short-sighted relief, as "at last realistic"), a young, likeable city-dweller of conventional culture finds himself stranded in a desolate country estate. His sole companions are the foreman, his son and his daughter – illiterate, barely articulate descendants of Scottish settlers who had inter-married with Indians. All conversation with the three having proved impossible, the young man, in order to establish some contact, takes to reading to them from an old English Bible he has found in the house. The blank pages at the end record the spotty lineage and history of the family, from the time they set forth from Inverness up to the moment when they lost their capacity to write. Spurred on by vague didactic notions, the young man actually does more than read to them: choosing the Gospel according to St Mark, he practices reading "as an exercise in translation, and maybe to find out whether the Gutres understood any of it."[1] The Gutres (or Guthries, as they were named originally) turn out to be the most attentive of listeners; in perfect silence they absorb every word that is read to them and when the Gospel is over demand that it be read (translated) to them again "so that they could understand it better." The worship they feel for the Book extends to its reader: "While he read to them, he noticed that they were secretly stealing the crumbs he had dropped on the table. One evening, he caught them unawares, talking about him respectfully, in very few words." The end of the story, for all its suddenness, should not come as a surprise. One Friday afternoon, the young man finds himself thinking (quoting?) aloud: "It won't be long now." His words are echoed by the foreman, standing behind him; his hour is indeed come. He is pushed towards the shed by all three Gutres (the Spanish transliter-ation of the Scottish surname has a particular ominous, guttural

15

sound to it) and, once inside, beholds the cross they have prepared for him.

If I have gone into this story at length it is not solely for the pleasure of repeating (and thus translating for my own means) a particularly haunting, near-perfect story. Perhaps better than others, this story by Borges exemplifies what his whole work stands for: a *mise en texte* of the scene of reading in Spanish America, and concomitantly, of a narrative practice. If all of Borges' stories ("Pierre Menard" being of course the most often cited in this context) endlessly tell us that literature – all literature – is a rereading, an open-ended exercise in the repetition of one, perpetually different text, "The Gospel According to Mark" goes one step further. Here, Borges' reader-scribes (or, more accurately perhaps, active listeners) are not, like Pierre Menard, European men of letters but Argentine peasants, *criollos* of old-country and new-country blood, who have forgotten how to read and write. Cultural paupers in a way, they are still dazzled by the Book and, deprived as they are of letters, can only enact their gruesome misreading. By giving his story a clearly Argentine setting, Borges seems to stress a salient aspect of Spanish American literature: its capacity for inventive (if, in this story, deathly) distortion. Rereading and rewriting the European book, this story tells us, can be a sometimes savage, always disquieting experience. The stance chosen by the Spanish American writer – one might call it a *pose*, were the word not so fraught with derogatory connotations – is the exact obverse of Mallarmé's dictum and, as such, refers back to it, like a parody. The Book is not the ultimate goal but a prefiguration: a dissonant concert of texts, often fragmented, of broken bits of writing, it is the substance for beginnings.

This fundamental aspect of Spanish American literature has been frequently studied in various of its manifestations, the most patent being fiction, the exercise of retelling *par excellence*.[2] In fact, the plundering of the European archive affects all genres in Spanish America, even those that, at first glance, would appear not to need the support of earlier texts. Travelogues, first-person accounts of various types, *testimonios*, diaries, autobiographies, all "genres" or hybrid modes of representation that would have the reader believe he is dealing with direct, unmediated accounts of real life narrated by real individuals, are no exception: these modes of structuring reality through writing that claim not to obey preconceived structures[3] are also dependent upon a textual (if sometimes unwritten) prefiguration. Dependency does not mean, here, the strict observance of a model or a slavish form of *imitatio* but reference to an often incongruous conflation of possible texts that the writer uses as a literary springboard, a way of projecting himself into the void of writing, even when that writing directly concerns the self. If the library is a metaphor central to Spanish American literature, then the autobiographer too is one of its many librarians, living in the book he or she writes and endlessly referring to books. Reading before being and being what he or she (mis)reads, the autobiographer too goes by the book. Indeed, the self-reflecting genres, purportedly the most referential, could prove to be the exact opposite.[4] When writing of the Mexican José Miguel Guridi y Alcocer, perhaps Spanish America's first modern autobiographer, a critic, possibly unaware of the full implication of his words, sweepingly dismisses Guridi's *Apuntes* (Mexico, 1802) as "the history of a simple existence that wants to be complicated, lived more in books than in real life."[5] What the critic fails to see is that for the autobiographer books *are* real life.

Reference to books, in self-writing, can take many forms. I shall here deal with the explicit, and consider a frequent strategy of the Spanish American autobiographer, the highlighting of the act of reading. Treated as a textual primal scene, it may be put on equal footing with those privileged features – the first recollection, the formulation of the family romance, the fabulation of lineage, the staging of the autobiographical space, etc. – that recur most frequently as basic autobiographemes. The encounter of self and book is crucial: reading is frequently dramatized, evoked in a particular childhood scene that suddenly confers meaning on the whole life. The starkest, perhaps most eloquent version of the scene may be that of Victoria Ocampo in the first volume of her *Autobiografía*: "I carry a book that has been read aloud to me and pretend I am reading it. I remember the story perfectly, I know it is behind those letters I cannot understand."[6] This childish mimicry might well be seen as the scene of reading *à l'état pur*, the basic gesture – the rhetorical pose – awaiting an object that will complement it and give it full meaning. As in pictorial self-portraits, the book takes on the importance of those objects – an easel, say, or a skull, or a set of keys – whose signification surpasses their scope as mere objects: they become attributes of the individual and tell his story.[7] In *Recuerdos de*

18 AT FACE VALUE

provincia, for example, Sarmiento delights in recreating a foreseeably self-centered emblematic scene of reading: like Hamlet, with whom he is prone to identify, he is the young man with a book in his hand. Sarmiento describes himself grudgingly minding the store while surreptitiously devouring books:

[T]his I did while selling *mate* tea and sugar, looking askance at those who came to draw me out of the world I had discovered to live in. In the morning, once I had swept the store, I would settle down to read and a Mrs. Laora who passed by on her way to church and then back again would always see, day after day, month after month, this motionless boy, untouched by any disturbance, his eyes fixed on a book. Shaking her head she would go home saying, "This cannot be a good boy. If those were good books he would not be reading them with such enjoyment."[8]

The scene of reading does not necessarily correspond to the first book read in childhood. The experience involves a recognition of reading that is qualitatively different from the reading practiced previously: a book – the Book of Beginnings – is suddenly singled out from among many others. A second version of Ocampo's scene, when the child is older and has learned to read, emphasizes the quasi-religious nature of this discovery. One summer, a French governess introduces her and her sisters to Fénelon's *Télémaque*. The book stands out for Ocampo from the "boring books" read in class, also from the moralistic novels of the Comtesse de Ségur and other childhood fare of the period; clearly marking a break from the quotidian, it commands enthusiasm and, above all, respect. In view of the exceptional character attributed to it, it is kept, once the reading is done, in a special place.

Each day, after the reading hour, Mademoiselle took the two volumes and instead of putting them in the drawer with the other books, would raise the chimney hood (it was never used in summer) and would hide this Olympian world, in which I dreamt of living, on the hearth. At the beginning the hiding place struck me as disgraceful but little by little I grew accustomed to this odd notion and even approved of it. Later on I would have found it shocking for Mademoiselle to hide these books anywhere else.

(p. 124)

Ocampo and her sisters know where the book is kept but refrain from reading it outside the ritual "reading hour." Although "there was no material obstacle" to reading *Télémaque* at other times, "an obstacle existed, of a different nature":

It came from the book itself, from its moldy pages, wonderful and defenseless. How could one act dishonorably with a book so noble? When Calypso, the nymph Eucharys, Télémaque and Néoptolème disappeared behind the hood, it was best to leave them there till the following day, even if the desire to continue reading and living in such dazzling company consumed me. (p. 125)[9]

Often associated with the scene of reading is a mentor – either an actual teacher or, more generally, a guide to the child's readings. In the nineteenth century, the figure is usually male for reading is associated with men and authority. Sarmiento, for example, recalls having learned to read at his father's instigation: "I owe thus to my father that love of reading which has been my constant occupation throughout the best part of my life" (p. 161). Women, because of their scant instruction, are not usually associated with the scene of reading nor are they acceptable figures of authority. Yet, while not connected directly with reading, they are not left speechless and early nineteenth-century autobiographies often present them as powerful (and useful) storytellers. A constant in Sarmiento's *Recuerdos de provincia*, when trying to reconstruct the history of his province of which no written record remains, is the phrase "cuéntame mi madre," evoking the oral testimony of the mother.

With the passing of time, the mentors associated with the scene of reading change. In twentieth-century autobiographies women do appear as meaningful figures of cultural influence and even, at times, of cultural authority. While attributing his discovery of books to two men, his godfather and his father, Enrique González Martínez, in *El hombre del búho*, celebrates his mother as an inspiring model of intellectual curiosity and freedom of thought. "During the family readings, so frequent at home, my father explained and classified while my mother interpreted in her own way and according to her emotions the book we were reading."[10] Reading, here, is not so much equated with power as it is with excess. *El hombre del búho* devotes memorable pages to the mother's lust for reading, pages glorifying a lack of moderation that the son was never quite able to emulate:

A student of my father's from the time she was very young till she married him, she acquired the habit of reading in her husband's company. Yet her favorite books she would read alone, quite sure of her judgment and satisfied with her choice . . . She read chaotically, at all hours, and, when a book interested her, it was not unusual for her to sit up all night to finish it,

drinking black coffee and smoking cigarettes, a habit she acquired in the
first years of her marriage. A long nap the following day cured her of her
sleepless night. She was avid for books, eager for all knowledge, and sorry
that life had not given her a more suitable opportunity to cultivate her
spirit with greater and better discipline ...   (pp. 582–585)

Going one step further, José Vasconcelos' *Ulises criollo* presents
the mother figure not only as reader and purveyor of books but as an
ideological matrix, the conscious guardian of a national culture.
Reading and mother are united in one of Vasconcelos' earliest
recollections: a woman with a book on her lap. In both González
Martínez and Vasconcelos, the bonding with the mother cannot be
ignored as a decisive influence in the scene of reading. An element of
passion, even of eroticism, is introduced, that renders the scene
considerably more complex. Sarmiento, who was tied just as
intensely and intimately to his mother as these two writers, never
could combine his two passions – mother and books – because his
mother could not read.[11]

It can be argued that the highlighting of the scene of reading is not
peculiar to Spanish American autobiographies but is, on the contrary, a commonplace of most autobiographies composed by
writers. It would be odd that it not be so, since, from the moment he
or she decides to explore the past, an author is bound to view any
experience from youth that might be interpreted as a promise of a
future vocation with a benevolent eye, and is therefore most likely to
dwell on it. Rousseau's early recollections are, of course, a good
example of this attitude: "I know not what I did before I was five or
six; I do not know how I learned to read. I can only remember the
first books I read and what effect they had on me. This is the period
from which I date the uninterrupted awareness of myself."[12] The
Spanish American experience is not essentially different. Its specificity is more a question of manner, made obvious in its need to
advertise itself, in its not infrequent flamboyance. Not only is there a
need, on the part of these writers, to recreate the scene of reading as
a set piece; there are additional markers, throughout these autobiographical texts, that (in much the same way as Brecht's Chinese
actor reminded his audience that they were in the theatre) alert the
reader to the fact that he is "in literature" – that the autobiographical text is, indeed, a literary construct. The importance given the
scene of reading in the autobiographer's youth may be originally
intended as a realistic ploy, destined to bring verisimilitude (and, in

retrospect, a small amount of precocious glory) to a writer's story. In fact, it works like a self-reflecting strategy that confirms the textual nature of the autobiographical exercise, reminding us of the book behind it all.

Reliance on books – not necessarily a conscious stance on the part of the autobiographer – may manifest itself in the simplest of forms: the illiterate Jesusa Palancares, in Elena Poniatowska's *Hasta no verte Jesús mío*, describes her rapture when her common-law husband Pedro, who could read *"muy bonito"* with "a lot of fire in his eyes," read out loud to her nightly in the tent they shared as soldiers of the Mexican revolution.[13] In other cases, the scene of reading may be simply alluded to, in covert fashion. When, tucked in the folds of Manuel Rojas' account of childhood, *Imágenes de infancia*, one finds a reference to Jules Renard's *Poil de carotte* – the only book explicitly mentioned in the text – in connection with a decisive experience, the purported non-bookish quality of the narrative is called into question by what amounts to a scene of reading *manquée*.[14] Conversely, the relation with books may appear fraught with uneasiness, as in the case of Pablo Neruda. Belittling his debt to literature, proclaiming a vitalistic, anti-intellectual position (which, ironically enough, appears to come from a book, *Leaves of Grass*), Neruda engages in a crusade against the book that his writing, and even his habits as a rare book collector, consistently question. Neruda's complex attitude towards books and literature is at the very core of his autobiographical venture. In spite of his declarations – "I do not come from a book / and my poems / have not fed off poems"[15] – his persona relies on texts for support as much as that of other autobiographers; not merely on that vague "book of nature" that Neruda disingenuously mentions but on precise texts written by others and, not insignificantly, by Neruda himself. While claiming to "unwrite" literature – the book's paper reverting to wood, the text reverting to loose words – Neruda, in *Confieso que he vivido*, cunningly rewrites his previous books of poetry and, specifically, his *Canto general*.[16]

A closer examination of the substance of the readings themselves is in order if one is to distinguish the peculiarities of this cultural gesture. If the Spanish American autobiographer might be seen as a modern-day Hamlet, a book permanently in hand, it is necessary to find out what, precisely, is in that book. A first look promptly reveals that these epiphanic discoveries usually arise from an indirect contact with the text. There is always a mediation: either the book is translated and thus at one remove, if not two, from Spanish – González Martínez discovers himself in a French translation of Goethe, Vasconcelos is smitten by an English translation of Homer – or it is read in the foreign original and translated, so to speak, in the very act of reading. Only in rare cases does the scene of reading involve a book in the language the autobiographer will later use to write his or her life story.

Probably sincere (although sincerity, in itself, is hardly a measure to gauge autobiography), the choice of the European book as a clue to textual (and vital) self-discovery shows, in addition, a fair amount of naive boastfulness. Like those confronted with the Marcel Proust questionnaire or asked to play the "Ten-Books-On-A-Desert-Island" game, the autobiographer would not be caught lacking, culturally disarmed, an intellectual simpleton in the eyes of others, thus the showy preference for "the classics." This desire to show oneself competent, a reader of the canon – not realizing that the canon, by the mere fact that one is reading it *from* Spanish America, translated into a Spanish American context, is no longer the same – might be seen as a result of conventional cultural colonialism, and indeed should, in part, be seen that way. Vasconcelos, wary as he was of exposure to cultural intermingling, does not hesitate to view his reading of the *Iliad* in English, at the turn of the century, as directly related to "the penetration of the new influence"[17] suffered by Mexicans in the frontier towns of Piedras Negras and Eagle Pass. However, beyond this evidence – the wholesale importation of European (rarely Spanish) literature and culture through the sponsorship of France – lie other, more interesting issues: what was *done* with those cultural imports, how were they received (how were they read) and, more importantly, how were they integrated, manipulated into different cultural artifacts.[18] Autobiography, again, seems not only to reflect this integration, carried out on all levels of discourse and in all genres, but to constitute an ideal field in which to observe it at work.

An early plunderer of the European archive, Sarmiento left many self-serving presentations of himself. One of them is particularly revealing: "[Sarmiento] does not go out, does not go to the theatre, nor does he gamble for his amusement. For the past half century he has been reading in French, English, Italian and Spanish, everything that can be read by a scholar. His library contains four great bookcases of English books and four huge ones of books in French."[19] In *Mi defensa*, his first autobiographical text published in 1843, Sarmiento claims that the clue to his progress as an individual, as well as to the progress of a whole nation, is "to read very well."[20] The Spanish text stresses the apprenticeship: "*haber aprendido a leer muy bien,*" to have learned to read very well. Sarmiento's life story (not unrelated to spiritual autobiographies albeit decidedly secular in spirit) might have been subtitled *The Reader's Progress*. But what can Sarmiento mean? Beatriz Sarlo and Carlos Altamirano, in a penetrating essay devoted to *Recuerdos de provincia*, interpret the expression to signify, beyond a comprehensive understanding of what is read, a means of achieving intellectual independence from the usual cultural mediators, mainly priests, who remained faithful to old ideas and traditional values.[21] Free of such hindering intermediaries, the good reader, self-taught, would come into contact with cultural goods he could claim for his own. There is indeed an eloquent cry for such unmediated access to culture in Sarmiento's *Recuerdos de provincia* (1850). Returning once more to his favorite scene of reading, the voracious young reader alone in the store, surrounded by bolts of material, Sarmiento recalls his encounter with the book as a major, providential breakthrough:

But there must be books, I kept telling myself, that deal especially with these things and will teach them to children. If one understands what one reads properly, one can learn without the need of masters. I then launched myself in search of those books and, once my mind was made up, found all I was looking for, and just as I had imagined it, in my own remote province ... Like Archimedes, I could cry, "I have found them!" because I had anticipated them, invented them, and searched for them.   (pp. 172–173)

Ridding himself of the short-sighted controllers of culture, Sarmiento is free to tackle his education directly and learn to "read very well" without mediators. Or is he? If we consider the nature of the books he is about to read – all foreign imports – we must conclude that the direct access of which he dreams is a fiction: he will have to become his own mediator, or rather his own translator. Significantly, translation is mentioned in the first autobiographical text, *Mi defensa*, immediately after the scene of reading, as, in a way, its complement. To read very well, for Sarmiento, is, basically, to translate:

To complete my report on these very disorderly studies that continue to this day, I shall add that, in 1829, while I was in hiding for political reasons, I was able to get an old *grammar* by Chantreau and some dictionaries and when I came back out I had translated for myself [*me había traducido*] many books; that for the past twelve years I have been watching over my pronunciation, which remains incorrect; that in 1834 I learned English in Chile, hiring a tutor for a month and a half to introduce me to the study of that language, which to this day I have not learned to pronounce; that in 1837 I learned Italian in my country and, in 1841, learned Portuguese here [in Chile] since I needed it for my work in *El Mercurio*.   (D, p. 9)

Note that Sarmiento himself gives the two activities equal standing: to read is "to translate *for myself*." The learning of languages allows not so much for a way out – Sarmiento cannot pronounce the languages he learns and communicates imperfectly with other speakers – but a way in, a means of incorporation. His apprenticeship of languages, or rather, of translation, is again recalled in *Recuerdos de provincia*, this time in an expanded, more eloquent version:

For Spanish-speaking peoples, to learn a foreign language is merely to learn how to read. At least one such language should be taught in grammar school. In teaching me Latin (which I know imperfectly) Friar Oro had provided me with a simple machine for learning languages, which I have used successfully to learn the few I do know. In 1829, ... while under house arrest in San Juan, I took up the study of French as a pastime. I had planned to study it with a Frenchman, a soldier of Napoleon, who knew neither Spanish nor his own grammar, but the sight of don José Ignacio de la Rosa's library made me greedy and, with a borrowed grammar and a dictionary, I translated twelve volumes, including Josephine's *Memoirs*, one month and eleven days after beginning my solitary apprenticeship. Let me give a concrete example of my devotion to that task. I kept my books on the dining room table and just pushed them aside so that breakfast, then lunch, then dinner might be served. My candle would go out at two in the morning but, when I was really absorbed in my reading, I would spend as much as three days at a stretch leafing through the dictionary. It took me fourteen years to learn how to pronounce French, for I did not really speak the language until 1846, after I had been to France. In 1833, when working in a store in Valparaiso, I set aside half of my monthly wages to pay an English tutor by the name of Richard and two *reales* a week for the neighborhood night watchman to wake me up at two in the morning so that I could study my English. I would stay up all night on Saturday and make it one with Sunday. Thus, after a month and a half of lessons, Richard told me that all I lacked was the pronunciation which, up to this day, I have not mastered. I went to Copiapó [where Sarmiento worked in a mine with other Argentine *émigrés*] and translated the sixty volumes of Walter Scott's complete works at the rate of a novel a day ... In Copiapó many still remember the miner who was always reading.   (p. 178)

To read, then, would be to translate – but to translate in what fashion? Sarmiento obviously gives the word a special meaning, implies a translation "for myself" of which no written record remains. But why, then, use the verb *to translate* and not, as one would expect, simply the verb *to read?* Could the two not be synonymous after all as a first glance at these texts would seemingly indicate? Further examination of Sarmiento's autobiographical texts shows that this is indeed the case, that whereas *to translate* does replace *to read*, the two do not coincide precisely in Sarmiento's mind but rather diverge from each other. If to translate is to read, it is to read with a difference: the translation perpetrated, one might say, by the reader does not copy the contours of the original but necessarily strays. Sarmiento's description of the method resorted to by his beloved teacher Friar Oro when teaching him Latin – what the good friar calls his "learning machine" – is most significant: Oro has the young boy translate from Latin into Spanish, teaches him to recognize the differences ("me iba enseñando las diferencias") and then to wander away from the text: "he enlivened the reading with digressions from the geographic canvas of the translation" [*la tela geográfica de la traducción*] (p. 71).

In a sense, one might say that to translate, in the way that Sarmiento understands it, is not "to read very well" but, conventionally speaking, *to read very badly*.[22] That Sarmiento reads if not badly at least differently is evidenced in the manic pace at which he claims he performs this exercise. A novice in French, he claims to have "translated" twelve French books in "one month and eleven days," a schedule that allows barely three days per volume, not counting the presumably frequent and necessary forays into the borrowed grammar and the borrowed dictionary. The pace adopted for his English "translations" is (incredibly) even more rapid: this time, after a very brief period of instruction at the end of which he is declared competent by his tutor, he "translates" Scott's remarkably turgid prose at the rate of one novel a day, attending all the while, however perfunctorily, to his duties at the Copiapó mine.

Sarmiento, it is true, was given to exaggeration but one suspects that, in this particular case, his record is basically truthful. He probably did skim through most of those volumes – time would not have allowed him to do otherwise – and patched together a translation (whatever he *believed* he was understanding, given his deficient command of the foreign language) that was a simulacrum of the original, a hastily put together textual artifact, a *different* book. However "correctly" Sarmiento may have thought he was reading, he was certainly aware that to read is to modify. Thus he describes his practice of reading as the task of "translating the European spirit into the American spirit, *with the changes that the difference in setting required*" (p. 181; my emphasis). Some of those changes were doubtlessly conscious; others worked on Sarmiento's reading without his knowledge.

Sarmiento sees his hasty reading of European writers as a necessity, a way of filling a void. In his spirited polemic with Andrés Bello while in Chile, to Bello's criticism of those who "having been initiated in foreign languages and not knowing, or not having studied, the admirable models our own language has to offer, rush to write according to the version they have read the most,"[23] he haughtily responds that, since Spain has little or nothing to offer in the realm of the humanities, it is imperative that her former colonies go a-borrowing. Sarmiento's strong bias against Spain is a well-established fact. On closer examination, his bellicose statements reveal, however, that what is under attack is not so much language and literature as an *attitude* towards language and literature: not the book itself but the way in which the book is read. The influence of Spain, claims Sarmiento, stifles the imagination through "the perversity with which the language .is taught, the influence of grammarians, the respect for the *admirable model*, the fear of breaking rules ... There is no spontaneity, only a jail whose door is guarded by inflexible affectation."[24] Sarmiento's judgment of Spain and of the influence Spain has had on Spanish American culture is characteristically couched in terms of books and reading: "We are a second, third or fourth edition of Spain, not like those books that are revised and enlarged in subsequent printings but more like the last copies of a bad engraving, glutted with ink and barely intelligible."[25] In sum, Spain has not only taught Spanish America to read the same book always in the same way (with "respect for the *admirable model*") but – Sarmiento carries the metaphor one step further – it has turned its docile colonies themselves into repetitious copies (bad texts) that have little to offer in the way of meaning.

This excursus into Sarmiento's views on Spain helps cast light on his notions on reading and translating. Reading in a conventionally respectful way, in Sarmiento's view, results in redundancy or paralysis, is a spiritually stunting experience. Reading in the manner that Sarmiento reads – patchily, filling in gaps more or less at random – makes way, instead, for an inordinate amount of intellectual freedom and creative imagination. More importantly, it allows Sarmiento to add to what he reads. As his grandson would say years after his death, "Sarmiento could never copy anything word by word (even less if it was his) because his superabundance of ideas made him always expand what was written."[26]

The consequences of reading expansively, digressively and even perversely are well illustrated in Sarmiento's works in general and in his autobiographical texts in particular. Freely studded with unexpected references, misspelled quotations, foreign word-dropping and not-quite-accurate attributions, these texts even propose at one point (not surprisingly, if one comes to think of it) a persuasive defense of plagiarism. This seemingly cavalier attitude towards the European canon on Sarmiento's part was denounced, is denounced even today, in the name of knowledge. Sarmiento, claim his opponents, does not *know*; what they fail to see is that he *knows differently*.

Appearing as they do in a chapter of *Recuerdos de provincia* crucial to the autobiographical strategy, Sarmiento's considerations on plagiarism are of particular interest. *Recuerdos*, it will be remembered, follows a genealogical schema. Building up a complex family romance, Sarmiento evokes, one by one, from chapter to chapter, illustrious figures – heroes with whom he identifies and through whom he extolls his own best qualities – to replace his ineffectual father. Somewhat perversely, these fabulous father figures are all relatives on his mother's side, as if the father's line had nothing to offer. There are, however, two notable exceptions, both connected to reading: Sarmiento's father's brother, José Manuel Eufrasio de Quiroga Sarmiento, Bishop of the province of Cuyo, who teaches the child to read, and Sarmiento's father's cousin, Gregorio Funes, Dean of the University of Córdoba, whom he never met but to whom he devotes passionately personal pages. A figure of considerable intellectual power, Dean Funes (like Sarmiento himself) was a man in transition, "halfway between the colony and the republic ... like the god Terminus of the Ancients, one face towards the future, the other towards the past" (p. 110). Also like Sarmiento – the unspoken identification of the autobiographer with his model builds up very effectively in this chapter – Funes was a great reader, a distinguished historian, a biographer, a "reformer of Colonial ideas" and (perhaps) a plagiarist. When writing his history of the colonies, the Dean, Sarmiento tells us, had the misfortune of trying to fill the void left by Spain in a way that was sadly misunderstood by his successors. Sarmiento chooses to perceive Funes as a victim and proceeds to defend his work with arguments that touch so suspiciously close to home they deserve to be cited in their entirety:

[T]he author resorts to the treasures of his erudition both in the chronicles written on this continent as in the European classics that only he possessed, not realizing that he wrote at a time when those classics were about to be within everyone's reach. So it was that the reader began to notice in the Dean's writings sentences, paragraphs, that had once sounded pleasant to his ears, pages that his eyes remembered having read. The charge of plagiarism was brought against Dean Funes, an accusation that for us is not so much a reproach as a clear indication of his merit. There are still distinguished writers in our new American literature who prefer to cast a good idea in the mold already given it by the classic expression of an illustrious author. García del Río is the most brilliant example of that school of erudition that presents fragments of good literature and choice thoughts, inlaid like precious stones, in its works. Before that, like an underlying layer, a sediment of good reading resulting from a wonderful flood, there was compilation, and the products of the intelligence of great authors from the past were appropriated by the champions of new thought. In Spain, Campmany belongs to this family of writers who translate French writings and put them into circulation, decked out in Spanish terms, under the guarantee of their own signature.

What we call plagiarism today was then erudition and wealth. I myself would prefer to listen once more to an author worthy of being read one hundred times over than to read the incomplete exercises produced by thoughts and styles still at an embryonic stage. Our national intelligence is as yet insufficiently developed to compete with those writers the world judges worthy of attention.   (pp. 127–128)[27]

Sarmiento does not seem to have indulged excessively in this "appropriation" that he so disarmingly (even convincingly) posits as necessary to a new literature. He does, however, practice it at times. His close reading of Pierre Leroux, for example, an author he claimed to carry often in his pocket,[28] shows up in the more or less direct transcription of some of Leroux's articles from the *Revue Encyclopédique* in the columns of *El Zonda*, the newspaper Sarmiento founded and directed in 1839.[29] Not surprisingly, even Sarmiento's self-writing offers examples of this textual cannibalization. The fourth chapter of *Recuerdos de provincia*, devoted to the near-extinct Huarpe Indians native to San Juan, appears to combine quotations from the historian Ovalle, duly acknowledged, with a very vivid, personal evocation of the Huarpe's hunting habits by Sarmiento. In fact, as Verdevoye points out, the whole sequence has been lifted from Ovalle's text: what appears to be the product of individual observation and rememoration on Sarmiento's part is, in reality, a rewriting.[30]

If at times he occasionally forgets to name the authors he quotes, like the Dean he so admired, at other times Sarmiento practices, perhaps unwittingly, what would later be one of Borges' favorite ploys, the game of false attributions. A good example of this is to be found in one of the epigraphs to *Recuerdos*: "It is a tale / Told by an idiot, full of sound and fury, / Signifying nothing" is erroneously attributed to *Hamlet* instead of *Macbeth*. The false attribution is telling, a slip worthy of note, since it reveals the image Sarmiento has of himself and wishes to impose on the reader of his auto-biography: not that of a weak murderer, burdened by contradictory feelings, but that of the misunderstood prince. Also telling is the very free translation that Sarmiento chooses to give of this epigraph: "Es éste un cuento que, con aspavientos y gritos, refiere un loco, y que no significa nada." Not *idiot* but *madman*; not *sound and fury* (usually translated in Spanish literally: *sonido y furia*) but *shouting and histrionics*. Sarmiento was often familiarly referred to as "el loco Sarmiento," Sarmiento the madman, because of his excessive behavior and his penchant for theatricality – a nickname of which he was well aware.[31]

Sarmiento's most notorious misattribution occurs in the epigraph to *Facundo*, the biography of the infamous provincial *caudillo* Facundo Quiroga. It is not a coincidence, I think, that two of Sarmiento's most flagrant "mistakes" appear in the epigraphs to the books where he seems to strive the most for personal figuration: *Recuerdos de provincia*, his own autobiography, and *Facundo*, the biography of his enemy and mirror image Quiroga and, it might be argued, an oblique portrait of himself. The conspicuous position of

these mistaken quotations, as epigraphs that forcibly call attention
to themselves while they announce the rules of the text, should not
be dismissed lightly.

Sarmiento refers more than once to the incident behind the
epigraph to *Facundo*, with a wealth of detail that leads the reader to
believe he attributed as much importance to the event – let us call it
the scene of quoting – as he did to the emblematic scene of reading.
The most familiar version of this scene is found in the preface to the
first edition of *Facundo* itself (1845). There we first read the epigraph
– "On ne tue point les idées" – then the attribution – Fortoul – then
the most digressive of translations: "Men are slaughtered; not so
ideas." Sarmiento then provides an autobiographical context for the
quotation:

> Towards the end of 1840, in a show of mercy, I was sent into exile. I left my
> country all battered and bruised from the blows received the previous day
> during a bloody Bacchanalia indulged in by drunken soldiers and hood-
> lums from the *Mazorca*, and as I passed the Zonda Baths, under the
> national coat of arms I had once painted, in happier times, on the wall of a
> room, I wrote the following words in charcoal:
>
> > *On ne tue point les idées.*
>
> When informed of the fact, the Government sent a commission charged
> with the task of deciphering the hieroglyphic, supposedly full of ignoble
> outbursts, insults and threats. Once they heard the translation they said,
> "So? What does it mean?"[32]

The episode is mentioned again in personal letters and, as might
be expected, in *Recuerdos de provincia*. There the incident is presented
more succinctly but in a striking way:

> On the 19th of November of 1840, passing the Zonda Baths on my way to
> exile, I wrote under a coat of arms of the Republic: "On ne tue point les
> idées" and three months later, in a Chilean paper, speaking in the name of
> old patriots: "All of America is marked by the glorious victors of Chaca-
> buco..."   (p. 200)

What follows is a lengthy quotation from an article on the wars of
Independence, a piece dear to Sarmiento since it marked the
beginning of his literary career. But it is the syntax of this quotation
that constitutes its most remarkable aspect. The verb – "I wrote" –
effortlessly joins two very distinct activities in a single gesture. The
writing of a borrowed quotation melds with the writing of Sarmiento's own text, the one merely preceding the other as a begin-

ning, a gathering of impulse for an act of writing that is incorporative by nature. Quoting lies at the origin of writing as translating lies at the origin of reading. The emphasis lies here on the intransitive: I write – my own words or those of Fortoul.

But are these really Fortoul's words? Only in the preface to *Facundo* is the phrase attributed to the French social thinker frequently read by Sarmiento. In other references to the incident the phrase is cited casually; it is evidently not Sarmiento's, for it is in French, but it has been "appropriated" by the fact that Sarmiento usually fails to name its true author. Critics have pored over this quotation to reach different conclusions as to its accuracy and rightful attribution, conclusions more often revealing of the critic's ideology than anything else. Thus while some denounce Sarmiento for glorying in the use of a phrase that is not his, others call attention to his misattribution. It should be Volney and not Fortoul, says one; it should be neither Fortoul nor Volney but Diderot, says another. The attribution to Diderot (which Paul Verdevoye argues most persuasively) is tempting and adds to the complexity of Sarmiento's appropriative gesture, for Diderot's original phrase is "On ne tire pas de coups de fusil aux idées": Sarmiento's misattribution would also be a misquotation. Interestingly, the phrase had already served as an epigraph: it had been used by Charles Didier in an article published in the *Revue Encyclopédique* with which Sarmiento, an assiduous reader of the *Revue*, was in all probability familiar. Thus Sarmiento would not only be perpetrating a false attribution and an inaccurate quotation: he would also be expropriating someone else's system of authorization, taking an epigraph from Diderot that had already served to channel the interpretation of a text by Didier and using it to direct the reading of his own. Misquoting (and its more benign variant, misspelling) can be an unexpectedly corrosive exercise.[33]

Sarmiento's quotation, precisely because it is incorrect, false, and impossible to classify, disconcerts the reader through its very defiance, its refusal to be assimilated. In that sense, it does indeed constitute a founding gesture and characterizes a particular way of reading, of writing, of imposing an image of self. And it suggests yet another possibility. When recounting the incident somewhat jocularly in a letter to his friend Quiroga Rosas, Sarmiento writes "On ne tue *pas* les idées."[34] Yet when he writes it on the wall before crossing into Chile, or on that other threshold, the first page of

Facundo, he writes *point*. That difference from *pas* to *point* – from the ordinary negation to a literary, somewhat archaic form – is not to be neglected, for it adds to the significance of Sarmiento's quotation and reveals it for the self-conscious gesture it in all likelihood is. The phrase may or may not be an "authentic" quotation – from Fortoul, from Volney, or from Diderot. What is important is that it *look* like a quotation, like a phrase written by another and not improvised by the self that takes on new meaning in a new context. Sarmiento first effects a complete decontextualization in which accurate authorship and precise wording are sacrificed, followed by a literary distancing confirmed by the lapidary *point*. It is only then, when he has freed and manipulated the quotation at will – when, in a sense, he has "unquoted" it – that he bends the phrase further by brutally adapting it, through a wilfully interpretive translation, to present-day reality, transforming it into a denunciation of Rosas' dictatorship: "Men are slaughtered; not so ideas." In turn, one might submit Sarmiento's free translation to yet another interpretive twist: authors are expendable; not so literature.[35]

Reading, translating, quoting and misquoting, borrowing and adapting, in sum cannibalizing texts written by others, are hardly bookish, or only bookish activities for Sarmiento. They condition the way he perceives himself as an individual. By this I do not mean that they furnish him with the means to improve himself intellectually, to become a more "civilized" man, as he himself would say. That aspect is indeed present – Sarmiento unquestionably believes, like his mentors of the *Revue Encyclopédique*, in "continuous progress" and in "perfectibility" – but it may well be the least interesting side of the reading process. Reading, as put into practice, nearly defiantly, in *Mi defensa* and *Recuerdos de provincia*, not only represents a view of literature, it is an integral part of Sarmiento's self-image and provides him with veritable ontological support: Sarmiento cannot be (or rather, cannot see himself being) without books. This is evident throughout his autobiographical writings in which references to the European archive are no less frequent than in Sarmiento's other, purportedly more "objective" texts. *Mi defensa* and *Recuerdos de provincia* perform a phantasmal translation of book into being.

This process, which, with time, will become systematic in Sarmiento, is set in motion in adolescence, practically from the time he enters the scene of reading. To read the other is not only to appropriate the words of the other, it is to exist through that other, to be that other. It may be argued that most children and adolescents resort to such projective fantasy and that the process should not be seen as particular to Sarmiento, to Argentine literature, nor to Spanish America. Indeed, the first manifestation of this transposition is rendered by Sarmiento in a humorous fashion as, precisely, a childlike reaction: "I memorized the history of Greece and immediately that of Rome, feeling myself to be, successively, Leonidas and Brutus, Aristeides and Camillus, Harmodius and Epaminondas, all the while selling *mate* tea and sugar" (p. 172). The foreign library gives the young Sarmiento in his provincial San Juan what films will give the characters in Manuel Puig's *Betrayed by Rita Hayworth* a full century later: a supplement of being from fantasy land. However, what does constitute a difference is that Sarmiento (who is not alone in this literary *bovarysme*) continues this process of vital translation and identification well beyond his childhood. An old man thinking back on the history of Greece to explain the ills of modern-day Argentina, he writes in 1875 that "one feels one is something only by comparison; only in that way can one live in this narrow world, in this second-rate country, in this decrepit body."[36] More importantly, Sarmiento turns the process of comparison and translation through which he constructs his autobiographical self into one of the basic tenets of his literary ideology.

Sarmiento's reading, or rather, Sarmiento's dramatization of his reading in *Mi defensa* and *Recuerdos de provincia*, clearly takes into account the contamination between life and text and turns it to his profit. Reading Middleton's *Life of Cicero* makes Sarmiento "live for a time with the Romans" and dream of becoming an "illustrious orator" – a project he made true in his public speeches and very definitely in his writing, unmistakably influenced by a rhetorical, more precisely oratorical, tradition.[37] Reading Benjamin Franklin's *Autobiography* marks him even more strongly.[38] Not only does Sarmiento translate himself into Franklin (or translate Franklin into himself) but the text of Franklin's *Autobiography* also serves as a generic mediation, allowing him to discover a literary tradition:

Franklin's *Life* was for me what Plutarch's *Lives* had been for him, for Rousseau, for Henry IV, for Mme. Roland, for so many others. I felt myself to be Franklin. And why not? Like him, I was poor, like him, I was studious and, if I worked hard enough at following in his footsteps, some day I would cultivate myself like him, I would receive an honorary doctorate like

him, and I would make a place for myself in the literature and politics of
America.   (pp. 176–177).
For Sarmiento, translating himself into Franklin is more than being
Franklin the exemplary figure.[39] It is also being Franklin the reader,
and very concretely the reader of Plutarch – the author who, for
Sarmiento, legitimizes the act of telling lives. So, in retrospect, the
translation of (or into) Franklin affords Sarmiento both a way of
being and a way of writing, allowing him to find a place in an
(auto)biographical tradition. In *Mi defensa* and *Recuerdos de provincia*,
the need to achieve being through literary reference results in a
strikingly precise exercise in textual self-portraiture. The autobiographer is bolstered by snippets from other texts, becomes
himself in the very act of referring to others, and most especially
when referring to other autobiographers: through quotations from
Montaigne he asserts his conviction that self-writing is acceptable,
through allusion to Rousseau and Madame Roland, his belief that
self-writing works in his own interest, through reference to Benjamin Franklin, that self-writing is useful to others. To remember
one's readings, and, more precisely, the way others have remembered themselves, is a way of remembering oneself, of being in one's
text. Self-writing takes the form of a cultural gesture.

Towards the end of *Recuerdos*, suffering from the anxiety of closure
that plagues most autobiographers – How to end my life story while
still alive? How shall I write down that asymptotic point where my
past and my present connect? – Sarmiento writes with uncharacter-
istic modesty: "The interest of these pages has already vanished,
even before my task is done" (p. 218). It is not really that Sarmiento's story loses interest; rather, it is Sarmiento who loses
interest in his story. He seems eager, in fact, to move on to
something else, leaving his personal anecdote behind. The way in
which he chooses to do so adds a twist to Sarmiento's scene of
reading, a final, dramatic flourish. *Recuerdos de provincia* seizes that
precise moment in which the individual, who has been bolstered all
along by reading, by translating, by quoting, by writing, gives way
to and is supplanted by his texts. *Recuerdos* ends on seven very short
chapters (of a total of twenty-five) containing what amounts to a
well-ordered, descriptive catalogue – in sum, a critical bibliography
– of everything Sarmiento ever published. These publications, the
text would indicate, portray the autobiographer just as faithfully as
the forebears he has evoked earlier on; they speak for him, and will

continue to do so, in his absence. "The spirit of an author's writings, when remarkable, is his soul, his essence. The man is overshadowed by its manifestation. The public is less interested in his private acts than in the influence those texts have had on others" (p. 218). The autobiographer's emblem – the book in his hand – has now become his epitaph.[40] "I am my forebears' successor," writes Sarmiento at an imporant juncture of *Recuerdos de provincia*. At the end he might have written, no less accurately: "I am succeeded by my texts."

Several facts doubtless contribute to explain the literary texture of this writing, remarkable even in Spanish America. Sarmiento lived at a time when cultural identity was tenuous at best and when reading, and even owning books,[41] gave the reader a distinct, if often illusory, sense of authority. Furthermore, being self-taught, he revelled, like most autodidacts, in exhibiting his readings and having them reflect not only his knowledge but his own sense of being. Yet the blatancy of Sarmiento's gesture, or the historical reasons that might explain it in his individual case, should not mislead us into thinking that it is unique. Sarmiento brings the self-constituting cultural gesture into the open by constantly alluding to it in one of its many forms. After him, the scene of reading will continue to mark Spanish American autobiographical writing,[42] either through its obsessive presence, as in the constant references to the European text that double Victoria Ocampo's autobiographical exercise (a sort of "I quote therefore I am") or through its forceful omission, as in Neruda's vehement protestations – "*Libro, déjame libre*" – in his memoirs and in his poetry. A mirror for the autobiographer, the book will, like a mirror, reflect, comfort, augment, distort: what it exhibits will be, nonetheless, the spectator's own image.

2

From serf to self: the autobiography of Juan Francisco Manzano

> ... speech only appears in the text in a fragmented,
> wounded state. It is present within it as a "ruin."
> Michel de Certeau, "Montaigne's *Of Cannibals*"

"The lady Doña Beatriz de Justiz, Marchioness Justiz de Santa Ana, wife of Don Juan Manzano, took pleasure every time she went to her famous estate of El Molino in choosing the prettiest Creole girls, when they were ten or eleven years of age; she took them with her and gave them an education suitable to their class and condition so her house was always filled with servants ... " ["La Sra. Da. Beatriz de Justiz Marqueza Justiz de Sta. Ana, esposa del Sor. Don Juan Manzano, tenia gusto de cada vez qu. iva a su famosa asienda el Molino de tomar las mas bonitas criollas, cuando eran de dies a onse años; las traia consigo y dándoles una educación conforme a su clase y condision, estaba siempre su casa llena de criadas ... "]¹

This casual anecdotal beginning, not unlike the opening of so many nineteenth-century novels, is deceptively innocent. For it is not, as might appear, the beginning of a novel told by a third-person narrator of which the Marquesa is the principal character; it is, instead, the beginning of the autobiography of the Marquesa's slave, Juan Francisco Manzano. Nor, as the Spanish original clearly shows, is it a particularly harmonious piece: unsystematic in its spelling, arbitrary in its punctuation, nonchalant in its syntax, this text is, quite obviously, *different*.

With the same carefree syntax and quirky orthography, Juan Francisco Manzano goes on to narrate what appears to be the first and only slave narrative to see publication in Spanish America. He tells how, on one of his lady's visits to El Molino, she chose "one María del Pilar Manzano, my mother" (p. 33) for chief handmaid;

how María del Pilar wet-nursed Manuel de Cárdenas y Manzano, the Marquesa's grandson; how the handmaid married Toribio de Castro, another of the Marquesa's slaves; and, eventually, as a culmination of this tortuous genealogy binding the slave to his master, how María del Pilar gave birth to a child of her own, the Juan Francisco who writes the *Autobiografía*. As was customary, the child was not given his father's surname but that of his master. In this way, the Marquesa's mundane visit to El Molino (an unexpected and ironic antecedent of Valéry's *marquise* sallying forth at five) becomes a founding, life-giving gesture: the aged, benevolent presence of Beatriz de Justiz must perforce open Manzano's life story since she is, quite literally, the power that, presiding over life and death, allows him to be born.

That the slave's life should depend so totally on a gesture from his owner, and that the slave's family romance should be so enmeshed in that of his master's is not, of course, unusual in nineteenth-century colonial Cuba: "remember when you read me that I am a slave and that the slave is a dead being in the eyes of his master," writes Manzano to his protector, Domingo del Monte.[2] In his *Autobiografía*, Manzano brings life to that dead being in the eyes not of his masters but of his readers. He replaces the mistress' founding gesture, even as he describes it, with another gesture, also life-giving, which he himself effects – his own writing.

The circumstances in which this autobiography was written, and the fortune of the text thereafter, are of singular interest. As a domestic city slave who taught himself to read and write against remarkable odds (I shall return to this issue, central to my discussion), Manzano stands out amongst his peers. Born in 1797, he became a poet of some renown, his slave status notwithstanding, and was encouraged in his literary ventures by the reformist, though not openly abolitionist Cuban intellectuals who gathered around the liberal publicist, Domingo del Monte, in the 1830s. One result of these contacts was Manzano's freedom; taking up a collection, del Monte and his friends obtained his manumission in 1836. Manzano's autobiography was another: at del Monte's request, in order to publicize the cause of abolition abroad, Manzano wrote a two-part autobiography narrating his life as a slave. The text was to be included in a dossier that del Monte was compiling for Richard Madden, the British magistrate who, as superintendent of liberated Africans, served as arbiter in the Court of Mixed Commission established in Havana in 1835.[3] Once completed, Manzano's life story was corrected and edited by a member of del Monte's group, Anselmo Suárez y Romero, himself the author of an abolitionist novel, *Francisco*, which was also to be part of the del Monte anti-slavery dossier. Manzano's text was then translated into English by Madden (not so Suárez y Romero's *Francisco*) and presented, together with a report, at the General Anti-Slavery Convention held in London in 1840.

In Cuba, Manzano's manuscript circulated clandestinely in del Monte's milieu, to the extent that "when someone mentions 'the autobiography' it is immediately understood that he speaks of Manzano's."[4] In this process, the second part of the manuscript was lost, perhaps destroyed: what remains is Manzano's account of his early life in bondage till his escape, at age nineteen, to a more lenient home. Thanks to the occasional slackening of censorship laws, Francisco Calcagno was able to integrate fragments of this first part in his *Poetas de color* (1887), a series of biographies of Black poets, but the text by itself was considered unpublishable while Cuba remained under Spanish rule. By 1898, it was all but forgotten. Virtually unknown for nearly a century, what remained of Manzano's autobiography, a fifty-two-page manuscript, passed on to del Monte's heirs and was eventually acquired by the Biblioteca Nacional in Havana; it was published for the first time in its entirety in 1937. Until then, Madden's somewhat biased English translation was the only version of Manzano's autobiography available to the general reader.

As may be seen from this account, Manzano's autobiography was an inordinately manipulated text – a slave narrative that, besides having dispossession for its subject, was, in its very composition and publication, dispossessed. It was written at the request of another (del Monte); it was corrected and edited by another (Suárez y Romero); it was translated and altered by another (Madden); it was integrated into another's text (Calcagno); and it was deprived of its second part. It was, in short, a text *used* by others over which Manzano had, apparently, little or no control. That the text was wielded to further a worthy cause, one close to Manzano's heart, does not lessen the importance of that manipulation.

Manipulation of one kind or another is a frequent enough phenomenon, of course, in North American slave narratives. The slave's story was usually told órally first, then discussed with the editor, then dictated to that editor, who would then read it back to its original storyteller for clarification. The transcribed text would then be complemented with other testimonies to support it and, of course, to condition its reception.[5] As often as not, the editors would add factual details or rhetorical pronouncements to the text so as to enhance its dramatic effect. This creative and well-meaning editing was not without its pitfalls since, as John Blassingame points out, "on occasion the narratives contain so many of the editors' views that there is little room for the testimony of the fugitive."[6]

Manzano's case is obviously different. At the time he composes his life story, he is – besides being a slave – a writer, a relatively well-established poet, and would not seem to need, as did so many North American slaves, the mediation of a white scribe to give shape to words he himself could only speak. Yet Manzano does need the white man's mediation – not for his text to be written but for it to be read. Inevitably, slave narratives are works in collaboration since, on his own, the slave lacks the authority to plead against his condition; his text must be incorporated into the white literary establishment (and thus validated by it) if it is to be heeded at all. It is always, in one form or another, a mediated text, one unavoidably fostering the *twoness* so many Black writers have described and so many members of minorities have felt. In Manzano's case, the principal mediators were del Monte and Madden, the instigator and the translator, whose interest in Manzano needs now to be considered in detail.

Del Monte played the role of literary mentor for Manzano well before the autobiographical project, when Manzano was writing poetry. This was not an exceptional role for him, and his magisterial influence was recognized by many young writers who sought his guidance. Even so, Manzano's reaction to del Monte's reception of his poems seems excessive. His letters reveal unconditional faith in the critic's literary opinion, unending gratitude for his help, and a near total reliance on del Monte that amounts to granting him absolute control over the poems: "Only the care with which Your Grace has devoted himself to polishing my verses, improving them in those parts where it was necessary, will grant me the title of 'half poet.'"[7] For his part, del Monte assumes the power granted him by Manzano. Besides dispensing literary advice, he arranges for the publication of the poems, in Cuba and abroad.[8] He also has Manzano attend his *tertulia* and read his work out loud. (Critics have isolated one such reading, turning it into a memorable emblematic fiction – Manzano, reading his sonnet, "My Thirty Years," before an audience of compassionate *delmontinos* who promptly start a collection to buy his freedom.) It is quite possible that Manzano played up the dependent nature of his relationship with del Monte in the hopes of gaining the critic to a cause far more important than the literary quality of his writing.[9] Not coincidentally, in his letter of 11 December 1834 to del Monte, after quoting from one of his poems where he compares himself to a leaf lost in the wind, and del Monte to a powerful tree, Manzano places his liberty, in addition to his poems, in the hands of his protector, reminding him of "the inclination to gain his freedom that, by natural principle, is in every slave."[10]

In a sense, both men had something to gain from each other; Manzano, as a slave and poet, for reasons that are self-evident; his patron, for reasons somewhat more complex. Del Monte, who held liberal views on slavery but was capable, when he felt threatened, of obfuscated reactions against Blacks,[11] surely found in the patient and submissive Manzano (whose patience and submission may have been strategic as well as temperamental) the victim that fit his expectations; Manzano became for him, as Richard Jackson puts it, somewhat of "a showpiece Black."[12] As such, he could indeed be counted upon to produce an autobiography that would be doubly useful; useful because it would depict the heinous excesses of slavery; and, more importantly, useful because it would reflect, however vicariously, the opinion of an enlightened middle class that wished to distinguish itself from its more obtuse contemporaries. The dossier containing Manzano's autobiography that del Monte was to give Madden was destined to furnish the English magistrate with "the exact state of opinion on the slave trade and on the condition of slaves held by the thinking youth of this country."[13]

It is unclear (and of course impossible to evaluate) to what extent Manzano deliberately conformed to del Monte's ideology. Jackson's contention that, in order to please his protector, Manzano "had to play down the threatening image of the rebellious slave while playing up the image of the docile and submissive slave," while not impossible, has little basis.[14] Equally plausible (although undoubtedly more bleak) is the conjecture that Manzano did not have to play down the "threatening image of the rebellious slave," simply because he did not have one: the system had perversely beaten it out of him, both through physical abuse and, more importantly, through the attribution of privilege. In oppressive situations, self-censorship becomes second nature; of the images the system had to offer, del Monte's ideal probably seemed the most desirable to Manzano and it may well have coincided, without too much conflict, with his self-image.

Only Manzano's letters remain of the correspondence between Manzano and del Monte, so that whatever written injunctions were given by del Monte, if any, are missing. Furthermore, Manzano's letters do not refer to any instructions he might have received from his mentor, nor does he provide details about what he is writing. He calls his project "the course of my life" or "the story of my life," and, quite often, refers cautiously to his autobiographical venture as "the matter," *el asunto*. Significantly, he uses the same euphemism to refer to the plans for his manumission, showing how writing and freedom – two projects "unfit" for a slave – were closely allied in his mind. What Manzano's letters do reveal, however, is a *change of attitude* towards his literary mentor, brought about by the autobiographical experience itself. Two letters referring specifically to the project allow one to measure that change. In the first, dated 25 June 1835, Manzano describes the actual beginning of his writing. I quote it in its near entirety for it is of consequence:

My dear Sir Don Domingo: I received Your Grace's esteemed letter of the fifteenth of this month and I was surprised that in it Your Grace tells me that three or four months ago he asked me for the story, I can't but answer that I did not receive notice so far in advance, for the very day that I received your letter of the 22nd I set myself to looking over the space occupied by the course of my life, and when I was able to I set myself to writing believing that a *real*'s worth of paper would be enough, but having written on without stopping, even when skipping at times four, and even five years, I have still not reached 1820, but I hope to end soon limiting myself to the most interesting events; on more than four occasions, I was close to giving up, a picture filled with so many calamities seems but a bulky chronicle of lies [*un abultado protocolo de embusterías*], all the more so since from a very young age cruel lashings made me aware of my humble condition; I am ashamed to tell this, and I don't know how to demonstrate the facts if I leave the worst part out, and I wish I had other facts to fill up the story of my life without recalling the excessive rigor with which my former mistress treated me, thus obliging or pushing me into the forceful need to resort to a risky escape to save my miserable body from the continuous mortifications that I could no longer endure, so prepare yourself to see a weak creature stumbling in the greatest sufferings, going from overseer to overseer, without ever receiving praise and being always the target of misery, I fear losing your esteem a hundred percent, but let Your Grace remember when he reads me that I am a slave and that the slave is a dead being in the eyes of his master, and do not lose sight of what I have gained. Consider me a martyr and you will find that the endless lashings that mutilated my still unformed body will never make a bad man of your devoted servant who, trusting in your characteristic prudence, now dares breathe a word on this matter, and this when the one who has caused me such misery is still alive.[15]

The awkward syntax of this letter, which I have attempted to reproduce in English,[16] is typical of Manzano's prose. It lends a sense of urgency to his writing, contributing effectively to its compelling quality. Manzano needed little encouragement to tell his story. How to tell it, as this letter illustrates, was another matter. For Manzano, the autobiography signifies access to a new scene of writing fraught with anxiety, very different from the relatively safe scene to which he was accustomed as a derivative poet. The questions he asks himself in this letter, the reflections self-writing inspires, the misgivings he experiences are all part of an auto-biographer's quandary. What shall I choose to tell? When shall I stop? Will they think I'm lying or exaggerating? And then, as the "bulky chronicle of lies" is out in the open before him, come the fears: I am ashamed of it; I wish I had other things to tell besides it; it will disappoint my reader (del Monte) who will no longer like me.

What is the nature of the *it* that disturbs Manzano to the point of shame? As is often the case with victims, he takes on the shame of his oppressor, has trouble naming the torture to which he has been subjected. But why would the telling of that misery disappoint del Monte when he had requested the piece? These ambiguities are not resolved but enhanced by the contradictory nature of some of Manzano's queries. On the one hand, he declares that he is limiting himself to the "most interesting" events; on the other, he wishes that there were *other* facts than those he is telling to fill up the story of his life. A second letter to del Monte, written three months later on 29 September 1835, is remarkably different. Again Manzano brings up the *asunto*, but gone are the anxiety and disarray that marked his first reaction to his mentor's request. Even the manner of the letter is different, the syntax less choppy, the tone more poised. Again, for purposes of comparison, I quote extensively:

[I] have prepared myself to write down for Your Grace a part of the history [*istoria*] of my life, reserving its most interesting events of it mine [*de mi ella*] for some day when, seated in some corner of my country, at peace, assured of my fate and of my livelihood, I may write a truly Cuban novel. For the moment it is best not to give this matter the spectacular development required by different occurrences and scenes because one would need a whole volume, but in spite of that Your Grace will not lack material, tomorrow I shall begin to steal hours from my sleep for that purpose.[17]

Manzano's attitude here could not differ more from that of the previous letter. Instead of queries and doubts, now there are decisions; Manzano speaks as the author of his text, in control of his writing, well aware of the fictional potential ("a truly Cuban novel") of his material. While the first letter gave full power to del Monte over Manzano's story, the second establishes a line between what has been promised to the critic ("your Grace will not lack your material") and what Manzano keeps for himself. The previous letter, marked by subservience, waived Manzano's rights to the text by "giving" it to del Monte; the second letter, marked instead by resistance, has Manzano keep the text for himself. Or rather, has him keep *part* of the text.

In addition, the second letter reverses the notion of *interest* that justifies the choice of material for the autobiography. In June, Manzano was writing down "the most interesting events" for del Monte; in September he is reserving "the most interesting events" for himself, for an eventual book he will write when he is free and feels fully at home. This does not mean, of course, that Manzano, in September, is removing those most interesting events recorded in June from his text and replacing them with other, less interesting ones. It does mean, and this I find of major importance, that in these three months of writing himself down, Manzano's concept of "the most interesting" has changed; that he is valuing *something else* in himself besides the story of his misfortunes, and that that most interesting *something else* is not for giving.

Since Manzano never wrote his "Cuban novel" (indeed he did not write much after the *Autobiografía*, save some poems)[18] he did not endow that something else with a visible form. That something else, I contend, is nonetheless there, marking the entire auto- biography, from the moment *resistance* to the other (or differentiation from the other) replaces capitulation before the other. From the moment Manzano announces that there is a part of himself he will not cede – a part that is *ungiving* – that part informs, through its very defiant silence, the rest of the writing.

A look at Richard Madden's translation of Manzano's text and a comparison of that English version with the Spanish original are useful at this point. Indeed, by working from Madden's text back to Manzano's, assessing the changes made by Madden and, more importantly, evaluating what Madden suppressed from the original because it in some way frustrated reader expectation, one can begin to identify the nodules of resistance in Manzano's story. After undertaking such a comparison in his 1981 edition of Madden's translation, Edward Mullen, while noting the suppressions and changes, surprisingly concludes that "Madden's translation is – with the exceptions noted – strictly that, a rendition into English of the original ... of an *originally authored text.*"[19] The statement is highly debatable, given the fact that one of the first things Madden does is, in fact, to "de-authorize" the text by making it anonymous. It becomes, to quote the title, *The Life and Poems of a Cuban Slave.* Madden's claims that this was done to protect Manzano, while most probably sincere, are not completely convincing. For, as has been argued, if Manzano's name has effectively disappeared from the title page, his initials appear in Madden's preface. Furthermore, Madden furnishes details from Manzano's life (how much it cost to liberate him, what trades he plied as a free man)[20] that make him easily identifiable: "The Spanish authorities did not identify him because they did not wish to. At that time, the only poet on the island that had once been a slave was Manzano."[21] It is highly likely, instead, that Madden needed to make the text anonymous in order to heighten what he considered its representativeness. Thus his translation was presented not as the life story of one individual but as the generic account of "the Cuban slave" and, even more ambitiously, as "the most perfect picture of Cuban slavery ever given to the world."[22] This claim that led to the excision of the particular (the amputation of the name; the cuts that would follow) tells us as much about Madden and his practice of reading as it does about the generic Cuban slave.[23] In a more general manner, the burden of representativeness cast upon certain texts is indicative of the way in which those texts, written by individuals from groups judged weaker or insignificant by the group in power, are often read. In such cases, neither the autobiographers, nor the personas they create, are easily accepted individually by a reading community which much prefers to perceive difference *en bloc*.[24] This imperative exerted on some autobiographical texts – a way of putting its author in his or her place – may also be observed in the way women's autobiographies are often read.

Madden not only made the text anonymous, he incorporated it into a book most of whose sections he had written himself. The order of Madden's book is as follows: two long poems denouncing slavery, "The Slave-Trade Merchant," and "The Sugar Estate," written by Madden; then the "Life of the Negro Poet Written by Himself" in a much abridged form; then a few "Poems, Written in Slavery by Juan ...," adapted into English by Madden; finally, a quite lengthy appendix containing a conversation between Madden and Domingo del Monte and sundry pieces against the slave trade, again written by Madden. Despite the book's title, calling attention to the slave, only about a fourth of the pages of the total text have been written by the slave himself, and they are dwarfed by Madden's doubtless well-meaning, although stifling, prefatory and concluding material.

There are other cuts in Madden's translation besides the supression of Manzano's name. Family names are often omitted, as are place names and dates. The order of some incidents is altered, perhaps, as William Luis persuasively suggests,[25] to present Manzano's suffering as a continuum of growing intensity and not, as does the text in Spanish, as an accumulation of brutal incidents interspersed with unexpected moments of peace and happiness. To have left these moments in place, argues Luis, would have lessened the effect Madden strived for, suggesting that the slave's misfortunes were mitigated by moments of happiness or, at least, relief. Whatever the reasons for this reordering, it ultimately does a disservice to the very cause Madden preached. His more linear presentation of events, while effectively stressing the progressive nature of suffering in the slave's life, sacrifices another of its characteristics, no less fearful – its arbitrariness. By alternating random moments of cruelty with no less erratic moments of kindness, Manzano's original highlights to perfection the utter helplessness of the slave, a pawn in the hands of his master.

Positive moments are downplayed, displaced or even suppressed in the English version. Other suppressions affect passages that must have been perceived as harmful to the "worthy victim" image desired for Manzano; passages illustrating Manzano's ambiguous stance with respect to other Blacks, his confused sense of allegiance, the dubious manifestations of his *twoness*. For example, Madden edits out Manzano's self-presentation as "a mulatto amongst blacks" (p. 68). He deletes a passing comparison of Manzano to Christ (replacing it with the phrase "like a criminal") in the description of one of his punishments (p. 52), he does away with the passage where Manzano speaks, with some smugness, of his status as head servant and of the way in which he was set as an example before the other slaves, sparking their envy (p. 59–60). He even eliminates an episode in which Manzano is "dangerously wounded" in the head by a stone "thrown accidentally by a black" [*me la dio un moreno sin querer*) (p. 42). Finally, Madden omits the enthusiastic (and not very sympathetic) passage in which Manzano, evoking an exceptionally long period in which the capricious Marquesa de Prado Ameno did not make him the victim of her ire, speaks of her fondly: "[I] had forgotten the past and I loved her like a mother, I did not like to hear the other servants calling her names and I would have revealed their names to her had I not known that she got angry t those who carried tales" (p. 68).

These editorial deletions, following a definite ideological pattern, are not, however, the most interesting. More revealing are other passages suppressed by Madden, those dealing more directly with Manzano's person – his urges, his appetites – eliminated for reasons one can only guess. Probably judged insignificant, as having no direct bearing on the exemplary story of "the Cuban slave," perhaps even considered frivolous by the somewhat staid Madden, they are, on the contrary, crucial to the understanding of Manzano the man and Manzano the autobiographer in his complex relation to writing and books.

Manzano's autobiography abounds in references to the body, which is not surprising, given the physical abuse his text describes. For Manzano, the slave, the body is a form of memory, the unerasable reminder of past affronts: "These scars are perpetual [*estan perpetua*] in spite of the twenty-four years that have passed over them" (p. 54). Yet that body does not belong to him; it is his master's to exploit, through hard labor, and it is also the master's to manipulate, for his pleasure. From early childhood on, Manzano's body is not so much exploited through hard work (a city house slave, he is only overworked when, in punishment, he is sent to the sugar mill) as it is used by his mistresses. His first mistress, the kind and grandmotherly Marquesa de Justiz, who has the child christened in her own daughter's christening robes, "took me for a sort of plaything, and they say I was more in her arms than in my mother's who ... had given her mistress a little Creole whom she called the child of her old age" (p. 34). Infinitely more complex but equally depersonalizing is the involvement with Manzano's body shown by his second mistress, the perfidious Marquesa de Prado Ameno. As his mistress' page, Manzano writes, "I was an object known as the Marquesa's *chinito* or little mulatto" (p. 61). Emblematic of her power over his body is an intricate ritual of dress. Madden's translation reduces to three lines the following detailed description of Manzano's first livery:

[T]hey made me many striped short suits and some white undergarments [*alguna ropita blanca*] for when I wore my page's livery, for holidays I was dressed in wide scarlet trousers of fine cloth, trimmed in gold braid, a short jacket without a collar trimmed with the same, a black velvet cap also trimmed with red feathers and on the tip two little rings in the French style and a diamond pin and with all this and the rest I *soon forgot the secluded life I had led in the past* ... She dressed me combed me and took care *that I not mix with the other little Blacks*.   (p. 37; my emphasis)

For Manzano, clothing provides a new identity while effacing the old. It makes and unmakes the man at random, conferring a tenuous sense of selfhood (a sense that is reinforced by isolation from his peers)[26] that is all too easily destroyed. If Manzano's years in the Marquesa de Prado Ameno's service are presented as an oscillation between good and evil depending on the mistress' whims, no less important is the alternation between the two forms of dress that the text so painstakingly details. On the one hand, there is the *ropa fina*, the finery that clothes his body inside the house and signals, to him and to others, that he is in his mistress' good graces. On the other, there is the fall from grace, the shorn hair, the bare feet and the *esquifación* or field laborer's hemp gown Manzano is forced into before being tied up and carried off to the sugar mill.[27] This change of dress was public, and one was stripped of one's identity in the presence of others; Manzano cleverly enhances this humiliation by recording the horror and disbelief in his little brother's eyes when watching the scene for the first time (p. 46). As Manzano writes eloquently, "the change of clothes and of fortune were one" (p. 55).

Isolated from the bodies of other Blacks, permanently disoriented by the frequent change in costume, Manzano's body is, quite literally, displaced. If one looks for the *space* allotted that body in the mistress' house, one will find it has none. Its place is always at the mistress' side or at her feet, but never out of her sight or her control: "[M]y task was to get up at dawn before the others awoke and sweep and clean all I could. Once I finished my duties, I would sit outside my lady's door so that, on awakening, she would find me immediately. I went wherever she went, following her like a lap dog, with my little arms folded" (pp. 39–40). The threshold – by definition a non-place, a dividing line – is the space assigned to Manzano's body, the *locus* of his exploitation. In it, the body is no longer a body but a tool and a buffer: "[I] stayed outside her door, stopping anyone who tried to enter, or fetching whomever she called for, or being silent if she slept" (p. 51). To be on his mistress' threshold, to be that threshold wherever she goes, intercepting undesirable contact, is the function of Manzano's body: "In the evenings *monte* was played in the home of the Gomes ladies and, as soon as she sat down, I had to stand behind her chair with my elbows spread out, preventing those who were standing from pushing her or grazing her ears with their arms" (p. 65). Indeed, the only place where his body escapes the control of his mistress is the common lavatory: "Regularly the common room was my place for meditation. While I was there I could think of things in peace" (p. 68).[28]

The lavatory as refuge, while clearly not an original concept, allows me to explore another aspect of Manzano's bodily manifestations, one that Madden deletes completely, and one that should bring me closer to Manzano's problematic relation with books and writing. Several times in his text, Manzano stresses his hunger, more specifically, his gluttony, giving it an importance that surpasses the cliché of the ever-hungry growing boy. "I was very fearful and I liked to eat" (p. 38) is the way he succinctly describes himself as a child. A way of repossessing his body, this voraciousness is also a powerful means of rebelling against limits:

It is not surprising that, always hungry, I ate everything that came my way, for which reason I was considered a great glutton, and as I did not have a fixed time for eating I stuffed myself and swallowed my food nearly without chewing and that resulted in frequent indigestions that had me frequently attending to certain needs and that got me punished ... (p. 39)

As there is no place for Manzano's body, there is no specific time for his eating. However, in the same way that he furtively claims a space for himself in the lavatory, which is a place of waste, he will, no less furtively, make leftovers his nourishment: "When they dined or supped I was quick to pick up everything they left uneaten and I had to be crafty about it for when they got up to leave the table I had to go with them" (p. 40). It is by building on this notion of the residual, neglected by Manzano's translators and, I may add, his commentators,[29] that I wish to approach his relation to books.

This relation is, of course, notoriously one-sided. Manzano's gluttony is only matched by his voracity for the letter, yet that letter is constantly denied him: books are unavailable, reciting by heart punished, writing forbidden. (Even when Manzano publishes, as he will later, he will do so by special permission.) The notion of an archive, of a cultural totality, indeed the very notion of a *book*, which inspired such awe in a Sarmiento, the "man with a book in his hand," are totally alien to Manzano. His is a very particular scene of reading, for he only has access to fragments, devalued snippets from an assortment of texts he comes across by chance, leftovers from his masters' cultural table:

Since I was a little boy I had the habit of reading whatever was readable in my language and when I was out on the street I was always picking up bits of printed paper and if it was verse I did not rest till I had learned it by heart.   (pp. 65–66)

Even before knowing how to read, the child is a collector of texts. Under the tutelage of his first mistress, the Marquesa de Justiz (who was herself a poet),[30] he memorizes eulogies, short plays, the sermons of Fray Luis de Granada and bits of operas he is taken to see. He becomes, very early on, a most efficient memory machine. As the young Sarmiento a few years later, his gift is exhibited before company, yet unlike Sarmiento, that gift is not allowed to follow its normal course. As soon as the young Manzano uses his prodigious memory for himself he is regarded with suspicion: "When I was twelve I had already composed many stanzas in my head and that was the reason my godparents did not want me to learn how to write but I dictated them from memory to a young mulatto woman called Serafina" (p. 38). Manzano is condemned to orality: not in vain is he nicknamed "Golden Lips." And, when his recitation of poetry is judged too disruptive, he is condemned to silence:

My mistress found out that I chatted too much and that the old servants in the house gathered around me when I was in the mood and enjoyed hearing my poems ... [She] who never lost sight of me even asleep she dreamed of me spied on me one winter night they had made me repeat a story surrounded by many children and maidservants and she was hidden in the other room behind some shutters or blinds. Next day for no good reason I received a good thrashing and I was made to stand on a stool in the middle of the room, a big gag in my mouth, with signs hanging on my chest and on my back I cannot remember what they said and it was strictly forbidden for anyone to engage in conversation with me and if I even tried to engage one of my elders in conversation he was to give me a blow.

(p. 41)

Lacking books, the "notebook of memory" (p. 41) will have to do. A repository for his models (the poems he hears, or occasionally reads, or picks up in the streets), his memory also stores the poems he continues to compose in spite of the double interdiction: he cannot write them down (for writing is beyond his reach) and cannot say them out loud (for reciting is forbidden). In the absence of writing, oblique ways of leaving a trace on paper must be found. I quote from an admirable passage describing the family drawing lesson, a lesson that Manzano cunningly spies on and turns to his profit:

[I] too would be present standing behind my mistress' chair and there I stayed throughout the class as they all drew and Mr. Godfria [probably Godfrey] who was the teacher went from one to another of those who were drawing saying such and such here correcting with the pencil there and fixing something over there, through what I saw and heard corrected and explained I found myself ready to count myself as a regular attendant of the drawing class I forgot which one of the children gave me an old brass or copper pen and a pencil stub and I waited till they threw away a draft and the next day after having looked around me I sat in a corner my face to the wall and I started making mouths eyes ears eyebrows teeth ... and taking a discarded draft which was untorn ... I copied it so faithfully that when I finished my mistress was gazing at me attentively although pretending not to see me ... From that moment on everybody started throwing all sorts of drafts to me in my corner, where I half lay on the floor.　　(p. 40)

Relying heavily on residue and mimesis, Manzano's drawing lesson reverses the order of the lesson of his masters. Fished out of a waste basket or thrown to him like a bone, the used up matter, discarded from above, is given new life and value as it is used below – in the corner, on the floor, in the serf's place. From copying drafts, Manzano will go on to copying script and to writing itself. During his short, happy time in the service of the Marquesa's son, Nicolás

Cárdenas y Manzano, he recognizes that the furtive memorization of his master's manual of rhetoric, taken up "to give myself learning," is unproductive since he cannot fully apply what he learns. Deciding to "teach myself something more useful" (p. 57), he teaches himself to write, in a manner no less striking than when he taught himself to draw, resorting to an equally inventive re-cycling of refuse. Buying pen and very thin paper, he rescues his master's crumpled notes and discarded scraps of writing and, flattening them out under one of his fine sheets, literally traces them "and with this invention before a month was over I was writing lines shaped like my master's script . . ." (p. 57). His master, "who loved me not like a slave but like a son" (p. 56), opposes these efforts and (in this respect, no different from his mother) "ordered me to leave that pastime, inappropriate to my situation in life, and go back to sewing" (p. 57). That this same master was "an illustrious protector of public instruction on this island,"[31] and, indeed, would later be president of the Education Section of the Sociedad Económica de Amigos del País, does not lack irony but does not come as a surprise.[32] Whereas Manzano sees writing as *useful*, his master (who sends him back to his sewing, a task, Manzano claims, he was not neglecting) considers it a *pastime* and time, within the slave system, cannot be *passed*, it must be *measured* in work.[33]

Identity and identification are words that occur nowhere in Manzano's autobiography except here, in the passage devoted to the writing lesson. Manzano tells how, in preparing his master's table, chair, and books every morning, he "began identifying with his habits" (p. 56); and, when summarizing the learning process observed above, he explains that "that is why there is a certain identity between his handwriting and mine" (p. 57). What is noteworthy, of course, is that Manzano does not identify with the master himself: he identifies with his reading, with his writing, with the *means* through which he, Manzano, will ultimately achieve his own identity. For there are two stories in Manzano's autobiography: one, complying with del Monte's request, is the story of the self as slave; the other, just as important if not more so, is the story of that slave-self as reader and writer.

His master's initial objection notwithstanding, Manzano would continue his writing with considerable success. From a modest cottage industry somehow run out of the Marquesa's home ("I wrote many notebooks of stanzas in forced meter, which I sold" [p. 66]), he would go on to publish with special permission (*Poesías líricas*, 1821; *Flores pasageras* [*sic*], 1830), on to del Monte's patronage, and on to moderate renown as a poet and as a playwright (*Zafira*, 1842). What strikes the modern reader about Manzano's poetry, however, is its desperately conventional, measured and ultimately *correct* style. It is mediocre Neoclassicism at its very worst, which, if one thinks of it, was to be expected. Manzano himself declares that his model was Arriaza, the contemporary poet who had translated Boileau; del Monte, who edited Manzano's poetry, was an ardent Neoclassicist; and Neoclassicism, after all, was very much the fashion of the day. Besides being the style Manzano read, heard and memorized, it was, I suspect, a style that afforded him comfort precisely because of its readymade formalism, its handy clichés, its lofty abstraction, its reassuring meters. Manzano's avowed liking for *pie forzado* – the prefixed "mold" of the poem (verse and rhyme) determining the writing itself – confirms, I believe, this suspicion. It is pointless to search these poems for poetic originality, personal confessions or reflections on slavery; ludicrous to find in them, as does one critic, "the cry of the *patiens ovis injuriae*,"[34] or, as does another, a "creative suffering."[35] Yet it is equally short-sighted to dismiss them because they are imitations.[36] Manzano's poetry, I argue, is original precisely *because* it is so imitative, because it is such a deliberate and total act of appropriation of the reading and writing that had been denied him.

In his poetry, Manzano models his self and his "I" on the voice and the conventions of his masters. His second wife, the nineteen-year-old free mulatto María del Rosario, "pretty as a gold nugget from head to toe"[37] becomes a conventionally abstract *Delia*. (A previous muse, sung in the 1821 poems, perhaps his first wife Marcelina Campos, receives the Catullan name of *Lesbia*.) Another poem, "A Dream," addressed to Manzano's brother Florencio, describes the latter as a "robust Ethiopian" – an ordinary euphemism for Blacks which would be used by white critics for Manzano himself. Manzano's poems relish artificiality: streams become nymphs, winds are zephyrs, heaven is the empyrean. Hyperbaton and prosopopeia abound, mannerisms and classical references are frequent; so are resounding, meaningless fillers. "His ear taught him the cadence of verse; his genius dictated to him the marks of good taste," writes Calcagno, intent on forcing Manzano into the stereotype of the uneducated, "natural" poet.[38] But those marks of "good taste" (another name for cultural convention) were less attributable to "genius" than to Manzano's extraordinary gift for mimicry, a gift so excessive it contained in itself its own undoing.[39] Manzano's poetry is so overdetermined by imitation, it constitutes such a comprehensive reservoir of clichés, that it unwittingly turns into parody. His only contribution to the theatre, *Zafira*, a play in verse, fared no better. It is a "Moorish" romance in the spirit of the period, as closely dependent on convention, thematically speaking, as were the poems in their choice of form.

After the poems and the play, a look at the *Autobiografía*, however perfunctory, cannot but disconcert the reader. For if the poetry gave the impression of being overwritten, the story of Manzano's life and of his self-discovery as a poet produces quite the opposite effect. The possibility exists that Manzano was helped more with the first than with the second: his poems were reviewed and edited by del Monte before publication whereas the manuscript of the autobiography, at least the one that was published in 1937, apparently did not benefit from editorial help. (Del Monte had charged Suárez y Romero with editing Manzano's text and Suárez apparently complied;[40] yet that corrected version, the whereabouts of which are unclear, was not the one that was finally published.) What a comparison of both, poetry and autobiography, shows is an unquestionable split, affecting Manzano's production as much as his self-image as a writer.

The lyric "I" of Manzano's poetry is a relatively comfortable rhetorical construct, one into which Manzano seems to fit without effort. His models, stored either in his memory or in his stray bits of print, are easy to call up and reassuring in their authority: they are, after all, the models of the master. However, when Manzano writes prose, and more specifically when he inscribes himself in his autobiography as a Black man and a slave, there is no model for him, no founding fiction – no *master* image – to be rescued from texts. In order to validate his autobiographical gesture and thus authorize himself, Manzano cannot pick and choose from his scraps because those scraps do not contain the makings of his image, or rather contain them, unwritten, as an absence. If those scraps may be used for poetic mimicry, allowing Manzano to speak with his master's voice, they do not lend themselves easily to the expression of an autobiographical persona they in no way prefigure. One can trace letters from the master's refuse; one cannot, however, trace a self for which there is no written model.

The *Autobiografía* as Manzano wrote it, with its run-on sentences, breathless paragraphs, dislocated syntax and idiosyncratic misspellings, vividly portrays that quandary – an anxiety of origins, ever renewed, that provides the text with the stubborn, uncontrolled energy that is possibly its major achievement. The writing, *in itself*, is the best self-portrait we have of Manzano as well as his greatest contribution to literature; at the same time, it is what translators, editors and critics cannot tolerate. "It would suffice to clean up this text, freeing it of impurities, for the clear and touching manner in which Manzano relates his misfortunes to reveal itself in all its simplicity," writes Max Henríquez Ureña.[41] This notion (shared by many) that there is a clear narrative imprisoned, as it were, in Manzano's *Autobiografía*, waiting for the hand of the cultivated editor to free it from dross – this notion that the impure text must be replaced by a clear (white?) version for it to be readable – amounts to another, aggressive mutilation, that of denying the text readability in its own terms. Of the "perpetual scars" marking Manzano's body, this could well be the cruellest.

3

The theatrics of reading: body and book in Victoria Ocampo ˋ

> I experienced everything through the transmuted substance of my body ... I had no other thing to offer under the species of linked words, under the bread and wine of the spirit we call literature. That, in sum, could well be the epigraph of every one of my texts ... The more I strayed from it, childishly heeding who knows what convention of the *hateful* *"I"*, the weaker my writing was – flabby, without substance.
>
> Victoria Ocampo, *Autobiografía*

Books, many books are mentioned throughout Victoria Ocampo's texts. If autobiographies are wont to highlight the privileged encounter with the written word as a symbolic beginning for their life stories, an acknowledgment of the very tools for self-definition, this highlighting usually occurs, emblematically, close to the beginning of their narrative. In the case of Victoria Ocampo, however, there is no such clearcut inception of the readerly into the life story; not one, not two, but many encounters with books are described in her text. The significant gesture is tirelessly repeated: one scene of reading brings on another, book follows upon book and discovery upon discovery, so that we are left with many beginnings; so many, in fact, that they blur into a dizzying continuum in which the bare gesture – reading – perpetuates itself as the self-sustaining motion of one, consistent autobiographical act.[1]

I have already referred to Ocampo's initial version of the scene of reading, recorded amongst her earliest childhood recollections. Under the entry "Book" she writes: "I carry a book that has been read aloud to me and pretend I am reading it. I remember the story perfectly, I know it is behind those letters I cannot understand" (I, p.81). I wish to dwell on the precise phrasing of this recollection for it contains many elements specific to Ocampo's scene of reading. Much like Sarmiento, she favors the Hamlet-like posture – the young reader with a book in hand. Yet in Ocampo's recollection of the scene the theatricals of the pose are stressed. She sees herself performing: *carrying* the book (as an actor would carry a prop onstage) and *pretending* to read. Distance is emphasized in the scene but so is familiarity: the child carries a book full of letters to which she has no access, but it is a book with whose contents she is quite familiar since it has been read to her many times.[2]

It may be argued that this parading with a book in hand is no more meaningful than any other example of childhood make-believe: as one might "play doctor," one "plays book." For that matter, Ocampo is not unique amongst autobiographers in playing this game: Sartre, to give one memorable example, recalls a similar imposture in *Les Mots*.[3] As a point of reference, the latter text proves useful to evaluate Ocampo's experience. Sartre's childhood mimicry has a precise model at its source: the child's maternal grandfather is a writer, has a library full of books and, when taking a book from a shelf, follows a set pattern of trivial gestures on which the child spies avidly. The first time the boy pretends to read from a book, he performs a "ceremony of appropriation": he opens the book "to the right page" as he has seen his grandfather do, fully expecting a revelation which, to his dismay, does not occur.[4] Moreover, for Sartre, books are a permanent and gender-affiliated presence: on the one hand, there are the serious "cultural objects" revered by his grandfather; on the other, the frivolous "colifichets" that fuel the erotic imagination of his grandmother and his mother.

Ocampo's posturing with the book in hand, while clearly imitative, differs from that of Sartre in that she has no clear reader, in her immediate entourage, either "seriously" male or "frivolously" female, on whom to model her own reading. No one adult in her childhood is associated with books in any exemplary way nor does reading appear to play a prominent part in family tradition beyond the conventional reading practiced by the well-to-do: "Despite the fact that, like Virginia Woolf's Orlando, I had 'bestowed my credulity' on writers from childhood, I had the misfortune of barely knowing professional writers or people who were interested in books" (II, p.71). When the parents' library is described, books are made to appear as ornaments, objects appealing more than anything to the senses (I, 94). The adults who read to her, hardly identified, do not seem to have any special connection to books beyond storytelling. A blurry French governess, Mademoiselle Guérin, is credited with teaching her the alphabet; *showing* may be a better term, since the learning process itself (French is Ocampo's first reading language) is presented as an undirected, spontaneous event; "I learn the alphabet I don't know how ... I learn French I don't know how" (I, 83). A favorite great-aunt, Vitola, is also mentioned as reading to the child in Spanish but little more is said.

It is obvious that we are not faced here with a situation such as, again, that of the young Sarmiento, born to parents of rudimentary culture, who taught himself to read and took pride in his status as an autodidact. The family into which Ocampo was born, in 1890, was both socially prominent and wealthy. Together with her five younger sisters, she received at home the privileged if restricted education of the upper-middle-class – training in languages and music, plus a smattering of general knowledge that conspicuously excluded Argentine literature, history and current events. Despite this limited formation, Ocampo is far from being culturally deprived. Yet it is clear, from the numerous passages throughout her autobiographical texts that echo that first recollection of the child posturing as reader, that books take on for Ocampo an importance well beyond the one her milieu is willing to assign to them. They are not marks of conventional culture nor are they means to achieve the formal education to which, as a woman, she has no right: " 'If she had been a boy she would have taken up a career,' my father would say of me, probably with sadness" (II, 16).[5] It is not surprising then that, like Sarmiento, Ocampo referred to herself as an autodidact:[6] she had to teach herself new ways of reading and of relating to a canon to which, because of her gender, she had limited access. The inordinate intensity with which Ocampo successively fills out the first version of her scene of reading, giving life to the childhood posturing and turning that posture into an expression of self, betrays a relation with books that goes well beyond – and even goes against – the tame and ideologically limited cultural landscape in which she was raised.

Ocampo has written extensively about her voracious childhood reading and I shall not go into it in detail here.[7] Although her appetite for books is constant, the reading itself follows different patterns. In early childhood there are the books one is read to from;

later on the "classics," read in the classroom and eliciting a prescribed response; finally, there are the books that one reads for oneself, those that Ocampo appropriates more directly and turns into vehicles of self-expression: "Books, books were a new world in which blessed freedom reigned. I lived the life of books and had to account to no one for that life. It was my thing. [*Era cosa mía*]" (I, p.177).

Like Proust's scene of reading to which Ocampo refers often, this private reading is a solitary ritual observing specific rules. However, reading does not escape contamination with the outside world and even seems to encourage it. If French and English books are devoured inside the house, the reading experience also incorporates the specifically Argentine surroundings, so that, in memory, the two live combined, in a constant interplay of the exotic and the familiar: the Brontës' Yorkshire moors will "forever smell of the Argentine summer and echo with the amorous duets of *hornero* birds and the resonant presence of cicadas,"[8] while "The Fall of the House of Usher" will always be associated with the mooing of cows and the bleating of sheep.[9] This very elementary contamination between what Ocampo will later set up as complementary and often interchangeable categories, *lo vivido* and *lo leído*, carries over into other domains. As *lo vivido* seeps into the book so at other times does *lo leído* parry the onslaught of direct experience and even replaces that experience. When Ocampo reads *David Copperfield* she has already lost her great-grandfather; yet it is Dickens' description of Steerforth's body on the beach, at the end of the novel – "I saw him lying with his head upon his arm, as I had often seen him lie at school" – that gives her her first "real" contact with death and with personal loss:

[I] wept also for myself. I wept for the childhood I knew was leaving me since I had already begun to look back on it; and I wept for the childhood that did not completely let go of me, that in vain resisted triumphant adolescence, as Steerforth's familiar posture, with its appearance of life, in vain resisted death. (I, pp.179–180)

From adolescence on, Ocampo will read most major events of her life through books. This is not to say that hers is a primarily bookish existence, lived in seclusion, nor that, because of books, to transpose the phrase Borges wrote of himself, "life and death are lacking from [her] life." Books do not do her living for her but they are, in a way, the space in which her life is enhanced and can be lived more fully than anywhere else. Referring to the modelling function of readings done early in life, Ocampo highlights empathy and identification. The theatrical terms she uses provide a helpful clue to the self-representational potential she attributes to books:

All imaginative and highly sensitive children are fascinated by certain heroes and tell themselves stories in which they play an important role in relation to their hero – they are pursued, loved, betrayed, saved, humiliated or glorified by him. Later, once that stage is left behind, they usually act out in life those scenes so often rehearsed in childhood. When the magnificent or terrible moment finally arrives, the reply comes naturally, on cue. Impossible to change it, impossible to get it wrong ... There have been too many rehearsals. It is no longer possible to choose another, it was never possible to choose another reply. Each being carries within himself the same scene, the same drama, from the moment he awakens to consciousness till the end of his days, and he plays out that scene, that drama, no matter what events or what characters come his way, until he finds his own plot and his own character. He may never find them. But that does not stop him from playing out his scene, bestowing on the events and characters least likely to fit his play the shape of the events and character that are his own. He was born to play but one scene and one drama, and cannot help repeating them as long as he lives.[10]

Reading is a vital performance, but a performance that continuously seeks new settings. "From my adolescence onwards," writes Ocampo, "I was dissatisfied with the books I was given. I began to read all those I could lay my hands on."[11] One of the first examples of this new, unfettered manner of reading that remains in her memory for its modelling impact is Rostand's *L'Aiglon*, a text that she hears and sees before actually reading it, much as she had heard the book she carried around as a child. At age fifteen, she sees a performance of *L'Aiglon* with Marguerite Moreno (who would later give her acting lessons) in the title role, and recognizes herself wholeheartedly in the young hero. The fact that the role of the Duke of Reichstadt was usually played by a woman – Sarah Bernhardt, in one of her most famous performances, and now Marguerite Moreno – must have had, one suspects, some part in this spontaneous reaction. However, there was more that bonded Ocampo to the protagonist:

I immediately recognized myself in the hero. Why? The whole thing seemed preposterous. The plight of Napoleon's son was not my own.

However, that sick boy (his ravaging consumption seemed to me then an enviable illness) was as much a prisoner at Schoenbrunn as I was in the house on Florida and Viamonte. He was a *pas-prisonnier-mais*. He could not go out riding without "the sweet honor of an invisible escort." His mail was censored. He was allowed to read only those books that had been chosen for him. Someone lent him books clandestinely:

> Le soir, dans ma chambre, je lisais, j'étais ivre.
> Et puis, quand j'avais lu, pour cacher le délit
> Je lançais le volume au haut du ciel de lit.

My bed had no canopy but it did have a mattress and under that mattress I hid my private library.   (p.100)[12]

Ocampo not only reads herself into a character but into a character *who reads*: like Hamlet, Napoleon's son is a prince with a book in his hand. However, unlike Hamlet, who reads with impunity, the young Duke's unsupervised reading, his only means of liberation, is an offense in the eyes of his guards. It is in this illegality, assumed defiantly as a liberating act, that Ocampo recognizes the mark of her own reading.

The theatrical nature of the experience is to be noted. Rostand's text is discovered not on the printed page but on a stage – through voice and representation, through active posturing. What Ocampo "reads" (and what she reads herself into) is, in sum, a performance: an actress playing the role of a character who rejects the role others would impose on him and turns reading into rebellion. If reading is performance, this particular reading of *L'Aiglon* is the performance of a performance. And it is also, of course, a translation; a passage not only from text to life, or from French theatrical convention to Argentine everyday experience, but from one gender to the representation of the other: the young Ocampo identifies herself with a boy but also with a woman playing the role of a boy.

The presence of the theatrical in Ocampo's scene of reading, from the posturing with the book as a child, through the dazzled recognition of self in *L'Aiglon*, to the unceasing search for her "own plot and [her] own character," reveals Ocampo's obsessive preoccupation with self-representation, a preoccupation that informs all of her work and reflects a gender-related cultural predicament. But this presence of the theatrical should also be seen quite literally, as the expression of a vocation – "I was born to *act*. I have theatre in my blood."[13] – that was thwarted early on, leaving its diffuse trace in her life and in her writing. Ocampo's life story casts her early on as a misfit, constantly at odds with the real-life roles society had to offer, roles that did not include, needless to say, that of actress or writer. Instead of public acting, for example, she is allowed recitation in private: a pale and insufficient substitute, it is allowed, even encouraged, as a decorous manifestation of talent. That Ocampo wished to go beyond those private spectacles and devote her life to acting, that she strived to achieve her goal by coaching with a reputed professional, that, when faced with strong parental opposition, she did not assert herself, appears in her autobiographical writing as one of her more poignant defeats; a defeat that occasional and very successful public performances in later years, as the *récitante* in Honegger's *Le Roi David* and in Stravinsky's *Perséphone*, doubtless rendered more unpalatable.[14]

Literature was not an easy career, even for men, at the turn of the century. The caricatures of the uncomprehending, self-assured bourgeois that pepper the texts of Spanish American *modernismo*, the discomfort shown by that bourgeois himself when he became a writer, as did the members of the Argentine generation of 1880, are proof of the unease with which society looked on the institutionalization of literature and on the professional status claimed by writers. For women wishing to write, the issue, foreseeably, was infinitely more thorny.[15] An adolescent, Ocampo complains vehemently to her friend and confidante of those years, Delfina Bunge:

Man of letters is a word that is taken pejoratively in our midst. "He is a man of letters" (or what is worse, "*she* is a woman of letters") means a good-for-nothing ... (Unless he's a professor and has a chair: they respect that kind of title.) If it's a woman, she is a hopeless *bas-bleu*, a *poseuse*, she borders on perversion or, in the best of cases, she is a badly put together Miss Know-It-All. Conversely, the word *landowner* [*estanciero*] has prestige. As in the fable, it means *veau, vache, cochon, couvée.*   (II, p.104)

For women, the dividing line between the permissible and the perverse, in areas pertaining to literature on theatre, clearly reproduces the separation between public and private. Theatrical performances are limited to domestic interiors – safe places where, precisely, one does not make a spectacle of oneself. The same applies to literary performances – reading and writing – albeit in a more complex way. Reading from a censored list is permitted, even encouraged but the censorship itself is arbitrary. Many books were on the family index but others, unaccountably, escaped it: *Anna*

Karenina, for example, and also Shakespeare and Dante because, "although all sorts of things happened there, they eluded censorship because of the rhyme, as operas did on account of the music" (II, 62). An autobiographical footnote, tucked away in an essay by Ocampo on Virginia Woolf, is expressive of her parents' shortsightedness. The father used to show early Max Linder films at home:

"[I]f there were love scenes accompanied by kissing, my mother ... planted herself before the projector, intercepting the image. We protested but she would not budge. As she couldn't guess how long the amorous outbursts lasted (these were silent movies and in covering the image she covered the subtitles), her shadow remained longer than necessary on the screen, just in case, and made us lose the gist of the story."[16]

For all its comicality, the passage is significant. The mother's purpose is clearly to censor all intimations of sexuality, in their graphic, physical representation. But in so doing she also obscures the words (those silent movie subtitles the viewer *reads* as if he were hearing them being *said*) and deletes the meaning of the story. The intercepting gesture inadvertently merges body and reading, the two main components of Ocampo's autobiographical writing.

As with the plays staged in private, Ocampo's first publication was very much an *entre nous* affair. Two of her poems, in French, were published anonymously in 1908; the Buenos Aires newspaper in which they appeared merely identified her as a young woman from a distinguished family. In no manner, however, was writing or even interest in literature to be personalized and made public, to be *signed*. In 1910, during an extended stay of the Ocampo family in Paris, the parents allowed their eldest daughter to audit courses at the Sorbonne and, as was fashionable, attend lectures at the Collège de France. Ocampo heard Bergson, Faguet, and was particularly taken by Hauvette's course on Dante. Also during that stay, arrangements were made for Ocampo to sit for different artists then in fashion, amongst them Troubetzkoy and Helleu. One of the artists, Dagnan Bouveret, struck by her love of books and by the passion with which she quoted from the *Commedia*, decided to place a small head of Dante on the table on which she leaned while posing. Ocampo wryly recounts the consequences of his idea:

[My parents] tactfully told him that his new ornament was not suitable for a nineteen-year-old girl and that it might seem pretentious or would be interpreted as a ridiculous show of *basbleuisme*. Dagnan answered that my love of Dante seemed to him to justify fully "the ornament" but that he was ready to erase it and replace it by some pansies or a laurel sprig in a vase. So he did. Thus we were separated, Dante and I, in effigy, and the vegetable kingdom occupied his place but could not (in my memory) "briser son absence." So much could it not shatter it that my first article, in *La Nación*, was a commentary of the *Commedia*. It was published ten years later – that is, after ten years of navigating against wind and tide.(II, 151)

If Ocampo did not become an actress she did become a writer, "against wind and tide" as she so enjoyed saying, against the Argentine literary establishment and against the better judgment of the social group to which she belonged. The displacement of one vocation by another doubtless affected her writing and her general demeanor within a field she would always perceive as not entirely her own. Despite the importance she would achieve in literary circles, both at home and abroad, despite the fact that she founded and for many years directed *Sur*, one of the most influential literary journals in Latin America, despite her self-assured stance when she advocated women's rights and founded the Argentine Women's Union in 1936 with two other women, María Rosa Oliver and Susana Larguía,[17] when Ocampo speaks of herself as a writer there is always malaise, a reluctance to accept herself fully in that role. As is well known, such self-disparagement is not uncommon in women writers of the nineteenth (even the twentieth) century.[18] In Ocampo's case, the deprecating gesture may also echo, unconsciously, the very class prejudice she believed she was battling – contempt for the professional writer and devaluation of "paid" work. But the gesture is further compounded by the fact that Ocampo the actress is always behind Ocampo the writer, or rather, that the writer is an actress in disguise, living out a *rôle manqué*. The text she reads will always be a partition waiting to be performed, a quiescent word in search of expression, a *chose possible*, as she notes much later, quoting Valéry: "the poem is an abstraction, a text that awaits, a law that has no life but in the human voice . . ."[19] So is the self perceived as a *chose possible*, another word – "I" – in search of its script. If the theatre cannot provide a suitable scene for the encounter of the two, then literature – writing as a performance of reading – will have to suffice.

Ocampo's living and writing her life through books and through authors has been routinely interpreted as a desire to identify with the male models offered by a patriarchal society.[20] While this interpretation is *in part* true it suffers from oversimplification and needs to be qualified on several levels. In relation to the literary *characters* with whom Ocampo bonds through her reading, such an interpretation falls short. For example, it ignores the young Ocampo's reading of self in *Corinne* and her sympathy for Madame de Staël, often mentioned in the second volume of her autobiography.[21] Furthermore, that interpretation – living through books as a way of identifying with male models – sidetracks the most interesting and intricate bonding of them all, that of Ocampo with Dante's Francesca.

Describing her first encounter with the *Commedia*, at age sixteen, Ocampo recalls the drastic nature of her reaction to "some passages from the *Inferno*":

The impression made on me by that reading is only comparable to what I experienced as a very young child when, in the sea for the first time, I was swept off my feet and rolled over in the sand by a magnificently impetuous wave. In all of my being I received the baptism of those *parole di colore oscuro*, as the poet himself so fittingly writes, and I emerged from that immersion staggering, my lips wet with bitter salt.[22]

Two years later, in a letter to Delfina Bunge in which she speaks of her attraction for the man she will eventually marry (with disastrous consequences), she begins by quoting from Canto v and adds: "These verses sing in my mind like a catchy tune" (ii, p.97). In spite of its adolescent pretentiousness (the eighteen-year-old Ocampo is courting literary approval from an older, budding *femme de lettres*)[23] the letter illustrates the process that Ocampo's subsequent writing will tirelessly repeat. *Lo vivido* and *lo leído* form a system of interconnecting vessels, flowing, being translated, into one another. One calls effortlessly to the other: the connection is automatic, "like a catchy tune." If the flow seems to favor at times one direction over the other, it is only because time or social circumstances so demand;[24] what is important is that contact, intermingling and mutual reinforcement between the two – life and literature – are unceasing.

Sustained by the *Commedia*, the third volume of Ocampo's *Autobiografía* stands out as the one that best expresses, celebrates even, this intermingling between literature and life in one passionate performance. Narratively speaking, this volume constitutes the high point of

Ocampo's story; devoted to the great love of her life and also (not by chance, as will be seen) to her literary beginnings, it also marks the passage from the private individual of the first two volumes to the more public adult of volumes four, five and six. Less digressive than the other volumes, book three is, in all senses of the word, the most *dramatic*: it dynamically sets forth a plot and plays the self into that plot as protagonist. From the Stendhalian echoes of its title, *La rama de Salzburgo*, it proclaims its literary texture and functions like a many-layered script through which Ocampo reads herself. Whereas the script is composed of many voices, the figure that holds those literary echoes together, the model that will center the performance and serve as an emblem for the autobiographical "I," is, once more, Dante's Francesca.[25]

Why Francesca? The reference to Stendhal's *De l'amour* in the title announces the text for what it indeed is, a narrative of *amour passion*, devoted in its near entirety to the account of a long, secret relationship with her husband's cousin, Julián Martínez. That in itself might justify the translation into Ocampo's life of Francesca, of a particular version of Francesca – Francesca the eternal lover, as popularized by nineteenth-century readings of Dante. The fact that the affair Ocampo narrates, with a mixture of passion and direct-ness rare in Spanish American autobiography, male or female, in a way parallels the episode in Dante (two cousins instead of two brothers) provides further grounds for the comparison. Yet neither the superficial resemblance, nor the clandestine character of the relationship, wholly accounts for the presence of Canto v in this text. Many other references to jealous husbands and doomed lovers (*Tristan, Pelléas et Mélisande, Anna Karenina*, the *Princesse de Clèves*) have their part in this concert of voices through which Ocampo writes herself.

More to the point, it is the illicit nature of this love that connects it to other transgressive gestures in Ocampo's life. On more than one occasion, when pressed by her lover to brave public opinion and leave her husband, Ocampo holds back for fear of parental rejection. This combination – vital attraction for the forbidden curbed by fear of authoritarian repression – immediately prompts the reader to rank this love with the other interdictions imposed by (or attributed to) parental, and by extension social, intolerance. Relegated to the limits of the permissible, like the child who hides her books under the mattress, the woman meets her lover in an apartment on the outskirts of the city. Ocampo inscribes the three forbidden passions – the theatre, literature and love – in the margins of convention.

As the coded language of flowers is ritualized in nineteenth-century novels, so books, from the very beginning and especially *at* the very beginning of Ocampo's relationship, convey meaning. When all other possibilities of exchange are barred, books become a privileged means of communication – better still, of conversation and confabulation. Before effectively becoming lovers, Ocampo and Martínez use reading as a clear substitute for physical contact:

I soon got into the habit of calling him, sometimes from my singing teacher's house. We spoke briefly. We recommended books to each other. We read Colette, Maupassant, Vigny. We set up rendezvous to read them at the same time. "At ten, tonight. Can you do it?" Twenty blocks apart, I at home, he in his house, we read. Next day we discussed our reading . . . On occasion we would make a date to meet in a bookstore, to see each other from a distance. We did not greet each other. We did not go beyond looks.

(III, p. 29)

In this fecund junction of love and literature and, more specifically, in the use of the book as mediator in the unfolding of love, the presence of Francesca in Ocampo's text takes on full meaning – not only as a passionate lover, but as a reader whose sign is the book. Francesca recognizes an expression of self and the *prima radice* of her feelings as she reads. Furthermore, in an important gesture of reflection, she recognizes the mediating qualities of the book itself: "Galeotto fu il libro e chi lo scrisse."[26] As with *L'Aiglon*, Ocampo reads herself into a figure who reads, and for whom reading is allied with interdiction. And, more importantly, she is reading herself into a figure who is aware of what the process of reading achieves.[27]

It is not impertinent to recall, at this point, the illustration on the cover of this third autobiographical volume. Although the role Ocampo had in the choice is hard to determine, all six volumes having been published posthumously, *La rama de Salzburgo* is strikingly different from its companion volumes. Whereas there are photographs on the covers of the others, there is an arresting full-length painting of Ocampo on the cover of this one – a sensuous, physically challenging Ocampo, the body very much in evidence, and *a book in her hand*. This is the very portrait by Dagnan Bouveret referred to earlier, the one from which a small bust of Dante was deleted by a parental ukase which had not succeeded, however, in deleting Dante from her mind. In a sense this cover, built around the absence of Dante, turns that absence into a presence, and *re-presents* Francesca: the painting binds love's body to the body of the book, defiantly expressing – as an actress on a stage – the union of the two.

"I lived Dante, I did not read him. I received baptism from certain verses; they had been written to name me. I took notes so I would learn to read him better" (III, p.98). If one discounts the mediocre French sonnets, turned out at some governess' bidding, writing for Ocampo had been until then only a possible sequel to reading, not its systematic complement. The scribblings in the margins of Dante now mark a transition. On the one hand, they are the logical continuation "in literature" of the haphazard private journal she has kept since adolescence; on the other, they prepare her for a more sustained, visible effort, the writing, in French, of her first book, *De Francesca a Beatrice*, which was published during this love affair. That writing should finally find its form and become a public gesture at this stage in Ocampo's life is not a coincidence. It is a way of completing the meaning of Dagnan Bouveret's painting, of exhibiting, through a now triple mediation – a book about a book in a language that is not her mother tongue – that which society denied her: to speak her body and to speak her mind.[28] "This book was a substitute for a confession, for a confidence" (III, p. 105). Significantly, *De Francesca a Beatrice* is dedicated to Ocampo's lover in a coded inscription, a subversive gesture that effectively succeeds in calling attention to itself.

If Dante's Francesca is the major mediating text that governs self-portrayal in *La rama de Salzburgo*, it is by no means the only one. Not surprisingly, this third volume of the autobiography, by far the most personal and stirring of all six volumes, is also the one in which the most reading gets done, in which the most quotations appear, in which literary reference is at its most dense. The very excess of feeling – "passion is beautiful only in its excess and can only be conceived in that excess" (III, p. 32) – is matched by the excess of voices that mingle in the text. Dante, yes, but Dante contaminated: not only read through French nineteenth-century readings but read in conjunction with Stendhal (the crystallization of love), Proust (the violence of retrospective jealousy), Shakespeare ("Make thee another self, for love of me"), Eliot, when all passion is spent ("What is actual is actual only for one time"), Péguy, when her lover is dead ("C'est le sang de l'artère et le sang de la veine / Et le sang de ce coeur qui ne bat déjà plus").

In a sense, one might apply the Stendhalian notion of crystallization not only to the love that is narrated here but to the process of narration itself, an accumulation of fragmentary quotes that gradually take on meaning. Indeed, this prolific annotation of life through texts is a ˌdilated process occurring at different stages. Resort to texts takes place at the time of the experiences themselves, for *lo vivido* goes hand in hand with *lo leído*, as has been noted: Ocampo thinks and feels "in literature." But it also takes place, even more conspicuously, at the time of the autobiographical act itself. Ocampo subjects her retrieval of the past to the very same contact with literature to which she had exposed life itself: memory of life also follows a path of texts. I give but one example. At the time of her relationship with Julián Martínez, Ocampo states, she had not yet read Proust. It is when she looks back on those years, in order to narrate them, that Proust's text, which she has since read, allows her to recognize and name, within that relationship, one of the sources of its undoing – her retrospective jealousy.

Resorting to literature, in that retrieval of the past, allows for something more: it permits a reinterpretation from afar in which literature is astutely used to give the self the best part, glossing over events that might reflect on it adversely, and channeling the reading of the autobiography away from potentially thorny issues. Again, I consider Ocampo's reference to Proust. Retrospective jealousy provides one of the more poignant scenes in this volume: Ocampo, being fitted for a dress, feels jealousy arise within her as the designer's assistant innocently describes for her in detail the body of the woman who had been Martínez's lover before her. The scene, subtly combining retrospective voyeurism and rekindled desire, is remarkably effective; so much so that, for a moment, it steers the reader's attention away from another, more immediate issue that affects the relationship in a manner no less adverse – the fact that Julián himself was jealous, not precisely of past lovers Ocampo might have had but of a very concrete man with whom she was flirting in the present.

In speaking of the publication of *De Francesca a Beatrice*, I purposefully compared it to an exhibition and meant it explicitly, in a near physical sense. Indeed, this is the sense in which the verb surfaces in the negative reactions greeting Ocampo's first literary attempt. The criticism to which she was subjected proved, at the very least, that her reading was unexpected. Ocampo showed her

manuscript before publication to two prominent figures of the
Argentine establishment, Paul Groussac, the acerbic French critic
turned self-appointed mentor of the Argentine intelligentsia, and
Angel de Estrada, the highly respected aesthete and *modernista* writer
who wrote for *La Nación*. Groussac, from his lofty magisterial stance,
dismissed the piece as pedantic:

[He] mocked my choice and assured me that if I really felt a literary itch
(an itch he clearly considered masculine) it was better to choose *"personal"*
topics. Personal? This good man did not understand that *Dante for me was a
personal topic.*   (III, 107)

For reasons precisely opposite,[29] Angel de Estrada also criticizes
Ocampo's piece and recommends caution:

You tell me that these pages are written this way because this is how you
feel Dante. I know, it suffices to read them. However, this is not what
makes the publication difficult, it is the excessively personal form, *utterly
straightforward* ... When women bared their shoulders to go to the theatre
and to balls, everyone screamed. Now there are fewer screams and he who
screams does so against all of society. It has become a general *state of body*.
But you are the only innovative woman who is on familiar terms with
designers of spiritual fashion and, being alone, you will reveal a *state of
mind.*"   (III, p. 106)

Despite the comparison with the world of fashion, highly revealing of a generalized opinion on women's writing, this judgment, in
an odd way, is not inaccurate. Estrada perceives something unto-
ward that smacks of exhibitionism, of unseemly revelation, of *excess*,
and not being able to name it precisely, he translates it into physical
terms: showing one's mind, if one is a woman, is as unacceptable
as, in the past, showing one's body. But then, showing body and
mind, through the reading of Dante, was precisely Ocampo's
purpose.
    When I speak here of body, as I have in the past pages, I am not
vindicating for Ocampo a notion of woman's writing based on
physical pleasure or physiological difference – a notion held by
certain French feminists which I find perilously close to essentialist
formulations of the feminine and do not happen to share.[30] Nor, of
course, am I celebrating Ocampo's body against her, considering *it*
in lieu of her writing, as not a few masculinist critics are prone to do
when dicussing women's texts and as some of Ocampo's male

friends and would-be suitors did. Ocampo tells the story at her
expense of the time when, as a young woman in Rome, she was
invited by a courtly Italian *senatore*, who shared her passion for
Dante, to see "his most precious treasure." "I imagined – she writes
– that it was some rare edition of Dante. He brought me, instead, a
plaster mold of Pauline Borghese's breast ... This man did not take
my love for Dante seriously. To hell with the senator and to hell with
the breast [*Al diablo el senador y el seno*]" (III, p. 15). Similar
misunderstandings, less ludicrous albeit more painful, abound in
Ocampo's life. Ortega y Gasset, sensitive to her physical attraction,
extravagantly sang her "feminine" virtues while subtly putting her
down intellectually in his epilogue to *De Francesca a Beatrice* (a book
he himself had published); Hermann von Keyserling never accepted
that Ocampo's passion for his books did not prepare a way into her
bed.[31] That there is a strong physical, both sensual and sexual drive
in Ocampo, the woman – what Drieu La Rochelle, her friend and, in
the early 1930s, her lover, called her *génie charnel* (II, p. 11) – is
certain: she manifests it often enough and in different ways
throughout the six volumes of her autobiography, never reluctant to
speak of erotic desire, of the physical urge to have a child by her
lover, of menstrual blood. Yet I read her references to her body in
the autobiography as signifying something more complex – something that surely includes the concretely physical but goes beyond it,
something more like a *presence* (the way one speaks of a presence on
stage) that society would have her repress and for which her body is
the most visible sign.

Ocampo speaks complacently of the more evident, even frivolous
aspects of that presence in visual terms, narcissistically referring to
the way in which others look at her, desire her, flatter her. Her sheer
size and good looks, those commanding proportions so imposing to
acquaintances and admirers in real life ("the Gioconda of the
Pampas," Ortega would call her) are translated in her autobiographical text into an overwhelming persona. Yet there is an odd
imbalance between that physical self-assuredness and the anxiety
of speaking found so often in these writings, an anxiety compounded
by a basic situation that repeats itself in the text: Ocampo, tongue-
tied (*callada, inarticulada, muda*, are her expressions) before a voluble,
eloquent writer. These interlocutors are frequently male but not
always: Gabriela Mistral, María de Maeztu, Virginia Woolf have
the same effect of cowing her into silence. Ocampo's description of

herself and Woolf, in the very first volume of her *Testimonios*, is an accurate reflection of these flawed dialogues:

Tavistock Square, this past month of November. A small dark green door, very English, with the number squarely placed in the middle. Outside, all of London's fog. Inside, upstairs, in the light and warmth of a living-room, the panels of which have been painted by a woman, two women speak of women. They look each other over, they ask each other questions. One of them is curious; the other, delighted.

One of them has found expression, because she has been able to find herself, magnificently. The other has tried, lazily, feebly, but something within her keeps her from doing so. Precisely because she has not found herself, she cannot move further.[32]

In life, Ocampo often compensated for that lack of eloquence with gestures. They were usually munificent (selling a tiara to pay for Tagore's stay in Buenos Aires, showering Virginia Woolf, who made fun of her in return, with extravagant gifts) and often overbearing. It was as if, when the writer faltered, the *grande dame* stepped in, asserting herself where the writer could not. This too easy shifting of roles worked its way into her writing, with infelicitous consequences: moments of rare literary effectiveness are succeeded by petty grievances or imperious statements, often bearing the imprint of class. In addition to her gender, and perhaps even more than her gender, it is this hesitation between two very different forms of self-validation – literary competence and social standing – that may well account for Ocampo's final lack of writerly *authority*. It certainly accounts for the way she is so often perceived by the least kind of her critics: as a rich woman, at once fascinating and exasperating, who writes.

At their best, Ocampo's *Testimonios*, essays on subjects ranging from current world events (women's rights, the Nuremberg trials) to everyday minutiae which she considered no less worthy (traffic in Buenos Aires, the smell and colors of trees), to her encounters with books and their authors (usually her most memorable pieces) turn her lack of eloquence into an advantage. In these scattered writings, the role of the witness is Ocampo's mask of choice: if she cannot easily speak, then she will testify to the words of others. Ten collections of essays, published under a title that emphasizes that testimonial stance, record her meetings, conversations, interviews with figures as diverse as Ravel, Mussolini, Malraux, García Lorca, Anna de Noailles, Nehru, Stieglitz. And, when the *Testimonios* do not

deal directly with live interlocutors – those figures Ocampo calls
"men-books-ideas" – they deal, for the greater part, with reading
and books. In all these encounters Ocampo plays Galeotto for the
reader: she is the go-between, transmitting the voices of others. The
Testimonios are, in a sense, mini-performances in which Ocampo, to
use a metaphor taken from the French classical theatre she knows so
well, plays the role of a *suivante* to the hero or heroine of her choice.[33]
Yet as in paintings in which the artist, while ostensibly painting
another, paints himself too in the corner of the picture, so Ocampo
uses these *testimonios* as vehicles for oblique self-figuration: these
texts are no less autobiographical, finally, than the autobiography
itself. Her own tendency to silence is replaced by the voices of others,
voices that will become, as she writes them down, her own voice.
Besides testifying to the people and events in her life, Ocampo's
Testimonios, as well as her autobiography, testify to her quest for
expression, to finding a *voice* for her *presence* so that her performance
will be complete.[34]

That Ocampo's choice of a writing language was so riddled with
anxiety surely contributed in great measure to her difficulties. Torn
between a native language which she was taught to consider
inadequate (Spanish words were not "words with which one
thinks")[35] and the second language, French, in whose comforting
cadences and prestigious rhetoric she seemed to perform best, she
would start out in literature by posturing as a "French" writer.[36] If
Ocampo would gradually come to master her own language, to the
point of attaining that seemingly effortless juncture of the spoken
and the written that Borges identifies as a typically Argentine
entonación,[37] a good part of her writing, and most importantly her
autobiography, would rely till the end on duplication as a necessary
vehicle for self-expression: Ocampo continued to write first in
French, then to rewrite herself in Spanish.

(A close examination of her style, throughout the six volumes of
the autobiography, sheds light on how the process worked. Ocampo
lived long enough to translate – to repossess – only the first three
volumes, which read admirably well. The other three were
published posthumously *as if she herself had also translated them*,
although it is clear, from the inferior translation, that someone other
than Ocampo performed the task. While a disservice, prompted
perhaps by a misguided sense of loyalty, the anonymous translation
of the last three volumes proves, through its flaws and by com-

parison with the first three, to what point Ocampo rewrote her texts and rendered her linguistic duplicity unnoticeable.)

Until the end, then, the process is the same – the appropriation of texts and voices of others. Self-expression is, necessarily, a process of *alteration*: one speaks through the voice of an *other* even if that other – as in the case of Ocampo's self-translation – is a simulacrum of oneself. Could one not compare the autobiographical venture, asks Ocampo resorting once more to the theatre, to what Jouvet says of actors?: "One enters a role, slides into it, one wields the text, one wields it cunningly, *surreptitiously one replaces oneself*" (VI, 11). The process of reconstituting this *altered* voice, the culling of literary fragments and "great" voices for the purpose of self-expression, brings to mind the method of Seneca's *hypomnemata*, as described by Foucault:

> The role of writing is to constitute, with everything that has been constituted by reading, a "body" (*quicquid lectione collectum est, stilus redigat in corpus*). That body must be understood not as a body of doctrine but rather – and following the so often quoted metaphor of digestion – as the very body of him who, on transcribing his reading, makes that reading and its truth his own. Writing transforms that which is seen or heard "into strength and blood" (*in vires, in sanguinem*).[38]

In this light, Ocampo's best-known cultural venture, the founding in 1931 of *Sur* (a review that was to be, for the next forty years, one of the most influential literary journals of the Spanish-speaking world), becomes another form of (distanced) self-writing, an extension of a presence that increasingly needed to be made public.[39] The concert of voices that Ocampo transforms *in vires, in sanguinem* for her own self will become her other body, that of the review to which her name is permanently allied.

I am aware that a successful argument could be made in favor of the dependent nature of Ocampo's reading. Such an argument would highlight the fact that the reading to which she turned in search of self-expression was taken mainly from a male-authored canon; the fact that Francesca, the readerly emblem of her choice, was a character in a text within that male-authored canon; the fact that the writers she befriended, as mentors, were mostly men. To this perceived dependency of Ocampo as a woman, one could add her excessive dependency, as a Latin American, on European models; a dependency evinced not only in the texts she quotes in her own writing but in the preference for the oddly anachronistic assortment of foreigners – Gramsci next to Denis de Rougemont, for example – that became the hallmark of her review. Beatriz Sarlo perceptively interprets this *"bovarysme* with regard to European writers" as a delayed response: "One might say that *Sur* is the review that Victoria Ocampo would have wanted to read as an adolescent and a young woman. It responds, more than twenty years later, to her unfinished struggle for initiation."[40] It is not, however, my intention to evaluate *Sur* in itself, as a cultural product of a period.[41] I wish to consider instead the first aspect of Ocampo's dependency, that affecting her reading, writing and composition of self as a woman.

It is true that male presences inform Ocampo's system of self-defining voices. If Ocampo does refer frequently to women – Woolf, Anna de Noailles, the Brontës, Mistral, María de Maeztu, Adrienne Monnier – either for their live presence or for their equally live texts, she never *quotes* these women, except in those pieces she devotes, specifically, to them. In other words, although sympathetic to women's texts – witness the admirable intermingling of Ocampo's voice and that of Woolf in "Virginia Woolf in My Memory"[42] – Ocampo does not incorporate them into that larger and freer system of quotations on which she relies for voice. There appears to be a contradiction here, one that betrays a conflict between two modes of self-representation.[43] On the one hand, there is Ocampo's desire to "some day write, more or less well, but *like a woman,*" because "a woman cannot unburden herself of her feelings and thoughts in the style of a man, anymore than she can speak with a man's voice;"[44] on the other hand, there is the fact that Ocampo most often speaks, if not *with* a man's voice, *through* men's voices. Ocampo never resolved this ambivalence; nor did she ever refer, she who was aware that her writing was marked not only by her gender but by her Latin American origins, to other Latin American women writers (Gabriela Mistral being the exception) embarked on a similar quest for self-expression. This silence should be read less as a sign of snobbery, I suspect, than as what could be called an "anxiety of sorority," a case of literary sibling rivalry.[45] Like Sarmiento, Ocampo creates distance around her, in order to be perceived alone.

The question is, though, do the voices appropriated by Ocampo continue to be solely men's voices? A possible solution to the predicament created by Ocampo's ambiguity takes us back to the

scene of reading; to Ocampo not only as reader but as woman
reader. Discussing Artemisia Gentileschi's painting within a male,
pictoric tradition, Mary Jacobus writes: "In order to see herself or
be seen she has to insert herself into a preexisting narrative."[46] The
same might be said of Ocampo who, as a reader and autobiographer
who seeks self-definition through reading, can only insert herself in a
masculine lineage of texts and a masculine system of representation
– the only one available to her – all the while wishing for another.
What might be judged Ocampo's weakness could well be, given her
time and her circumstance, proof of her resourcefulness. Lacking a
voice of her own and a feminist system of representation, she
repossesses voices of the male-authored canon and, by the sheer fact
of enunciating them from a feminine "I," succeeds, much in the way
Pierre Menard did when rewriting Cervantes, in differentiating her
text. The constant misunderstandings between Ocampo and the
"men-books-ideas" she seeks so passionately (and inadvisedly) to
dialogue with, the unfamiliar slant given by her comments to
canonically "correct" texts, the feeling, so often experienced by her
reader, that her quotations, while impeccably accurate, are
somehow off-key, are all symptomatic signs, I believe, of that
difference. A different way of reading it is also a different way of
reading oneself into being. "The alterity of feminist reading is
posited, not simply in opposition to masculinist reading, not simply
as a move that carries off familiar readings and puts them to strange
uses, but rather as a move that installs strangeness (femininity)
within reading itself," writes Jacobus.[47] The alterity of self-
figuration through reading, I would argue, is a move introducing a
similar uncanniness in the autobiographical venture. It is not
surprising then that, behind these readings that Ocampo appropriates in her autobiography in order to compose her own voice, lies
a question, a *want* that echoes throughout her text and is never
satisfied: "I am the *other*. But what?" – "Soy lo *otro*. ¿Pero qué?" (I,
p. 61).

PART II

Childhood and family tales

... family tales told so often about one that eventually one has the illusion of remembering them.

Leonard Woolf, *An Autobiography*

Sweet home without style, produced
abruptly from a single piece
of rainbow-colored wax.

César Vallejo, *Los heraldos negros*

Now I am another, I cannot remember that child
even if I try. As I observe him from myself, I can't
tell what he is like. Something of him remains in me,
many objects that were once in his eyes.

Felisberto Hernández, *El caballo perdido*

4

Childhood and exile: the Cuban paradise of the Countess of Merlin

> One writes of such things in order to transmit to
> others the world view that one carries within.
> Ernest Renan, *Souvenirs d'enfance*

Of the many fictions the autobiographer resorts to in order to achieve being in the text, the one dealing with the family past, and childhood in particular, would seem, at first glance, the easiest. It is removed enough from the moment of writing to be seen as a self-contained unit that the adult can deal with in a detached yet not unsympathetic way. It is endorsed by the most elementary and unquestionable of legalities, that of the birth certificate, and finally, in accordance with a narrative convention that sees topology and genealogy – the where and the where from – as necessary beginnings to the telling of lives, it is pretty much inevitable.

However, this has not always been the case. The importance given childhood in literature, autobiographical or otherwise, is, as is common knowledge, relatively recent:[1] lives – or rather the stories of lives – had other beginnings. As in Epinal engravings, children were depicted less as themselves than as miniature grown-ups, just ripe for adulthood. Prior to the nineteenth century, self-writing had little use for the subject's first years, except as a pre-history of the self. The life stories written in Spanish America before the nineteenth century are no exception; references to childhood in Colonial times are indeed so rare that when they do appear the modern reader tends to overread them. Thus, for example, when one reads in Sor Juana Inés de la Cruz's autobiographical *Respuesta a Sor Filotea de la Cruz* (1691) how she tricked her sister's schoolmistress into teaching her to read at the age of three and how she stopped eating cheese, her favorite childhood food, because it supposedly made people

79

stupid, the temptation is great to forget the purpose of those charming recollections. In truth having little to do with childhood, they are there to bolster Sor Juana's explicit line of self-defense (her thirst for learning is in the nature God gave her), not to delight the reader with well-chosen details that anchor, if only fleetingly, the small world of a mischievous and determined little girl.[2] The modern reader, curious about childhood, finds it, anachronistically, even where it is not.

As a significant element of autobiographical writing, and indeed as a means of launching a life story, childhood recollections are slower to develop in Spanish America than in Europe. It is interesting to note, for instance, how the early Spanish American autobiographers who read Rousseau's *Confessions*, while acknowledging the general influence of the master of Geneva, seemed loath to follow him closely in the recounting of a childhood which they clearly perceived in a different light. In his autobiographical *Apuntes* (1802), the Mexican José Miguel Guridi y Alcocer shows clear signs of having read Rousseau's *Confessions* and puts to good use what Starobinski describes as the two predominant "tonalities" in the text, the elegiac and the picaresque.[3] However, Guridi rushes through the beginning of his life at a precipitous pace; out of the eighty *apuntes* that make up the eight *legajos*,[4] he devotes only four to those early years. The elegiac element is there, as the adult looks back on his childhood, but only in embryonic form; it is the subject of allusion more than of full development, as if the autobiographer did not yet feel completely free to dwell on childhood or expand it in any creative way. Guridi's reference to his early years is practically limited to the following passage:

The first ten years are the sweetest part of life and our simple pastimes then, unimportant though they may be, are more delightful than those we enjoy later. When, for example, will the finest and best bridled horse give the same pleasure as a stick held between one's legs on which to gambol around? What splendid banquet will equal in taste the bread, the jam or the fruit eaten then? When will parties, amusements, or the possession of the greatest wealth match the fun of spinning a top and playing hopscotch, or give us the same satisfaction as owning two toys, or having a doll that closes its eyes or lifts its arm when we pull on a string?

How pleasurable the feeling of those innocent childhood pastimes, of that first period in one's existence! Happy age, delectable moments of life, you pass all too swiftly but leave your traces forever engraved in memory![5]

Guridi intuits the potential of the childhood story, its capacity to charm the reader through its use of evocative trivia. However, unlike Rousseau, he is unwilling, or unable, to make full use of it. In a similar way, the Chilean José Zapiola y Cortés' entertaining memoir, *Recuerdos de treinta años (1810–1840)*, while strongly influenced by Rousseau,[6] is spare in its recollections of childhood as indeed in its composition of self. Juan Bautista Alberdi, in Argentina, while openly avowing his debt to Rousseau in his *Autobiografía*, hardly follows in his mentor's footsteps when speaking of his early years. Rousseau's name comes up at decisive moments in Alberdi's life story, is permanently associated with his discovery of literature, and a direct and poignant reference to the *Confessions* serves to qualify Alberdi's birth: "My mother ceased to exist when I was born. As a result I can say, like Rousseau, that my birth was the first of my misfortunes."[7] Yet after a few fleeting references to childhood, Alberdi, even more rapidly than Guridi, plunges into an account of adult life fully geared towards the autobiographer's performance as writer and statesman. Sarmiento himself, another reader of Rousseau, while referring in a little more detail to his childhood (and while definitely imitating the style of the *Rêveries* in the chapter of *Recuerdos* devoted to José de Oro) feels the constant urge to read into that childhood the characteristics of the public man he was to become.[8] Rousseau's validation of childhood and adolescence, in the *Confessions*, meets with mixed, mostly negative, reactions in Spanish America – at least in public. While Luis Montt criticizes it for its inconsequence – "the Gil Blas-like adventures of a vagabond youth"[9] – Lucio V. Mansilla denounces it for its cynicism.[10] One senses that, while reference to Rousseau's *Social Contract* poses no problem for the autobiographer, reference to the *Confessions* must be brief, or masked, or needs to be couched in somewhat derogatory terms.[11]

Childhood, then, was slow to be accepted, both by writers and readers, as an organic part of Spanish American self-writing. Of the many possible explanations for that delay, two appear worth considering.[12] First is a question of generic hesitancy, to which I shall return but which merits a first mention here. The Spanish American autobiographer, especially in the first half of the nineteenth century, is hard put to define himself as a writing subject within the yet unstable limits of budding national literatures. Often a direct participant, either in the struggle for independence or in the process of consolidation of the national state, he usually perceives the autobiographical venture, ill-defined for the moment as a genre, as a didactic and not wholly disinterested task. Beside the purely political memorialist intent on righting his image for posterity and thus exacting, in Gusdorf's words, "a revenge on history,"[13] there is the writer statesman, postulating himself as an exemplary figure, a civic hero doubled by a moralist whose life story will prove useful to his descendants and future compatriots.[14] Spanish American autobiography, at its inception, is basically a public story: public in the sense that it tells what can and should be told, and public because, more than satisfying the individual's need to speak of himself, it serves the public interest. There is little or no room in these texts for the *petite histoire* (such as the trifling episodes childhood usually offers) and a great desire, instead, to become part of a more important History in the making. Indeed, in some cases, what is announced as the story of an individual soon becomes, by metonymy, the story of an emerging country. Such of course is the case with Sarmiento, who writes in *Recuerdos de provincia*, "I was born in 1811, the ninth month after the 25th of May" (p. 160). The reference to the first insurrection against Spanish rule as a way of dating his birth unambiguously establishes a genetic, quasi biological link between Sarmiento and his newly independent country.[15] In authors who conceived self-writing as a form of service – "I never wrote but with a practical result in mind," observes Sarmiento,[16] and the phrase might be shared by many – it is not surprising that childhood, an uncertain period of life at best, often pleasing for its very inconsequence, be given short shrift.

Characteristically, in the debates over literary specificity and generic definition that distinguish that early part of the Spanish American nineteenth century, history and fiction are inevitably held up against one another. Autobiography, although not named directly, is perceived as a form of history (Guridi called it a *legajo*, Sarmiento a *documento*). The *petite histoire* of childhood and family tales – the stuff of a life, so to speak – is seen as pertaining to fiction and, more precisely, to historical fiction. Vicente Fidel López, one of the fathers of Argentine historiography, himself the author of an *Autobiografía* and of historical novels, is eloquent on the subject:

In my opinion, a novel may be strictly historical without having in the least to trim or to modify the truth of well-known facts. In the same way that there only remains of the lives of men the memory of their capital achievements, there only remains of the life of a people the memory of the great vicissitudes of its history. Its ordinary, *family* life, if I may call it so, disappears, for it is like the human trace that disappears with death. However, since it is true that next to the *historical* life there has always been a *family* life – in the same way that every man leaving behind memories of himself once had a face – the clever novelist may reconstruct that lost part with his imagination, freely creating the *family* life while strictly respecting the historical life, combining one with the other to reproduce the entire truth...[17]

Perceived as fiction – a reconstruction, as López sees it, by the imagination – the *family life* is acceptable in the historical *novel* but not in history itself which is where Spanish American auto-biography, for the moment, aspires to belong. The nagging sense that the "I" is a historical artifact and should be presented as such for purposes of self-validation underlies and will never quite dis-appear from Spanish American autobiographical discourse. It will eventually find itself expressed in a more subtle fashion and, with time, will even be successfully combined with a more generous rendering of the *petite histoire* of childhood and family life.

A second attitude that surely contributes to the slow development of the childhood story is the Spanish American autobiographer's changing awareness of the past. To this matter too I shall devote further comment; the issue should nevertheless be brought up at this point, if only summarily, since this changing awareness obviously affects the way in which the individual, when looking back on life in order to write it down, decides to parcel out time and place emphases. Autobiographers in the nineteenth century set out pri-marily to record, and less frequently to reminisce. Nostalgia, when it is there, is a rare luxury in these lives of active political participa-tion; it is an attitude kept in line and controlled by a calculating adult wary of, or having no time for, unbridled self-expression, at least in an autobiography. As illustrative of this point, one should note that Alberdi, while controlling his emotions towards the past in his *Autobiografía*, does not hesitate to dwell longingly on his youth in his letters – that is, in a different, more "private" genre.[18] In autobiographies, the past is clearly conceived as being at the service of the present: the "now" is clearly more important, to these achievers, than the "then," the "what I am" preferable to the "what I was."

The subordination of the past to the present and even, in a continent much given to utopias, to the future is an imperative in early nineteenth-century Spanish America. It is therefore not sur-

prising that the literature of those early years, even while touched by
French Romanticism, more than dwelling on loss tends to conceive
itself in terms of gain and, in the true spirit of the Enlightenment,
makes progress its goal. When, for example, Andrés Bello, in his
silva, "A la agricultura de la Zona Tórrida" (1826), exhorts Spanish
America to return to nature after the turmoil of the wars of
independence, it is to nature as agriculture, the source of future
prosperity – the classical topos – and not to nature fostering longing
and reverie. In addition, when the past comes up in texts of this
period, it invariably tends to the monumental. A composite of
remote (sometimes unfamiliar) myths interwoven with quasi-
contemporary exploits – such as, for example, the carnivalesque
admixture of José Joaquín de Olmedo's ode to Bolívar (1825) – the
past is a cause for celebration, not for nostalgia. As such it bypasses
personal reminiscence and, importantly, it avoids the recent, more
quotidian past. In the early nineteenth century there is no equiv-
alent of Hugo's "Tristesse d'Olympio" in Spanish America. Nor, for
that matter, is there a true poetry of ruins: Heredia's "En el teocalli
de Cholula" (1820), harking back, it too, to pre-Columbian times, is
less a mourning for that past than a denunciation of those "barbaric" times in the name of "civilized" modernity. Meditation on
the past, in general terms, seems only justified when it leads to an
aesthetics of reconstruction – an aesthetics in which the individual
has yet to find a place. Historically, this should not come as a
surprise. The immediate past of these writers is usually rooted in the
lapsed order of the Spanish colony and, as such, may seem too close
for comfort. Remembering it in personal terms (much less longing
for it) might entail an affective evaluation of that past and the world
it stood for, a risky venture that the Spanish American writer may
not be ready to tackle. That recent past, in which he was born or to
which he has close ties, is outmoded.[19] As such, it is the one he needs
the most to forget.

> ... a plant from Havana, a plant from my country.
> When I smelled its perfume I trembled and wept
> a heavy tear on its petals.
> Condesa de Merlin, *Viaje a La Habana*

There is a way of distancing yet not avoiding the evocation of a
personal past in nineteenth-century Spanish America, a way, not

voluntarily chosen, that validates nostalgia as more than a solipsistic exercise. It is the literature of exile (to be sure also a genre of European Romanticism) in which the past is perceived as an irrecoverable world, a *patria* out of reach in time and space, only recaptured through the detailed recreation of writing. It is indeed through the nostalgia of exile, a chink in the unblemished surface of the monumental past, that the *family life*, as López called it, appears in the text. I shall not stop at the abundant examples of this reminiscing stance in poetry, its favorite mode of expression; José María Heredia's "Vuelta al Sur" and Juan Antonio Pérez Bonalde's "Vuelta a la Patria" are only two of many,[20] perhaps the most eloquent. In prose, and more specifically in autobiographical writing, its manifestations are more interesting in that (unlike the more conventional nostalgia found in lyric poetry) they are more detailed, and certainly more individualistic. They introduce an element of pleasure in the recreation of the past – a relish in the telling akin to that of gossip – that allows for fuller versions of the family tales. A good example, early in the nineteenth century, is *Mis doce primeros años* by María de las Mercedes Santa Cruz y Montalvo, better known as the Condesa de Merlin.

An exile from Cuba, although not for political reasons, Mercedes Merlin (as she signs herself in her letters to her compatriots) writes in France what may well be the first account of childhood in Spanish American literature. Written in French, and soon thereafter translated into Spanish, the book, *Mis doce primeros años*, suffered the misfortune that so often befalls such hybrids: considered neither French nor Spanish American, it remained unclaimed by either literature. The fact that the author was better known for her social than for her literary graces – she held a well-frequented *salon* in Paris during the monarchy of Louis Philippe, was a patroness of music, and wrote a life of Malibran – may account in part for the benign neglect from which she suffered as a writer.[21] The fact that she was a woman, at a time when writing, especially in Spanish America, was seen as a man's privilege, doubtless contributed an extra measure of oblivion.

The first of two autobiographical texts, *Mis doce primeros años* (1831), records the author's childhood from her birth in Havana in 1789 till her departure for Madrid, in 1802, to be reunited with a mother she had hardly seen since birth. As Adriana Méndez Rodenas convincingly argues, the text may be seen as an exercise in historiography *sui generis*, an "arch-text of origins" that coincides with – or rather antedates – Heredia's vision of Cuba from afar.[22] What I shall consider here, however, is the way in which this text, as an autobiography, differs from other Spanish American autobiographies of the time. One of the reasons for this difference is that *Mis doce primeros años* was written by a woman; the other, that it was written *outside* Spanish America. The look from afar affects the autobiographical stance: the "I" writes from another place. This truism, while applicable to autobiographical writing in general, attains material reality in the case of the exile. He or she writes, quite literally, from another country, from another culture, or from another language. The attempt to recapture a past that is marginal to the present of self-writing makes for a dislocating exercise: self and past are mutually exclusive, they have been torn asunder. The past can only be integrated into the present through an exercise in longing.

I do not speak here of those cases of temporary exile (Sarmiento is a good example) in which the author, hopeful of return, strives for a dynamic recreation of the past that will link up, quite naturally, with the present and open a door to the future. In cases such as these, exile – the place where the "I" writes itself – is not considered permanent but is rather a passing phase. The exile I am interested in here, that of the Condesa de Merlin, is of another nature. It is not transitory but definitive and, one might add, self-defining. Mercedes Merlin finds her identity as a writer *in* exile and *because of* exile. Only from the otherness she has, quite literally, espoused – she takes on her French husband's name and writes her memoirs in French – can she gain access, obliquely, to the scene of writing. Only by accepting loss (an idea totally repugnant to many of her ambitious male contemporaries) does she regain, on paper, her country and her childhood. The recreation of family life, which Vicente Fidel López saw as a reconstruction through imagination, becomes a reconstruction through the faculty that most resembles it, the faculty to reminisce. Indeed, Merlin opens her recollections on a reminiscing note.

What the reader is about to read is not a novel. It is the simple story of my childhood recollections and the result of chance. One summer afternoon, as I wandered alone over the countryside, immersed in sweet melancholy, I felt transported, little by little, into the past. There I searched for those moments when I thought I had glimpsed the image of happiness, and my country and my childhood came up quite naturally in my mind. It was like a sweet dream and, wishing to prolong it, I took up my pen when I returned home and drew up this quick sketch of my first impressions in life.

In dedicating it to my friends, I feel I am taking them into my confidence. I only ask of them a little sympathy in return. Far be it from me to pretend to be an author.

I think because I feel, and I write what I think. That is all my art.[23]

This introduction opts for a Romantic aesthetics of recollection in its most elegiac vein. Like the other Spanish American auto-biographers of the period, the Condesa cherishes her Rousseau: "Rousseau and his writings made me lose my mind" [*me trastornaban la cabeza*] (p. 111).[24] Unlike her male counterparts, however, she pays little attention to Rousseau's self-vindicating streak (for which she has little use), and is therefore better able to hear, in her exile, the voice of longing and reverie. Her autobiography is the prolong-ation of a vision, a *dulce sueño* that writing helps keep alive. In addition, the introduction differs vastly from autobiographies of the period claiming too to be "confidential." In most of the latter, the term "confidential" is not so much a reference to what is being told as it is a narrative ploy, a means of seducing the reader by privileging him as a recipient. Sarmiento and Alberdi use the term, as had Benjamin Franklin before them.[25] Mercedes Merlin's recol-lections set out to be a confidence and keep their promise (insofar as a published text can be confidential) by narrating the quotidian in a *ton mineur* that courts the reader's sympathy more than his admir-ation. Finally, the Condesa's opening statement, by belittling her own importance and that of her text – she is not an "author," her text is but a "quick sketch" – deviates from the monumental "I," that self-conscious historical creature nineteenth-century auto-biographers are prone to choose for their *persona*, and allows for the natural introduction of the *petite histoire*. The fact that the Condesa is a woman, more visible socially than intellectually, surely accounts for this self-deprecating pose, not infrequent in intelligent women of means whose education has been neglected and who, one day, discover their literary vocation in a male-oriented literary scene. (Victoria Ocampo, in twentieth-century Argentina, is a prime example of such an attitude.)[26] In sum, it is the woman's dubious stature as an *author* that paradoxically affords her greater freedom in the autobiographical venture. Not subjected to the strictures of the genre – because of her gender she has no stature as a writer and no pretensions to historical documentation – Mercedes Merlin is free to indulge in what her male Spanish American contemporaries tend to repress.

The story the Condesa has to tell, if limited to facts, seems hardly the idyllic childhood her introduction has prepared for us; instead, it suggests a story of childhood uncertainties and abandonments, a bit of Dickensiana from the tropics. Mercedes Santa Cruz y Montalvo is the first-born child of the extremely wealthy Count and Countess of Jaruco, themselves barely more than children when their daughter is born:

I was born in Havana. My father, the descendant of one of the first families in the city, on leaving childhood found himself the possessor of an enormous fortune. He fell in love and, when he was fifteen, married my mother who had just turned twelve, was beautiful as the dawn, and exhibited all the natural charms that heaven, in all its munificence, can bestow on a human being. Their first daughter filled them with joy and, one might add, with surprise, especially my mother who had barely left off playing with dolls. Thus she was not in the least disappointed when told I was a girl . . .

(pp. 22–33)

This playful attitude – paternity and maternity as nursery make-believe – is not without distressing results. When a dying relative of the young father summons him to Europe a few months later, he sails from Cuba with his wife, entrusting the child to the care of her maternal great-grandmother, a loving matriarch she calls *Mamita* and whom she will come to idolize. Supposed to last six months, the parents' absence prolongs itself throughout the better part of Mercedes' childhood. More than eight years would pass before the child was to see her father, who reluctantly returned to Cuba in 1798, on a mission; it would be even longer before she saw her mother, who never went back to the island. The Count and Countess had acquired a taste for Madrid, had set up house there, and had started a new family.

Mercedes Merlin does not record her reaction to her parents' abandonment, stating, rather improbably, that "[m]y happiness had been pure and without clouds from the day I was born till the day I was separated from *Mamita*" (p. 60). In the absence of father and mother, *Mamita*, as so many portentous Spanish American matriarchs – the *mamás viejas* or *mamás grandes* of Spanish American literature – becomes the origin, the genealogical source that justifies the child:

> [A]fter having found positions for her eleven sons and consolidated their fortunes, she commanded love and respect from those surrounding her. I remember being present at several family reunions in her house where one might count ninety-five persons, standing side by side. I was the last link in the chain. (p. 24)

The father's temporary return breaks that chain, separating the child from *Mamita*. What follows in *Mis doce primeros años* is a story of separation, interruption and seemingly thoughtless, therefore all the more poignant, neglect. Arbitrariness seems to rule Merlin's family romance. Although the father "seemed to want to compensate for his past indifference by generously granting all my desires" (p. 28) he sends Mercedes off as a boarder to the convent of Santa Clara, believing *Mamita* too lenient a guardian. The text registers the child's sense of entrapment within the rigid community, the pleas to her uncompromising father for release, the passionate friendship with a lonely, romantically mysterious nun who helps her escape back to *Mamita*, the new separation that is imposed on her. One last, decisive gesture from the father – to take the child to Spain to her mother – cleaves this life in two and marks a watershed in the text. Signifying the greatest uprooting, it takes alienation to a point of crisis; at the same time, in the child's eyes, it is a token of the greatest reconciliation. Thus, separation will continue to mark this text, scattering a self in the making, disrupting any attempt at coherent self-composure. The place of origin is at odds with the family romance. Cuba (with its synecdoche, *Mamita*) is synonymous with the abandonment of the parents. Conversely, reunion with the parents is synonymous with the abandonment of Cuba. The acceptance of one simultaneously precludes the possibility of living out the other, banishes it from the present to a distant, *other* time.

At the beginning of her narrative, when referring to her parents' crucial abandonment, Merlin resorts to euphemism as a form of denial: "This first event of my life had a huge influence on my education and my destiny" (p. 23). As the text progresses, the autobiographer's urge to embellish wanes and her straightforwardness when describing the true dimensions of her plight increases. However, if *Mis doce primeros años* finally does spell out the

child's deprivation, the figure of the father himself, and indeed that
of the mother, appear untainted. Writing thirty years later, the
daughter dissipates blame, interprets shortcomings in a favorable
light:

The rigor he had used with me was not really his, did not agree with his
character. My age was so close to his that oftentimes when in my company
he found it difficult to play the role he felt he should be playing. He finally
came to recognize the mistake ... But my father could not bring himself to
admit his injustice to me in my presence; if I interpreted his feelings, it was
because of the increased love and the extreme generosity he showed me.

(p. 77)

   Merlin's first move, complying with the unwritten rules of
decorum, is to conceal in part, or at least to excuse, a lack. Yet her
story is more explicit than meets the eye, more explicit than perhaps
even she is aware of. The first part of her recollections, corresponding to the years spent in Cuba, covertly brings up other voices that
do tell obliquely of that lack, that subvert the very image of restored
family harmony that *Mis doce primeros años*, on one level, strives to
create. Surprisingly spare in its depiction of secondary characters,
the text focuses nonetheless on five characters, characters who have
remained sufficiently present in Merlin's mind for her to devote to
four of them what amounts to a brief but no less eloquent secondary
story and, to the fifth, a full-blown narrative.[27] That the Condesa is
using these characters – four slaves and a cloistered nun – as partial
projections of herself, and their stories as self-reflections, as "allo-
biographies," to use the term coined by Richard Butler,[28] is
obvious: through the telling of these "others" – five victims of
authority whose plights, in some way, she makes her own – she is, in
fact, revealing her own untold story.
   A set piece relying on the more obvious clichés of the period, even
in its unlikely epistolary form, the romance of Sor Inés is the least
interesting of these secondary narratives. The confession of the
mysterious, melancholy nun who helped Merlin escape from the
convent is a story of thwarted love and repeated adversity, rich in
melodramatic touches, fatal gestures and ominous signs. It does,
however, start out with a theme – paternal injustice and neglect –
that is everpresent, if masked, in the Condesa's own life story.
Despite the superficial similarities between the nun's story and
Merlin's life, there is a very basic difference: instead of passing over

the father's behavior lightly, or making excuses for his unthinking intolerance, the story of Sor Inés, compensating with alacrity for what remained unsaid in Merlin's autobiography, is quite explicit on the subject of the father's cruelty.

The episodes concerning slaves are of greater interest, in that they are taken very directly from the child's everyday experience. It is not my purpose here to evaluate, as have others, Mercedes Merlin's ambiguous stance towards slavery.[29] What does seem important is the way in which she resorts, perhaps unwittingly but nonetheless systematically, to a group whose place in society was essentially uncertain, whose freedom of movement was nil and whose very identity depended on a higher authority, to play out her own basic comedy of origins and make visible its fissures, its contradictory texture.

Three of the slave episodes are constructed according to a similar triangular pattern. The father and the slave are at opposite extremes; between them stands the child, systematically playing the good role, systematically interceding, correcting flaws and restoring harmony. In the first story, she asks her father to free a runaway slave and her wish is granted. In the second, she begs her father to allow a young and sturdy female slave to work in the drying house and not in the sugar mill itself so that she not be separated from her baby; again the wish is granted. In the third, prior to her departure from Cuba, Merlin intercedes yet again, in favor of her nanny, a slave who had already once refused her freedom, when it was offered her, to remain close to her charge. On this occasion, the favors asked of the father are manifold; not only that Mama Dolores be granted her freedom once more but that her children also be freed, and, in addition, that they be given a house and a bit of land. Mercedes herself, like a miniature lady bountiful, supervises the building and furnishing of the new house. Before leaving for Europe, she has the satisfaction of seeing Mama Dolores' family reunited and eternally grateful to her for her generosity.

In all these incidents Merlin gives herself the best role. Self-aggrandizement is not absent from the autobiographer's designs as she retells these exemplary episodes that bring to mind the actions of the Comtesse de Ségur's near-perfect little girls. Beneath this gloss of virtue, however, the child's participation in these incidents suggests another meaning. All three episodes may be read as projections, and corrections, of some flaw in her family situation.

The first shows an individual deprived of his freedom by a figure of authority; the second, a mother who begs not to be separated from her child; the third (significantly enough, on the eve of the child's departure from her homeland), the vicarious restoration of the family romance. Compensation and satisfaction are achieved here not through dreams and fabulations but by projection and displacement. In showing how the child could mend the lives of others, the autobiographer only reveals more glaringly the unmendable quality of her own. As for the remaining slave episode, it follows a somewhat different pattern: it is the recollection of the child's encounter with a distraught female slave mourning the death of her baby and it is the one break Merlin cannot mend. The fact that this fourth episode reproduces the fantasy to which neglected children resort in order to punish their parents – imagining their own death and their mother's inconsolable grief – seems to confirm the compensatory nature of these episodes.

The Condesa de Merlin's desire to restore harmony goes beyond this oblique and creative tampering with her own family romance. It is not by chance, after all, that her most flamboyant charitable intervention – that of freeing her nanny's family and reuniting its members – takes place just before her departure from Cuba: the gesture is emblematic of a more general strategy of reconciliation and embellishment that operates throughout the text. Like her nanny's family, Cuba must be "fixed," restored before departure:

I wanted no one to be dissatisfied with me when I left Havana, so while my father occupied himself with the preparations for the trip, I took care of the affairs of my heart. I had only debts of gratitude to pay ... The memory of our past pleasures only brings longing to our souls; the memory of our sorrows only renews those sorrows; and both pleasures and sorrows, elusive even when they occur, appear later on in our imaginations as ancient paintings, half-faded and altered by time. However, when memory takes us back to the little good we have done, we recover the same sweet sensation, alive and identical in every way to how it was then.   (p. 87)

This virtuous meddling, interpreted in retrospect as a successful means to protect a happy past from the erosion of time, allows a very provident child to stock up on pleasant memories that the autobiographer will later put to good use. For it is not that, like her master Rousseau, the Condesa calls up only the good from her childhood forsaking the bad; it is simply that, thanks to the manipulation to which she has subjected her past, there is no bad. The childhood past in Cuba *must be* happy. Thus, in a sense, the opening lines of *Mis doce primeros años*, where the Condesa claims to find "an image of happiness" in her childhood and in her country of origin, are not inaccurate in spite of the facts themselves. The autobiographer here sets out to find the goodness she herself has taken the precaution to store.

The traumatic departure from Cuba, "at the age where habits have such tender roots" (p. 91), marks the end of the Condesa's childhood and its continuation in the realm of the imaginary; it signifies the difference between living (in) Cuba and imagining Cuba from afar. It also marks, most importantly, the beginning of the child's interest in books, practically nonexistent while on the island: "I barely knew how to read or write" (p. 97). This interest develops, quite literally, as she is borne away from her homeland. On the ship she "expressed the wish to continue studying French" (p. 94) and was coached by an officer in her readings of Racine; once in Madrid, she read everything her mother would allow, especially Madame de Staël. Little by little, Cuba would become a literary construct for the Condesa. Forty years later, when writing *La Havane*, the autobiographical account of her first trip back to Cuba since childhood,[30] she would reconstruct her island less from direct observation than from notes provided at her request by Cuban writer friends, from unacknowledged borrowings from *costumbrista* authors and from her own memories.[31] Rediscovery came to her less from what she saw on that trip than from what she read, remembered and imagined.

The elegiac, clearly literary character of the Condesa de Merlin's recreation of the homeland in *Mis doce primeros años* was not lost on the more insightful of her compatriots. In Havana, Domingo del Monte, reviewing the newly published French version, praised the text for "that sweet love of the homeland . . . which we consider the purest feeling of the heart,"[32] and accurately placed it in a literary tradition, pointing out its affinities with other elegiac texts. These other texts were not Spanish American (nor even Spanish), for the Condesa's nostalgic reminiscing and intimate tone lacked Hispanic antecedents; they were, instead, Chateaubriand's *René* and Lamartine's *Méditations*. Paradoxically, however, del Monte chides the author for the inevitable consequences of the very elegiac aspect he praises: he calls attention to the text's inaccuracies and anachronisms, even when he finds them to a point "excusable given the time that separates the observation of the subject from the painting of the picture."[33] What del Monte does not see is that *Mis doce primeros años* must perforce be anachronistic: it recreates what has been (or what the author imagines has been), not what is.

In spite of this auspicious beginning, *Mis doce primeros años* was not a widely read text in Spanish America and has indeed slumbered, practically unheeded, except by the very few – writers like Cabrera Infante, Carpentier, Arenas – who on occasion pay its author homage. More than thirty years would go by before childhood recollections of this kind gained acceptance in Spanish America as a way of structuring the past. Even then, this acceptance was achieved outside autobiography: the immense popularity of a novel, *María* (1867) – incidentally, a text also dealing with harsh paternal authority and powerless individuals – would be responsible for giving the nostalgic recreation of the childhood paradise literary standing in Spanish America.

Successive generations of readers have hailed Jorge Isaacs' novel as one of the highlights – perhaps the most brilliant – of nineteenth-century Spanish American fiction. Critics unanimously agree: *María*, they believe, arrived in a most timely way to legitimate a specific literary discourse, that of Romanticism. Most of those critics, however, have stopped short at this conclusion, unwilling to explore the reason for *María*'s phenomenal success or to discover, precisely, what the novel gave legitimacy to. Thus the enormous impact of the novel has been reduced to the fact that it was a well-told story of ill-fated love, more or less in the tradition of Benjamin Constant, made all the more poignant of course by the foreseeable death of the heroine. As a result of this reduction, the general criterion to judge *María* has been invariably lachrymose: tears are shed and those tears in some way ratify the novel's excellence. No one has stopped to consider other possible implications of this mournful stance, nor to inquire further into the reasons for *María*'s favorable reception. For *María* is indeed a legitimating text – not merely of the Romantic sentimental novel, Spanish American style, but of an ideological posture that exceeds generic boundaries and affords a new look at the past. If tears flow in *María* – and they do: the author himself invites his readers to weep – they flow for more than a lost love. From the beginning, multiple

signs point to a larger loss, one for which the death of the loved one
(the María of the title) is but a token: it is the loss of a childhood
paradise and, more concretely, the loss of the family home. Isaacs'
novel, in a masterly gesture, incorporates the *petite histoire* of the
immediate past – of his own immediate past, as we know, although it
is not my purpose here to read *María* as an autobiography – and
succeeds in giving it the stature of myth.[34]

The *petite histoire* that Isaacs recreates through the evocation of his
first-person narrator is, like that of the Condesa de Merlin, embellished by longing and desire. The unsavory aspects of the family
romance – notably the harshness of a thrifty father who cannot
tolerate weakness and loss – are glossed over, never taken at face
value; the ambiguous crisscrossings of desire and emotion within
the family circle, striking even in those pre-Freudian times, are
defused (or perhaps rendered blatant) by the sheer innocence with
which they are evoked.[35] The past was good, the text tells us again
and again, working against the evidence that it clearly was not,
patiently building a lyric imposture of incredibly seductive power.
And that past reconstructed so diligently coincides – unlike the
monumental recreations of Olmedo or even the prestigious gallery
of forebears proposed by Sarmiento – with the most immediate,
individual, past, the one left behind days, hours before. There is no
future in *María* or rather its future is its past: from the very
beginning the text is a protracted farewell.

Unlike the Condesa de Merlin in her enhanced recreation of
childhood, Isaacs has an eye for evocative trivia and knows how to
anchor nostalgia with detailed, if selective, precision. He is a master
of what Richard Coe calls *curiosa nostalgica*: "the minutiae of daily
life, familiar to anyone of that generation but now unknown and
unrecorded, are details of a manner of existence which was fundamentally acceptable and therefore *right*; and so their passing can
inspire nothing but regret."[36] Thus the eminently satisfying recreation of objects, meals, everyday occupations and petty rituals
gives structure to this idyllic past and, at the same time, makes it
ageless. Protected from chronology, the past in *María* is akin to that
cyclical time Bakhtin observes in ancient literatures: "an idealized,
agricultural everyday life, one interwoven with the times of nature
and myth."[37]

Isaacs' urge to reconstruct the childhood paradise does not stem,
as does that of the Condesa de Merlin, from geographic exile. Yet

the theme of exile pervades this text: on an anecdotal level, it is significantly connected to the figure of the father and, on a metaphoric level, it is to be traced in the many forms of loss and banishment alluded to in the novel. One of the very real losses artfully concealed by textual legerdemain is a decisive *material* loss: the father suffers a financial setback the results of which (although only hinted at in the text) definitely jeopardize the family's security, its social standing and signal the replacement of one form of production by another. It is this reversal that shatters, as much as the tragically thwarted love story and perhaps even more, the family's harmony, threatening to banish its members from the patriarchal paradise.

I mention Isaacs' novel because I believe *María* has considerable bearing on Spanish American attitudes towards the past. Vindicating the *family history* in its most minute, though far from insignificant, detail, *María* provides a concrete, Spanish American mold for the timeless *topos* of paradise lost. It marks the inauguration of the patriarchal archive and makes the writer its guardian and record-keeper, establishes him, as it were, as an official *memorator*. Let it be remembered that *María* was published in 1867, a time of political and cultural reorganization throughout most Spanish American countries that led to a conversion from old to new ways of production. If not a period of political turmoil, it is – under the patina of order and progress – a period of deep, often disquieting, social and economic transformations, the ideological consequences of which will be decisive in the shaping of Spanish America. But it is also, after times of strife and anarchy, a period of relative calm, conducive to an ideological reassessment of the most recent past. *María*, with its prettified recreation of the family romance, comes as a consolation and a relief. As if endowed with talismanic power, it reassuringly provides the means to look at that past and to relish what it has to offer – which is, after all, what has been stored in it from the very beginning. Writing one's childhood can be a form of investment, a capitalistic gesture; husbanding the products of the past, as embellished by memory, can result in an act of power, an attribution of privilege. Indeed, the family tale is not unlike a personal fortune, to be shared with peers and preserved from outsiders. Not surprisingly, it will also often lead to a dreamy exercise in collective narcissism, a gazing into an officiously selective mirror that only flatters the onlooker and his look-alikes.

5

A school for life: Miguel Cané's *Juvenilia*

Let us tighten the circle and watch over it.
Miguel Cané, *De cepa criolla*

As much as a desire for conservation, defensiveness may inform the
need to remember the past. Under the patina conferred upon them
by nostalgia, childhood and family tales can be provocative ideological statements, especially at times when the autobiographer
perceives himself – and the peers he would have share his more or
less fantasized communal experience – to be threatened. A particular case in point is that of the Argentine writers of the generation
of 1880 (Lucio V. Mansilla, Miguel Cané, Lucio Vicente López,
Eduardo Wilde, Eugenio Cambaceres), a loose group whose reason
for being owes as much to chronology as it does to social class.[1]
Prosperous bourgeois for the most part, these writers occupy
prominent and powerful positions in Argentine public life: they are
diplomats, politicians and jurists, and simultaneously devote considerable time (and a sustained, often perplexed attention) to the
practice of literature. In their writings, they cultivate a fragmentation that is as much aesthetic as it is ideological; shunning generic
categories, they also shun a univocal authorial attitude that might
prove too explicit and thus confine them to a single image. The
literature of the 1880s in Argentina is much given to creative
digression – a fireside chat, a well-told story, a pleasant recollection,
a well-placed joke. Writing for friends and family (*Entre-Nos*, the title
of Mansilla's collection of *causeries*, aptly qualifies the literary
production of the whole generation), these writers, not surprisingly,
often refer to a past shared with their readers and, again not
surprisingly, make autobiography one of their preferred modes of
expression. More importantly, several of them devote works to their

97

childhoods. Lucio Vicente López, the son of the historian, looks back to childhood in his strongly autobiographical novel, *La gran aldea*. Two others make their greatest contribution in the form of childhood memoirs: Eduardo Wilde writes *Aguas abajo*, published posthumously in 1914, and Miguel Cané writes *Juvenilia* (1882). Of these two, Wilde's text is the more seductive; however, for reasons that exceed literary merit, I shall postpone it in favor of Cané's *Juvenilia*, a text which, like *María*, earned immediate (and, in Argentina, undying) popularity.

Although a childhood story, and a nostalgic one at that, *Juvenilia* does not celebrate the homestead nor does it dwell on family life. Paradise lost is no longer rustic (the idyllically preindustrial valley of Cauca, in *María*) but urban (the city of Buenos Aires as it evolves from sprawling town to bustling metropolis). Nature, as a setting for childhood nostalgia, has been replaced by culture, family has been substituted by a broader (though, as we shall see, no less intimate) community. Within an already protected cultural construct (what Angel Rama would later term *la ciudad letrada*), Cané carves out another, more protected space whence to celebrate childhood, the prestigious Colegio Nacional de Buenos Aires where he spent six years as a boarder.

The schoolboy story is, of course, a set piece, one that would earn increasing popularity in the nineteenth and twentieth centuries as a childhood picaresque, benign or mordant according to the author's point of view. It is important to note that the genre (if one may call it that) had not manifested itself in Spanish America before Cané. One comes close to it in those sections of Guridi y Alcocer's *Apuntes* devoted to his early days in the seminary, one of them suitably entitled *Travesuras y gramática*, that is, pranks and grammar. But Guridi, eager as he is to go beyond those carefree years in order to highlight his later victimization by the Mexican ecclesiastical establishment, does not devote full attention to that period of his childhood. Incidentally, till late in the nineteenth century, seminaries, imbued with the spirit of scholasticism, would have been the only places in Spanish America affording the closed *locus* necessary to schoolboy sagas. The fact that these institutions usually bred unimaginative conformism or resentful dissent made them highly unlikely locations for an idealized recreation of the childhood past. That, besides the scant attention devoted to childhood stories in general, may explain both the enduring scarcity of such pieces and the praise that greeted Cané for what was unquestionably, given its context, a highly original text.[2]

There is no evidence that Cané had read Thomas Hughes' *Tom Brown's Schooldays*, published in 1857, but we do know, from his frequent references, that he was quite familiar with Dickens and especially partial to *David Copperfield*. Kipling – with whom the paternalistic and xenophobic Cané might have shared more than one attitude – had yet to write *Stalky and Co.* (1890). If I think of *Tom Brown* and of *Stalky*, it is because *Juvenilia* presents remarkable affinities with them, even if it does not share their narrative techniques. A conservative text, it indulges in the celebration of the formative years as a privileged period from which the boy emerges a better man, a potentially worthy citizen, and the possessor of (as Kipling put it) "Truth and God's Own Common Sense, / Which is more than knowledge."[3] Like those two related texts, *Juvenilia* shies away from any sign of disorder and ignores anything that might threaten the constructive quality it seeks for itself. This is not Musil's *Young Törless*, this is not Vargas Llosa's *Time of the Hero*; even the violence or mindless childish brutality that does appear in Hughes and in Kipling (the better to be overcome of course) is absent from Cané's benign and calculatedly good-humored re-creation.[4]

Juvenilia was published in 1882, in Vienna, when the author was thirty-one years old. The reader may have difficulty keeping this fact in mind, given the exaggerated aura Cané bestows on his recollections and the sense of distance and longing with which he evokes them. The first page suffices to set the regretful tone:

I confess in all truth that when setting down these recollections from my schoolboy days I only intended to while away long and lonely hours, many of them spent, as is now the rule in my life, far away from my country. Melancholy hours, unpleasantly weighted down by nostalgia, they would light up with the inner light of reminiscence as I evoked the memories of my childhood and my pen summoned smiling scenes from the past, driving away the shadows as birds are driven away from ruins by the oncoming morning light.   (p. 27)

This, thinks the reader, reinforced in his impressions by the heavy-handed *ubi sunt* motif that appears throughout the introduction, is the work of a man well along in life who resorts to pleasant memories as an antidote to end-of-the-road "shadows."

But the reader is wrong of course. Cané is in his prime and is only going back thirteen years into his past; *Juvenilia* is not a product of old age, as is the case with many regretful recollections, but Cané's second published volume and, it could be argued, his first real book.[5]

Several reasons might explain Cané's distancing strategy. The first and most obvious is of an aesthetic nature: setting these memories beyond reach, far into an irrecuperable past, is clearly a meliorative technique. It is also a self-serving one, implying that the author rereads the past in the light of a rich, accumulated experience and comments fruitfully on life's lesson. The image of the wise old man is enhanced by that of the philosopher.[6] Other, purely biographical reasons for Cané's lofty attitude should also be kept in mind. For example, Cané's many achievements in the public sphere – doctor in jurisprudence at twenty-one, member of Parliament at twenty-three, Postmaster General at twenty-nine, Ambassador at thirty – may well have made him feel like the elder statesman he impersonates so well in *Juvenilia*. Finally, the fact that he wrote the book on one of his many diplomatic missions, far away from home, must surely have reinforced the psychological distance between the present-day adult and the child left behind. All these reasons doubtless play a role in Cané's choice of his reminiscing stance. However there are other, perhaps less evident reasons for this authoritarian, *fatherly* posture: a close reading of *Juvenilia* gradually discloses, within this apparently simple and pleasant little book, an ideological position that is not so simple – and, at times, not so pleasant.

Cané's entrance to the Colegio Nacional occurs days after his father's death. This particular timing, the first chapter tells us, was in fact chosen by the young Cané:

I was to begin school three months after my father's death. The sorrow at home, the constant reminder of our grief, my mother's silent weeping made me wish to shorten the wait and I myself asked to begin as soon as the funeral was over.   (p. 39)

The weight of Miguel Cané senior's death on his son, and on his son's book, is of singular importance. A man of letters himself, a good friend of Alberdi and a member of the ground-breaking generation of 1837, the father died without having fulfilled his promise as a writer and a scholar, a fact resented by the son who attributes it to the confusion of the period in which he lived.[7] In a laudatory piece entitled "My Father" – a text viewed by Cané as a prologue of sorts to *Juvenilia*[8] – the son evokes his father in a striking way:

My positive memories begin with my father's death. It came in 1863, when I was twelve years old. Although his countenance, his expression, his tone (sometimes severe, sometimes loving) at different moments of his life come up in my mind like a clear, spiritual vision, the final image of him was so violent that, each time I try to recall the lively after-dinner conversations, brimming with intelligence, each time I try to conjure my father's face – his expressive eyes alight with enthusiasm as he spoke of art and literature, of emotions experienced in his travels, of the turmoils of his agitated life – a veil of shadows covers everything. What prevails is the lifeless, fatigued, inert face of the end, the labored breathing and, finally, the supreme stillness of repose.[9]

"My Father" culminates in a poignant note: "a thought haunts me constantly like a dream of vanished happiness: Oh to have lived the life of the mind and the life of the heart at my father's side!" (p. 22). But Cané's celebration is also an impassioned effort to excuse the father's shortcomings. This exquisite man of letters and protector of the arts never published a book; all he wrote "were fugitive pieces, impressions jotted down in passing, scenes from his travels, improvisations of the moment," while dreaming of writing "the national novel, the one that is yet to be written, the one we shall not see, the one our children will write" (pp. 20–21). Cané's portrait of his father could be seen, not inaccurately, as a summary of his own performance. He too produced ephemeral pieces, had a project for a national novel, *De cepa criolla*, which he left unfinished, and also wrote (as did most of his contemporaries) in a fragmentary way. Yet unlike his father he did produce one complete, coherent, well-rounded book – *Juvenilia* itself.

Adolfo Prieto argues persuasively that in the latter part of the nineteenth century, Argentine autobiographers often express a sense of displacement, even failure, when measuring their lives against those of their illustrious forebears, notably of their own fathers.[10] Basing his view on the autobiographies of Carlos Guido y Spano and Lucio V. Mansilla, both of whom had inordinately strong father figures to look up to,[11] Prieto proposes that self-irony and flippancy be seen as a way to attenuate pressure, as a diversion from the demands the autobiographer feels are imposed upon him.

Less convincingly, however, Prieto argues against a similar reading of Cané, disengaging him (and also disengaging Eduardo Wilde, again questionably) from the anxiety of paternal influence. In neither writer, Prieto claims, is the father figure so cumbersome that it justifies the self-irony and humor of the texts.[12]

Yet *Juvenilia*, that most charming of texts, those "childish adventures from a happy, self-mocking adolescent epic,"[13] is seriously and indelibly marked by the father. The fact that *Juvenilia* commences with the father's death and that Cané, immediately before undertaking his childhood memoirs, feels the need to write "Mi padre," conjuring the dead man's "lifeless, fatigued, inert face" as if to give it new life, shows how strongly the two – father and *colegio* – are linked, at least in his mind. In addition, it shows how necessary it was for the son to come to terms, in some way, with the figure of authority he had just lost, before embarking on a cultural adventure that would lead him, precisely, to emulate that figure.

As presented in *Juvenilia*, the school experience is a continuation of the father's lesson and at the same time a way of blotting out his death. If Cané claims that his positive memories begin when his father's life ends – that is, when he enters school – it is because (as the Condesa de Merlin and Isaacs before him) he has chosen to store only the good, or else he has chosen what amounts to the same, to read his past only in a flattering light. The positive character of *Juvenilia* is twofold. On a first level, these memories are positive because, read retrospectively as an antidote to the father's death, they are humorous and pleasant. If there is some allusion, in the first three chapters, to the child's loss and to his loneliness as "the new boy," it is rapidly and effectively amended by the comic trivia of boarding-school life – students' inventive efforts to avoid early morning call, inedible institutional food, stratagems to deceive masters, and other anecdotes of the sort, typical of the genre. The book continues much in the same vein, poking fun here and there at students and masters, its structure assured less by progression than by the accumulation of humorous incidents and pranks.

On another level, Cané's book is positive – and I return here to the general constructive thrust that connects *Juvenilia* to *Tom Brown's Schooldays* and *Stalky and Co.* – because it narrates an instructive experience, one that, in Cané's precise case, accomplished the formation that his father did not live to give him. The Colegio Nacional, for Cané, will quite literally stand *in loco parentis* and, more concretely, *in loco patris*. It is no accident that Cané dwells with such longing on the two rectors who most influenced him, the old and loving Dr. Agüero, who believed his boys could do no wrong, and the younger, physically and intellectually dynamic Amédée Jacques, brought in during Bartolomé Mitre's presidency to take charge of the institution. The sympathetic description of the good Dr. Agüero is an example of the tribute Cané pays to his memory:

As Dr. Agüero grew increasingly frail, it became customary for a student to sit up with him every night. Dr Agüero did not go to bed; in a huge Voltaire chair (the old man never suspected it was called thus!), he slumbered at odd moments, giving in to fatigue. We had to read to him for a couple of hours till the monotonous voice (or perhaps the tediousness of the subject matter) made him doze off. How well I remember that room, feebly lit by a light made softer by an opaque lampshade, the silence only broken by the cry of the night-watchman and, at dawn, by the stealthy steps of some fugitive returning to the fold! We would always read him the life of a saint from a book with green covers that invariably held a twenty peso bill on page 101. All the students at school knew that it had been placed there deliberately by the good Rector who, every morning, would naively check its presence at the mentioned page and delight in the good morals of his little children, as he called us.

More than once did I awake with a start on the sofa, placed close to him, where I had stretched out fully clothed. He would pat my head and say with a voice full of affection: "Sleep, child, it is not yet time." Time was five o'clock, when I would go to an adjoining room, light a fire (always with pine wood) in the brazier, and serve him *mate* till seven. Then he would say: "Go to such-and-such a cupboard and take the plate you'll find there. It's for you." This was the reward, the prize for the night-watch, and we all knew by heart what it was; an apricot and a biscuit that he had us eat slowly, one after the other, the apricot last.

Never once did it cross our minds to protest against that service. The custom had such an affectionate, patriarchal quality to it that we considered it a duty owed an old and sickly father by his sons.   (pp. 58–59)

Agüero is the lenient father whose authority is on the wane; being a man of the cloth, he stands for an outdated educational system. Jacques, on the other hand, is the dynamic figure of authority, the demanding French *normalien* charged by the President of the Republic to update the *colegio*: "the state of education at school was deplorable until its direction was taken over by the wisest man to ever set foot on Argentine soil" (p. 61), writes Cané hyperbolically.

A more enlightened father than Agüero, Jacques preaches positivism triumphant – "the philosophy of the really superior men of science of all times" (p. 82) – where his predecessor had expounded the bland version of scholasticism left behind by Spain. But the tacit comparison of these two father figures implies more than the contrast between two systems of learning. In a subtle way, it also opposes two periods, two cultural systems and two areas of cultural influence. If the paternalistic and bumbling Agüero is a remnant of Colonial times, the challenging and cultivated Jacques – who at a moment's notice can replace any master and teach any subject – is a model for Cané and his generation, a new version of the French *honnête homme* that students will seek to emulate.

In spite of its autobiographical nature, *Juvenilia* can hardly be seen as the story of one individual. The "I" does occupy the center of the narrative, but it is a center to which others are most readily admitted. Very few passages maintain the prolonged use of the first person, the "I" rapidly giving place to an all-encompassing, very seductive "we." A good measure of the book's success lies precisely in the adroit use of that plural: it created the illusion that *Juvenilia* had happened to everybody when, in reality, it had happened only to Cané and a handful of men.[14]

Underlying the pleasantly evoked childish escapades, underlying, too, Cané's blurry family romance,[15] is the permanent awareness of class bonding. Gradually, and none too subtly, a network of prestigious connections grows before the reader's eyes. An exercise in communal reminiscing, *Juvenilia* is also an exercise in purposeful name-dropping. Schoolmates are mentioned more for what they have become than for what they were: "the boy who sat next to me, Julián Aguirre, a native of Jujuy and at present a distinguished magistrate" (p. 73); "my friend Valentín Balbín, a distinguished engineer today" (p. 88); "I was friendly with one of the older boys, nowadays a doctor and a member of Parliament, one of the most authentically Argentine types [*uno de los tipos más criollos*] and one of the kindest hearts I have known in my life" (p. 44). The most conspicuous example of this self-validating strategy through prestigious association with power and authority, is to be found in Cané's account of his most serious prank. Having incited the class to rebel against the vice-rector, he is severely punished by Monsieur Jacques and expelled. And so,

... fifteen minutes later I found myself ignominiously expelled with all my goods and chattels – that is with my little trunk – outside the school door. It was half-past eight at night. I thought things over. My family and all my relatives off in the country and I without a peso in my pocket... what to do? The predicament I found myself in seemed of vast proportions and David Copperfield a pygmy by comparison; I believed myself lost forever in the eyes of society. I wandered for an hour, naturally without my trunk which I had left in the vestry of San Ignacio, and finally collapsed on a bench in Victoria square. A man went by, recognized me, asked me some questions and, taking me affectionately by the hand, led me to his home where he had me share a room with his sons, who were friends of mine. He was Don Marcos Paz, then President of the Republic, and one of the purest and kindest men to be born on Argentine soil.

Some of Jacques' enemies, wishing to profit from my violent expulsion, urged my mother to bring criminal charges against him. My mother, who only thought of my future, vigorously refused and went to see Jacques herself... [A]fter much pleading, she wrested from him a promise to take me back as a day boy provided I passed my exams with a grade of "fair." Luck and my own effort worked in my favor: I passed those first-year exams with highest honors and was readmitted once again as a boarder.

(pp. 71–72)

Cané makes it a point to show that his readmission was the result of his individual hard work and not of political pressure; but at the same time he takes care to indicate that the possibility of that pressure – of which Jacques, the foreigner, would have been the victim – lay very much within his reach.

Cané is conscious of this class bonding, conscious too of the fact that as he weaves his childhood tale he is also telling a bigger story, that of a select institution. This Colegio Nacional, a choice breeding ground for a young élite thanks to the overhauling effected by Amédée Jacques at Bartolomé Mitre's request, this place where meals were punctuated by readings from the exemplary biographies of national heroes contained in Mitre's *Galería histórica argentina*, gave a privileged group "the preparation that paved the way to all intellectual roads" (p. 157). *Juvenilia* is a success story, not of an "I" but of a cohesive "we" produced by the Colegio Nacional. Written during a time of threatening social change – xenophobia directed towards immigrants was, overtly or covertly, one of the great themes of the period – Cané's book may be read, and indeed should be read, as a rallying cry to the successful happy few; to the elegant, intelligent boys from "civilized" Buenos Aires who, throughout the pages of *Juvenilia*, outwit their dullard provincial schoolmates, make fun of their ignorant Italian or Spanish servants, and seduce dark-skinned *chinitas* on their clandestine outings. Not so much an elegiac musing over lost youth, *Juvenilia* is a paean to future growth. Mentally reviewing the past in his introduction, Cané notes how some of his schoolmates have disappeared from view or have not fulfilled their potential. Comfortingly enough, these are only exceptions, destined to enhance the achievements of others:

> Not all have disappeared and some stand out with honor in the present national scene. If these pages were to fall under their eyes, let their ties to the school, weakened by the years gone by, grow strong once more; may these memories be a source of pleasure for them as they bring back the happy hours of childhood ...
>
> Let us all, through a common effort, give new life to the Colegio Nacional that nurtured us intellectually, let us banish religious issues from its classrooms and, if we do not have Jacques to place at its head, let us raise to that position of honor a man whose spirit is open to the powerful evolution of the time, a believer in science and in human progress.   (pp. 57–58)

The rallying call is blatant in this appeal to the old-boy spirit. Yet Cané complements this explicit invitation by a more private bonding with his peers, one that is implicit in the elegantly disengaged attitude he cultivates throughout his texts. Like so much of the writing of the period, *Juvenilia* disparages its own importance, claiming for itself the *ton mineur*. Ironically, for one who would later institutionalize the study of literature in the University of Buenos Aires and who also ardently defended copyright laws, Cané belittles his presence as a writer in *Juvenilia*. He calls his text "a chat" (p. 139), notes that words "appear" effortlessly under his pen, refers to his recollections as "destined for my friends' eyes only" (p. 29), succeeds in conferring to *Juvenilia* the intimacy of gossip. Cultural allusion – so important to (if often misunderstood by) a Sarmiento – becomes a coded language, a private means of communication not devoid of irreverence, sanctioned by a gentlemen's agreement. Used less to bolster an argument than to establish a self-satisfied complicity, these frequently incomplete allusions (a quotation, a reference, with no indication of source that might help a lay reader) are pleasure objects, luxury items rarely elaborated but recognizable to the connoisseur. They have the charm of witty, if frivolous, tattle:

"the old man's horse desperately begged for light, like Goethe on his deathbed" (p. 30).

Of all the texts written by the members of the generation of 1880, Cané's autobiographical account seems to have been the most fortunate; because of its quaint and apparently innocuous stance, because it is routinely included in high school *curricula*, because it defends "values" in a manner sympathetic to many, it is certainly the one that has earned the greatest popular appeal. In Argentine schools today, the great-grandchild of the immigrant whom Cané feared and sought to keep at a distance through the class bonding process illustrated in *Juvenilia*, reads and identifies with the "I" of *Juvenilia*. One would like to think that the irony would not be lost on Cané.

6

The search for Utopia: Picón Salas looks forward to the past

It is wonderful to speak of the past in a land like
Venezuela where the future holds so little hope.

Picón Salas, *Odisea de tierra firme*

If the recreation of childhood, colored by idealization and nostalgia, comes into its own in the second half of the nineteenth century, it does not always appear in Spanish America in what one might call a pure state. Notwithstanding prestigious and well-received examples such as Renan's *Souvenirs d'enfance et de jeunesse*, Anatole France's *Le Livre de mon ami* and the greatly successful *David Copperfield*, to which should be added, this side of the Atlantic, *Ismaelillo*, the enormously influential book of poems calling attention to childhood that Martí wrote to his three-year-old son, many Spanish American auto-biographers of the twentieth century continued to make quick work of their early years, intent as they were on aggrandizing the adult. In Peru, for example, José Santos Chocano, in his autobiography subtitled "The Thousand and One Adventures," strategically suppresses childhood from his story. The chapter bearing the somewhat grandiose title "El hombre que no fue niño" – the man who was never a child – begins, without a jot of self-irony, in the following fashion: "The man who was never a child. This might seem like a frivolous phrase striving for literary effect when it is merely the stark expression of a fearful reality. My childhood was the War of the Pacific."[1] In other instances, while childhood is recovered, it is usually inserted in a larger context, presented as the first installment of what is usually a lifelong story. Such are the cases of Enrique Gómez Carrillo, José Vasconcelos, Enrique González Martínez, Victoria Ocampo, Pablo Neruda and María Rosa Oliver, to give but a few examples, all of whom devote initial sections, if not initial volumes of their autobiographies to their childhood years. In these examples, nostalgia is not usually the primary impulse that triggers the evocation: given the thrust of these endeavors – to bring the narrative up to present-day adulthood and up to the now of self-writing – the autobiographer often gears his childhood towards the future, bypassing elegiac elements that might weigh the story down.[2] This seems to be particularly the case with texts that are strongly marked by an adult political commitment, such as Neruda's memoirs or María Rosa Oliver's autobiographical trilogy, texts in which childhood events, and reactions to those events, are reread from an explicit political ideology.[3]

According to the spirit in which childhood is called upon – as the first stage of a life or as an entity in itself – the manner and even the form of the evocation may vary. It will vary, too, according to the figure the autobiographer sees himself cutting before the public at the time of his writing.[4] Unlike, precisely, Renan and Anatole France who, at the height of their careers, thought nothing of devoting an entire volume to childhood and revelled in the evocation of, as Renan puts it, "the faraway sounds of a vanished Atlantis,"[5] Spanish American writers with some degree of visibility, especially those playing a role in the political scene, have been less prone to allow themselves such a luxury. Indeed, a look at some of the Spanish American autobiographers who have treated their early years as independent, self-sufficient units, giving in to pleasurable nostalgia, is instructive. Significantly, these writers (Wilde, Delfina Bunge, Norah Lange in Argentina, Benjamín Subercaseaux, María Flora Yáñez, Luis Oyarzún in Chile) are not primarily public figures (in the sense that Sarmiento and Vasconcelos are) nor do they aspire, as Sarmiento put it, to "bequeath a statue" through their self-writing. Less bound by the pressure of representation, they tell the underrated *petite histoire* of childhood, deal with it in itself and not as the first chapter in a lifelong story, and do not turn it into a vehicle for an ideological statement that goes beyond it. This does not mean, to be sure, that these texts are devoid of ideological implications; the telling of the age of innocence, as even the refreshingly unsophisticated Condesa de Merlin has shown us, is far from innocent. It is simply that their authors do not feel the pressure to have that childhood point to a public adult they have not become.

If it is true that most public figures in Spanish America shun or feel uncomfortable with childhood stories *per se*, there are notable exceptions. Few indeed have evoked their childhood past more insistently, few have indulged more in the quasi-solipsistic poignancy of that evocation, than the Venezuelan Mariano Picón Salas, whose activity in the cultural affairs of his country and magisterial reputation in Spanish America were unquestionably part of his public persona.[6] The exceptional character of Picón Salas' exercise – the public man indulging in a quaint private tale – is, however, illusory. I shall attempt to show that, while dealing ostensibly with an individual story, the childhood recollections of this public figure have other implications. Like *Juvenilia*, and even more than *Juvenilia*, it is as much an ideological construct as it is a childhood tale.

Mundo imaginario (1927) marks Picón Salas' first sustained attempt to retrieve his early years, an attempt repeated and given its fullest expression in *Viaje al amanecer* (1943). Even *Regreso de tres mundos* (1959), the third of Picón's autobiographical exercises covering his adult life, devotes a first, highly evocative chapter to adolescence. Besides these clear-cut autobiographical texts dealing with childhood and early youth, the whole of Picón Salas' work – from his first book, *Buscando el camino* (1920), to the essays published before his death in 1965 – might be seen as a permanent allusion, usually manifest, at times covert, to his early years in Mérida. If indeed Picón Salas' purpose, when writing *Viaje al amanecer*, was "to liberate myself from the burden of stubborn ghosts in order to 'travel light' [*seguir 'ligero de equipaje'*], as in Antonio Machado's poem, on my pilgrimage throughout the world,"[7] the reader wonders whether those memories of paradise lost did not, in fact, have the opposite effect;[8] whether they did not weigh him down permanently, tinging his vision of the world with a sense of the irrecuperable that would significantly affect his ideological position as essayist and teacher.

For Merlin and Cané the childhood world was a closed order, one that beneficial recollection had perfected by carefully erasing all signs of disruption. For the Condesa, it was the closed Colonial order of Cuban society; for Cané, it was the elitist structure of the Colegio Nacional. In Picón Salas there is a similar need to select a privileged enclosure for the childhood story, only his setting, if no less isolated, is more ample in scope: it is the conservative city of Mérida, high in the Andes, out of touch with present-day Venezuela, and "where in the days of my childhood one still lived as calmly as in our Colonial eighteenth century."[9] Thus, from the very beginning, Picón's memories are given a setting which is in itself a relic and which naturally fosters the protection of the past.

This particular choice of place, at first glance, seems natural enough. Picón Salas was born in Mérida and so were most of his forebears, both paternal and maternal. Besides this genealogical link, the autobiographer repeatedly stresses a nearly physical tie, as strong as, if not stronger than the genealogical, with the mountainous landscape itself: "To be an inhabitant of Mérida meant to be permanently looking up. As if inquiring after a patient's health, people would ask each morning how the *sierra* was doing that day [*cómo había amanecido la sierra*]."[10] Picón claims, as a defining trait, his enduring "habit of being a deep-rooted *merideño.*"[11] Mérida, Picón's first memory of Mérida, is the substance that bolsters his self and one that he must keep retelling: as in a palimpsest, the memory resurfaces, in fragmentary fashion, in every page he writes. The fact that this obsessive reference to a Mérida past appears also in texts that are not primarily autobiographical, prompts the reader to reread Picón's autobiographical rendering of childhood in light of, and in dialogue with, those other texts.

Picón Salas' beginnings as an autobiographer are not simple: his initial movement is to distance himself from the past by cloaking the childhood story in the guise of fiction. From its very title, Picón's first attempt at speaking of childhood reflects this attitude: *Mundo imaginario*, a realm so far removed from a supposedly "untellable" present self that, like a tale belonging to another, it appears to be imaginary. Falling back on the first person plural to disengage the "I" even further from a personal past – adopting that "more massive, more solemn and less defined person"[12] that will become annoyingly frequent in his later writing – Picón describes the substance of *Mundo imaginario* as "that portion of our personality, already assimilated and dissolved, viewed from the outside with pity, or perhaps irony, and which is all our egoism allows us to show strangers."[13] Thus Picón purports to narrate what, in autobiographical terms, amounts to a nonentity: it is a discard, a portion "assimilated and dissolved," that the writing subject only recognizes in the realm of the imaginary.

The distance established by Picón with regard to his past and, more generally speaking, with regard to autobiography may be observed in many of his early first-person pieces. It is important to note, in passing, that most of Picón's self-writing was either done in exile or is connected, in some way, to exile. The metaphor of the journey appears in his titles, runs throughout his work, auto-biographical and otherwise. An echo of the classical *topos* figuring life as a journey, the metaphor punctuates the very real wandering (*errancia*, Picón has called it, coining a felicitous neologism) that fundamentally marked his life.[14] But whereas the literature of exile, especially when autobiographical in nature, is prone to indulge in homesickness, Picón, in his first book written outside Venezuela, would have his reader believe the contrary. In *Mundo imaginario*, written during the author's first and perhaps most decisive period away from his country, he jauntily proclaims that, as a "modern man," he has refused "to give in to nostalgic rambling [since] that dwelling on the past so dear to Romantics is forever dead."[15] Thus *Mundo* not only claims to present a "dissolved" person but to do so dispassionately, with no feeling for that person's past.

Four years later and while still an exile in Chile, Picón published *Odisea de tierra firme*. A collection of short pieces, subtitled *Relatos de Venezuela*, it combines fiction and history and constitutes, in Picón's words, a "nostalgic document, the elegy of a man who, from afar, saw his country in chains." It is "neither polemical nor pamph-leteering belonging rather in that poetic region where the absent homeland projects its distressing emotional image and man evokes his land and his dead, summoning and exorcising the past."[16] These are passionate terms, to be sure, that belie Picón's proclaimed indifference towards the past. Now it may be argued that *Odisea* is not really an autobiographical text and therefore should not be judged by the same measure applied to *Mundo imaginario*: one may choose after all to channel nostalgia into one's fiction while repress-ing it, for whatever reasons, in one's autobiographical writing. But the hybrid nature of *Odisea* challenges this neat separation. Indeed, it is an exercise in fiction, but the unity of the legends, stories and family chronicles that compose it is provided by a protagonist – a new version of the *memorator* – who, however fictitious, bears a definite resemblance to Picón Salas himself.[17] The coincidences are not just factual; the name chosen for the protagonist of *Odisea de tierra firme*, Pablo Riolid, will also be that of the autobiographical "I" in *Viaje al amanecer*.

This hesitation between viewing the past "from the outside" and evoking it nostalgically "from the inside" marks Picón Salas' self-writing from its very incipience. The process might be summarized in the following way: In the first step, *Mundo imaginario* – an autobiographical text – distances itself from its subject matter by stressing its recourse to the imaginary, by scorning nostalgia, and by purporting to be an "exterior" view of the author's past. In a second step, *Odisea de tierra firme* – a non-autobiographical text – takes off in the opposite direction, vindicating nostalgia and the recuperation of a "time past" that has much in common with the author's, but saving face, as it were, by attributing that nostalgia to a fictional character. Finally, *Viaje al amanecer* combines the two modes. It rescues the protagonist of *Odisea*, Pablo Riolid, and, as a matter of course, has him narrate Picón's own life story and become an autobiographical persona. That Picón, in the prologue to the reedition of *Viaje* for his *Obras selectas*, sees the book *both* as a cathartic exercise and as the product of a "nostalgia for that lost world [that] is one of the leitmotifs of my writing,"[18] is proof enough of his distinctive ambivalence towards the past. A closer analysis of *Viaje al amanecer* allows one to read that ambivalence, beyond fluctuations of a purely personal nature, on a concrete rhetorical and ideological plane.

As was the case in *Mundo imaginario*, Picón's first gesture in *Viaje al amanecer* is to thwart all attempts to set the past in a precise chronology. *Mundo* had already made fun of date-seekers: "I was born in Venezuela and, for the benefit of notaries – although I'm not expecting an inheritance – I'll say it was around 1901."[19] In *Viaje al amanecer*, the diversionary tactic is more elaborate and Picón takes pains to spell it out in his foreword. Drawing on the old Spanish saying that refers to time immemorial – *en tiempos de Maricastaña* – he postulates Maricastaña as "goddess of time" and dedicates his book to her. It would be more apt to say, however, that the divinity to whom Picón sacrifices and under whose sign he places these childhood memoirs is less a goddess of time than of timelessness. Picón's *Viaje al amanecer*, while not devoid of chronological markers that permit a superficial insertion in history, persistently works against history, mythologizing memories and projecting them onto a "fantastic past":

Maricastaña personified all the generations whose members trod these worn-out bricks, tied up their horses to the pillars of the verandas when they readied for war or prepared for the long journey to Caracas or Bogotá, and whose solemn portraits ... seemed to look at me frighteningly in the darkened sitting-room. There was one very old leather seat, kept in the study as a relic, on which colonel Riolid had rested his bad leg. After having gone as far as Peru on Bolívar's campaigns he returned to live and die in Mérida, scandalizing our prudish family with his barrack-room vocabulary, his taste for cock fights, his turbulent spirits that made him believe that all things could be solved in shoot-outs and the number of illegitimate children he had fathered with provisional concubines who sought him out and meekly asked for his blessing. Stories of Mérida and whatever had occurred in the immense and scattered land of Venezuela, the wars, the earthquakes, the devil's apparitions so frequent in Mérida's legends, all this found its place in a fantastic past, precisely the one in which Maricastaña had lived.[20]

Viaje al amanecer announces itself as a huge, timeless archive, one not so much destined to elicit recognition from the reader (as was the case, for example, with Cané's *Juvenilia*) as to dazzle him with the near miraculous aura of the unattainable. As Picón notes, "I prefer Poetry to History" (p. 7). Indeed, it is the product of this "Poetry" that he offers the reader – the heavily stylized, purposefully aesthetic souvenir he calls, with dubious quaintness, "the distant blue flower of childhood days" (p. 5). Picón's evocation of his first years reads like a collection of verbal *bibelots* to which time has not been kind.

As if to underscore this sense of a private collection, Picón frequently resorts to images of enclosure. The city of Mérida provides a closed space because of its geographical situation and its haughty standoffishness. On a lesser scale, so do the mahogany wardrobe full of "faded and fabulous objects" through which mother and child rummage; the tight circle around the kitchen fire in which old servants tell chilling "Spanish legends transformed by Indian fantasy" (p. 4); the square yard behind the house where a treasure is supposedly buried; and, finally, the family home itself, perceived by the child as an extension of the old wardrobe, a bric-à-brac collection of undistinguished yet beloved mementos to be avidly explored. Within these enclosed spaces the autobiographer sets out before the reader precious bits and pieces of his childhood, enumerating them in apparent disarray, as if mimicking the disorder of the heterogeneous yet highly prized collections the child found around the house. But for all its seeming fragmentation, *Viaje al amanecer* follows a coherent plan, proposing, through these scattered recollections that touch more on the surroundings of the self than on the self, an oblique yet effective diagram of the individual.

Viaje al amanecer is divided into three parts, aptly called, in accordance with the travel metaphor of the title, *etapas*, that is, stages in a journey. The first, by far the longest and most important of the three, is a celebration of origins, its title being, in itself, a patriarchal founding fiction: "El abuelo, el solar, la casa" ["Grandfather, Property, Home"]. Eschewing any systematic attempt to trace the personal growth of an individual (although retaining a general sense of development, hence the metaphor of the title), the text dwells on a series of figures rescued from childhood days that have, in some way, marked the autobiographer. A pious spinster, a fanciful mason and gravedigger, a wise old peasant, prepare the way for the grandfather of the title, whose death closes the first stage in the narrator's childhood years. While dwelling on these figures, this first section of *Viaje* remarkably bypasses elementary family ties: father and mother are barely mentioned and do not figure much in Picón's gallery. While not denying the psychological implications of this absence, I propose it be seen in other terms. Given the general thrust of these childhood memoirs, this absence seems necessary if only for aesthetic reasons. As Picón announces in his preface, in true programmatic fashion, he strives to clothe the substance of his evocation in "the gold and azure of myth" (p. 4) – an operation more easily practiced, perhaps, on figures already having some extraordinary dimension that renders them imposing, than one one's own, too familiar, parents. The figures evoked by Picón Salas – all of them, including the grandfather, colorful characters aggrandized by legend or gossip – share two very distinctive traits: they are all originals of some kind and, more importantly, they are all storytellers. Picón's memory rescues them in the very act of narrating, of remembering a past that lies beyond his scope.

The first in the series, Josefita, a distant relative taken in by the family, whose room Picón shares as a very young child, appears at first sight as a stereotypical if quirky old maid. Nightly, the child's last image before going to sleep is that of Josefita by candlelight, clad in a nightgown "so white and so long that it seemed the ideal garment for a soul in Purgatory" (p. 12), either praying to the Sacred Heart or going over her feet with a needle to dig out parasitic fleas. But Josefita is more than a stereotype. Slowly in Picón's description, this faded figure whose past reads like that of so many Romantic heroines (Clarín's Doña Berta comes to mind) takes on quasi-allegoric proportions as the embodiment of a period.

Together with the few pathetic belongings that metonymically allude to her – a daguerreotype that features her as an Empress Eugénie look-alike, a lock of hair cut from her dead fiancé's head, a macramé mat, and that symbol of nineteenth-century piety, the Sacred Heart – she stands for an order destroyed by the civil wars in Venezuela. Pious, impoverished Josefita is a lonely witness to a Venezuela still close to the Spanish colony; like Mérida, the city where she finds shelter, she is "conservative, pro-Spanish and anti-Federalist" (*conservadora, goda y antifederalista*) (p. 13). For the child who listens avidly to her stories and whose fantasy she nourishes, Josefita is a powerful link to the past:

She lights the small *corozo* lamp in celebration of the Sacred Heart of Jesus, a Jesus who, with his flowery beard, may well resemble her 1860 fiancé and, in that semi-darkness of my first years, gives me time and legend. (p. 15)

Beyond their "poetic" appearance, the figures evoked in *Viaje al amanecer* determine the direction of a precise archeological venture on Picón's part. It is not by chance that one of the figures evoked with most relish is Apolinar Gaviria, also known as *Sancocho* (hodge-podge), the town mason who doubles as town gravedigger. But there is more to Sancocho's digging than the ritual burial of Mérida's dead. Every so often, when called to repair something in the Picón household, he appears with a host of illegitimate sons to whom he delegates the actual work. While his offspring mend and build, he betakes himself to the backyard and, with Picón's grandfather's permission – "this was one of the secrets of the house" (p. 17) – he attempts a restoration of another kind, digging for a legendary *entierro*, a buried treasure from Colonial times that he will never find. This obsessive and perpetually inconclusive excavation, the goal of which grows ever more remote – "since the earth moves ... the treasure must have changed place" concludes Sancocho philosophically – provides a choice metaphor for the restorative tactics of *Viaje al amanecer*. Like Sancocho digging for an elusive lost treasure – a foundational story – the "I" digs into the stories of others (Josefita, el Mocho Rafael, his own grandfather) and plays at finding a treasure of his own.

The precise locations selected for the archeological venture, and the ideological bent given by the adult to his reconstruction, are worthy of note. On the one hand there are privileged spaces, inner *sancta*; on the other, primitive, unkempt areas. The patrician Josefita's memory functions within the individual seclusion of her bedroom *cum* chapel; that of the respected grandfather, in the more institutional (though no less private) library and study – an *escritorio* that is also a *locutorio* where the grandfather holds forth on the past (for the benefit of his grandchild) or on the present (to taunt the friendly opponents who come to argue with him). Instead, Sancocho and el Mocho Rafael, embodiments of that "man of the people" in whom Bakhtin perceives a remnant of the idyllic novel,[21] belong outside, in a "precivilized" space:

> If, during my early childhood, "Sancocho" or "el Mocho Rafael" personify what might be called the barbaric imagination, my grandfather exemplifies the cultivated imagination. In all three of them there was evasion, a taste for fantasy and discovery, for the telling of extraordinary things. And, as much as in my excursions out to the backyard, I delighted in venturing into my grandfather's study.   (p. 24)

In his very first book, *Buscando el camino*, Picón had devoted vignettes to both his grandfathers. On the father's side was Antonio Picón Grillet, the conservative *hidalgo* and *godo* living in the past, of whom Picón wrote that "in the big house, surrounded by his children and grandchildren, he was like a small fatherland [*como una pequeña patria*]. From his lips I learned the cult of heroes." On the mother's side was the liberal and more tolerant Federico Salas Roo, whose "Spanish gentleman's soul was filled with French wit."[22] Only the second has lived on in the pages of *Viaje*, a choice that may seem at first surprising since Picón had previously set both grandfathers on equal footing: "In the portraits of my two grandfathers, I read a double sermon on life."[23] But *Viaje* strives less to evoke family members *per se* (another reason, perhaps, for the relative absence of father and mother) than to recreate, through reminiscence, a community of storytellers. Of the two grandfathers, the one on the mother's side – "the one who told such pretty stories" (p. 46) – obviously fits the category better than the old conservative, more interested in historical records than in creative fabulation. In *Viaje al amanecer*, everything the maternal grandfather touches, in Midas-like fashion, turns to fiction:

> Time, landscapes, cities and adventures, whose mysteries had been partially revealed to me in the illustrated weeklies of the seventies and even earlier that were kept in the study, came up in his entertaining chats. Before Salgari's novels, before even being able to read fluently, I savored in his stories something like an oral art of prose.   (p. 33)

Finally, *Viaje* is less a recollection of facts than a recollection of the manner in which people told these facts, less an evocation of people than an evocation of their voices – or rather of the voices that the autobiographer, like a stage director mobilizing a cast of shadows, would have his characters adopt. The first section of the book, ending as it does with the grandfather's death, is also in a sense the end of the true childhood tale, for there is no storyteller – except the autobiographer himself – left to tell it:

Deprived of my grandfather's company, of the charm and liveliness of his stories, I feel a cycle of my inventive childhood drawing to a close. I now enter a darker and more frightening period. In my sleepless nights I hear my grandfather pacing the corridors, thumping his cane on the stone floors. Thick night, mother of all invention, is out there in the courtyard, lurking in the silent and scared watchfulness of shadows and stars.

(p. 47)

The first line of recollection that structures *Viaje al amanecer*, the one centered on stories and storytellers, thus ends abruptly. As if reflecting this disruption – the provisional loss of the family tale – the second, transitional *etapa* focuses on signs of catastrophe. Loss and early sorrow are subsumed in one memorable event, the announced sighting of Halley's comet that has all of Mérida, and the child in particular, convinced that the world is coming to an end. A period of instability, spiritual trials and budding eroticism, this *etapa* is handled by the autobiographer with benign irony since Picón, like other embellishers of the childhood tale, cannot tolerate upheaval. Fittingly enough, Picón has this section end on the very day Halley's comet finally makes its appearance, with a family banquet (prepared beforehand in case the world did *not* come to an end) symbolizing peace restored and, one might add, timelessness regained:

[A]s Halley's comet, harrassed by the clouds, moves away and is lost to our sight, we go to the dining room. From my grandmother, occupying the high chair at the head of the table, down to me, a starry-eyed nine-year-old, the family finds seats. Thick chocolate, redolent of vanilla, cinnamon and nutmeg and beaten by Clorinda's Indian arms, is savored with ritual solemnity. Surprised for a moment by the appearance of the mysterious guest, the house now returns to the slow rhythm of generations. One can talk once more – as if coming out of a dream – of the brindle cow that gives ten quarts of milk or of the roan horse belonging to one of my uncles which turned out to be an unbeatable trotter. I myself return to real things, to the land and its people, now that the first terrors of my childhood are past.

(p. 70)

The last stage in these childhood memoirs may be, in a sense, the most revealing. Picón's autobiographical itinerary had started out with foundational fictions rooted in genealogy and geography: as the subtitle put it, "Grandfather, Property, Home." It now closes with other fictions, of a different nature. Cultural myths and ideological constructs provide a closure for the childhood story and, at the same time, mark the passing of the autobiographer into a community that lies beyond the limits of Mérida. The child no longer seeks support in voices but in the different versions of a well-established cultural text. Books now replace the oral narratives of Picón's storytellers; Fénelon's *Télémaque* edges out peasant legends; and artistic manifestations, even of dubious quality, fire the imagination more than family keepsakes. The visit of a Spanish company, despite the comical hubbub it gives rise to (women getting their best finery ready, priests thundering against the evils of the theatre, the leading lady entering Mérida astride a white horse) and despite the mediocrity of its repertoire, brings culture home to the child: "From the classical seashores and the sacred woods of Greece, Iphigenia and Electra had come to the Andes, even in the shrill verses of don José Echegaray" (p. 81). As the culturally established, written fictions supersede the homey voices that recreated the past, so societal myths and cultural patterns of behavior are brought to bear on the adolescent. The father, a blurry figure up to this point, takes on new proportions, fashioning his son's life in accordance with the self-satisfied fictions of the liberal bourgeoisie of the period. Sons of good families should learn foreign languages, especially English; they should study in Caracas and participate in Venezuela's progress; they should adapt to a paternalistic code of behavior, insidious beneath its mild appearance, which the following incident illustrates to perfection:

Like all Venezuelan adolescents, I have bought a gun and tuck it into my belt each time I set out across the fields, on my spirited roan, to visit Teresita. However, after a mysterious intervention from my father when he saw me losing weight, neglecting my studies and disappearing unexpectedly from the house for days on end, I found out that Teresita was marrying a settler who was taking her far away, somewhere in the tropical region of Los Guáimaros . . .

"Do not see her again; do not set a bad example for those simple people,"
my father told me.   (p. 100)

The passage, with its patronizing overtones, brings to mind Isaacs'
María (Efraín's visits to his father's sharecroppers, his condescending flirtation with one of their daughters, his *señoritismo* towards
peasants in general). This similarity should not come as a surprise:
after all Isaacs' novel is, amongst many other things, an effective
mise-en-scène of the cultural codes on which the landowning Colom-
bian class based its conduct. Fifty years later in Venezuela – or, for
that matter, in many other parts of Spanish America – things had
not changed all that much: rural paternalism continued to be as
benevolent as it was ruthless. Moreover, fifty years later, Picón
Salas had most probably read *María*. There are indubitable echoes of
Isaacs' Romantic adolescent loner, carrying with him the last image
of the world of childhood he is so attuned to, in the young Picón
Salas who leaves Mérida for the big city and the outside world:

From where the road rises again I get the last image of my town with its
peaceful white houses, its church spires, the trees showing up over its
garden walls. Goodbye, Mocho Rafael, goodbye, Teresita, goodbye, Catire
Bravo! Other boys – as society changes – will listen to other stories and deal
with other characters. They will not be afraid of the devil, nor of Halley's
comet's next visit, nor of signs of the end of the world; they will always
enjoy (and why not?) butterflies, and birds, and the light of Mérida. By
then I shall be dead and should like them to remember me.

(pp. 101–102)[24]

It is not unusual that memoirs dealing with the subject's early
years present the end of childhood not only as the end of a stage of
life but as the end of a way of life for a community. Or perhaps the
situation should be presented the other way round: viewed in
retrospect, a historical change of some magnitude affecting the
community to which he or she belongs may be recognized by the
autobiographer *post facto* as the determinant factor that brought a
period of his or her own life to an end, an "external" sign of closure
that ratified, or perhaps even caused, personal change. *Viaje al
amanecer*, in this respect, is no exception. A look at the historical
changes that Picón identifies as having precipitated his entrance
into adulthood is pertinent since it allows us, in turn, to construe
retroactively the full ideological import of Picón's childhood
memoir.

The last pages of *Viaje* register signs of change less portentous, perhaps, than Halley's comet though no less indicative of imminent consummation. Venezuela's economy undergoes radical modification. If the world in general was not coming to an end, Picón's world certainly was, and so too the mythical Mérida his pages had recreated:

Some North American engineers start to drill for oil and people from all over the country rush to the makeshift camps on the shores of lake Maracaibo. This will be the wealth of the twentieth century. Oil needs lawyers to denounce it, technicians to drill for it and move its machinery, draftsmen and office clerks to draw, with steady pulse and good penmanship, the curve of its millions. Many young men from peaceful Mérida also head for the vertigo of oil wells. In our erstwhile calm mountains, things seem more hectic, more daring, less educated.   (p. 101)

Menos bien educada, writes Picón Salas, and the Spanish refers as much to a decline of formal education as it does to a more general lack of courtesy and values. The development of the oil industry, backed by North American capital, will often be perceived in Picón's later works as marking a definitive scission, dividing Venezuela into a *before* and an *afterwards*, an event finally more evil than was the appearance of Halley's comet in the minds of Mérida's prudes.

These changes in the economy, compounded by a general sense of cultural insecurity, drive Picón into a defensiveness which, ironically, is not unlike the one he criticized in his forefathers. In *Regreso de tres mundos*, his memoirs as an adult, Picón refers disparagingly to those "inflexible groups" in Mérida who "seemed to huddle together and retreat more and more into their parsimonious formulas and ancient habits before the violent tide of egalitarianism carried them away,"[25] Fear of invasion will drive Picón to a cultural haven not new in the history of Spanish American ideas. Although not explicit in *Viaje al amanecer*, a work labelled by its author as more "poetic" than "historic," the nature of this ideological refuge becomes clear in other texts by Picón Salas; in retrospect, it exposes a telling manipulation of his childhood past. One such text, complementary to *Viaje* and illustrating Picón's attitude towards the "new" Venezuela, is "Caracas," a 1957 piece later included in *Páginas de Venezuela*. Faced with what he perceives as an invasion of foreign values, Picón, in "Caracas" (as in numerous other texts), resorts to a particularly hackneyed version of *arielismo* to criticize

North American intervention and to counter the temptation of materialism. Much like a latter-day Rodó, he sees himself as a *magister*,[26] one who didactically calls attention to national moral corruption in the hopes of shaking a Venezuela that, not unlike Mérida, is forgetful of its roots and its manners. Like Rodó, too, Picón's criticism, and the solutions he proposes, are markedly short-sighted – even more short-sighted, one should add, when one thinks that the presence of the United States in Spanish America was no longer a threat, as in the days of the Uruguayan master, but a reality.

"Caracas" traces the evolution of the Venezuelan capital from 1920 till the moment of Picón's writing, recording the momentous alterations the city has gone through. With the Spanish American's flair for describing reality through somewhat distorted European models, Picón claims that the Caracas of the twenties was a "Stendhalian" city, living out its last days in a state of joyous insouciance: "The models that the *criolla* society looked up to were still French and Spanish, which amounts to saying that life had less haste and more charm. The great plutocracy that was to develop and consolidate itself later did not yet set up so many antagonizing barriers of fortune amongst people."[27] Perhaps less a city for Fabrizio del Dongo than a belated *modernista* paradise, a provincial capital indiscriminately dazzled by cultural trinkets from Europe which it inventively combined with its Spanish Colonial heritage, the bustling Caracas described by Picón Salas would drastically alter its mode of life with the advent of new industries. Picón, with the eloquence of one given to terminal visions, mourns for the old Caracas much in the way that, in *Viaje al amanecer*, he mourned for Mérida and for his own youthful years. The dictatorship of Juan Vicente Gómez, favorable to American investors, had sounded a death knell.

Evocation, in "Caracas," has a prelapsarian quality that definitely brings to mind the embellished reminiscences of *Viaje al amanecer*. The description of what came after – for Picón, the loss of culture, of education, of tradition – is foreseeably couched in negative terms: "People who were not even trained to be rich, skipping all social and cultural stages, suddenly found themselves with an enormous mass of millions," giving rise to "infectious bad taste" and to "wealth without style or roots" (pp. 240–241). Whisky-and-soda replaces "Mediterranean liqueurs," lunch is accompanied by "innocuous PepsiCola," Spanish-style *tertulias* and family reunions are substituted by "Yankee-style parties in country clubs": unfortunately it is at such trivia that Picón stops to exemplify, like a senescent grouch, the change in the times.[28] Less the "social historian" he sees himself as being, less the master of liberalism and social awareness he thinks he is – Picón's reaction against his ideological upbringing, while sincere, hardly goes very deep – Picón is, above all, a *costumbrista* with a good eye for colorful detail and a tendency to dwell on surfaces.[29] At its best – say, in the nostalgic evocation of Mérida's quirky characters in *Viaje al amanecer* – this *costumbrismo* can be effective, a rather unusual cross between Ricardo Palma's *tradiciones* and the García Márquez to come. At its worst – as in the narrow-minded presentation of modern Caracas or the prettified evocation of the Caracas that was – it suggests outdated quaintness. The *magister* at times is replaced, to his detriment, by the small-town gossip. As Gusdorf writes, "memory defines our roots and also confirms a few of our limitations."[30]

Yet Picón is, above all, a teacher. Although the substance of his writing may be anachronistic or lacking in insight, it is expressed in the rhetorical mold of the lesson and should be seen – even his autobiographical pieces – in that spirit. The education, or rather re-education of the no longer well-educated Venezuela seems to be his naively grandiose goal. An earnest effort to recuperate "values" in order to fend off disturbing influences, combined with an unconditional propensity to facile utopianism, shapes everything he writes. The following excerpt from "Caracas," as complete a summary of his teachings as any, is an eloquent example of this didactic thrust:

Ten years ago we thought that [Venezuela] would hopelessly prolong all the styles and economic patterns of the state of Texas. We wondered if the impact of the United States would not consume our small, racially mixed civilization; if we would not end up being too healthy or too optimistic; if the old ideal of dignity [*señorío*] and serenity in the Hispanic manner, "the tragic sense of life," would not be replaced by the dynamism of the rancher or the Texan millionaire; if *criollo* individualism, yielding to a collective norm, would not adopt the habit of men's clubs as in the United States; if iced water, sports, food without spices, comic books, and total comfort would not tame our pride and our Hispano-Caribbean quasi-disdain – that mixture of Spanish stoicism in the manner of Seneca and ruggedness in the manner of Guaicaipuro that was so frequent in some old Venezuelans. But maybe European immigration, principally from Italy and Spain, is already

modifying that process and will hopefully accentuate, as in Argentina, a
new Latinity.   (p. 249)

Hispanism and Latinity are key words here. They refer back to
Rodó, of course, and to the fabrication of a *mundo latino* eloquently
propounded in *Ariel* as a sustaining fiction, a continental antidote to
the North American threat in Latin America. But unfortunately the
word also evokes, at the time Picón writes (and it is hard, although
not impossible, to believe that Picón, in 1957, would not be aware of
it), certain Spanish American nationalistic movements uncomforta-
bly close to fascism that, from the 1930s onward, used *latinidad* and
the defense of all things Spanish as rallying concepts. Ironically,
Argentina, the very country Picón cites, was a perfect example of
such a reactionary reading of the cultural myth.[31] Advanced by
Rodó at a time of uncertainty, real political threat and much Big
Stick bravado, *latinidad*, if an artifice, worked as a new, dynamic call
to unity and action. Taken up by Picón Salas more than half a
century later, when the notion has served its purpose and come back
full circle, *latinidad* smacks of defensiveness and enclosure and ill
serves the author's apparently liberal stance.

What, within this framework, is the place of *Viaje al amanecer?* My
contention is that, sustained by Picón's didactic thrust, the childhood memoir itself becomes part of the "lesson," one more instructive chapter in the quest for Latinity. The book invites a double
reading: it recalls a childhood past and, at the same time, provides
ideological ammunition to face the future. Thus the conservative
city of Mérida, haughtily absorbed in itself, is not only the repository of the lost paradise of childhood; it is a haven for a Spanish,
goda tradition, a sanctuary of *latinidad*.[32] In this light, certain aspects
of *Viaje* that have already been discussed – the child often yielding
center stage to characters in some way representative of a heritage,
or the highlighting of storytellers as curators of the past – become
otherwise significant. So does the sense of timelessness in Picón's
Mérida (the realm of Maricastaña) and even the deliberate alternating of present and preterite within the narrative itself. This calculated use of anachronism seems particularly well suited to the
conservative function ascribed by Picón to his mythical city:

The site was beautiful and mild and families prospered. People did not
come in search of El Dorado but in search of peace: this was a place in
which to settle down, not a place to leave behind. These families inter-

married, built great mansions in stone as close as possible to the town square, were composed of priests and saints, military men, virtuous ladies and even some Messaline possessed by the devil. They have been signing deeds, passing on inheritances, making out wills and fighting over boundaries for the past three centuries. With a certain amount of boastful and objectionable pedantry, they purport to be the most Spanish of all the people living in this vast and scattered Venezuela. Time, for he who is born in Mérida, is dense and stratified, quite unlike the nervous and forgettable time one finds in more modern places. The past would merge into the present and people who had lived three centuries ago, or who only lived in the generous fantasy of some *merideños*, were the stubborn witnesses, the phantoms of our everyday life.   (p. 7)

In light of Picón Salas' "lesson," the title of his childhood story benefits from an unexpected twist. One would have thought that the metaphor of the title, the journey towards dawn, indicated a journey back, a quest for the autobiographer's origins. That may be the case, but it is not all. Given the prophetic strains that Picón adopts for his magisterial stance and the heavily salvational qualities he attributes to *latinidad*, the dawn of the title refers both to the past and to a future ever out of reach. Picón himself is not unaware of the double thrust in his writing, indeed he describes it at the very beginning of *Regreso de tres mundos*: "Personal life or History is nothing but the longing for the world we left behind and the fervent utopia, constantly corrected and amended, of that other world we would like to reach."[33] Neither as a teacher nor as a social historian does Picón Salas seem to realize the consequences of this double vision: it implies permanent evasion, a refusal to look the present in the eye – and in the "I." Nor does he seem to sense what is apparent to his reader: his individual, poetic world of the past, ending with the demise of the "old" Venezuela, and his utopia for the future, beginning with the "new" Venezuela (the better to replace it) are so perilously close to each other, so bound by a common lack of motion and a common belief in purportedly timeless "values," that they tend to meld and become one. Yesterday's idyllic Mérida gives birth to tomorrow's consoling *latinidad*; paradise lost is paradise regained. The autobiographical venture of *Viaje al amanecer*, in spite of the dynamic promise of its title, is less a voyage of self-discovery than an invitation to communal stasis.

7

A game of cutouts: Norah Lange's
Cuadernos de infancia

I remember myself in the sun of childhood, steeped
in death, in beautiful life.
Alejandra Pizarnik, *Textos de sombra y últimos poemas*

Picón Salas is not alone in turning quaint memories of his childhood
into effective ideological constructs; nor is childhood the exclusive
domain of conservative ideologists such as he. Looking back on her
early years in *Memorias de una cubanita que nació con el siglo*, Renée
Méndez Capote, in the spirit of the Cuban revolution, rescues
figures from her childhood that have been routinely ignored by
official historiography.[1] In the same vein, and striving to form a
similar, populist archive, the Chilean Manuel Rojas' *Imágenes de
infancia* (1955), devoted to the author's first years, is a childhood
picaresque doubling as a celebration of the working class. But at this
point I wish to turn to another type of childhood evocation, not only
to underscore, by contrast, the ideological manipulation to which
childhood may be subjected, but to explore a different, more
experimental and less frequent variant of the childhood tale in
Spanish America. I speak of childhood recollections such as
Eduardo Wilde's *Aguas abajo*, Norah Lange's *Cuadernos de infancia*,
Felisberto Hernández's *Tierras de la memoria*, texts whose primary
purpose is less the conscious recomposition of childhood for history
than the fragmentation of those supposedly idyllic years. Whereas
these texts may be seen historically, as evidence of the way in which
a subject perceives itself at a given time and in a particular context,
their chief interest lies in the fact that they reflect not only a
conception of the world but, more precisely, a conception of
literature. Not incidentally, recollections of this type are usually
written by authors of fiction; they are also the ones that come closest

to vindicating childhood, as did the Romantics, for epistemological reasons, although admittedly in a very different vein. In texts such as these, the evocation of early childhood, the first discoveries and experiences that anchor a child's growing sense of identity, serve as self-reflecting artifacts: through them the subject, aware of its textual fabric, reenacts its own, scattered composition. These texts should be considered not only in an ample cultural context but within the framework of the author's fiction: they are often pre-texts, precursor narratives, the childhood tale functioning like a generative matrix of fiction as well as life.

Published in 1937, and marking a significant turning point in the author's career, Norah Lange's *Cuadernos de infancia* is such a text. An early member of the *ultraísta* group loosely gathered around Borges in the Buenos Aires of the early 1920s, Lange achieved distinction as an avant-garde poet. Her incursions into fiction, to which she turned shortly thereafter, were less fortunate and suffered from affectation. As Lange herself would say years later, her first two novels, although mediocre, had the value of all learning experiences: "I realized I could do what I wished with language."[2] Considerable time would elapse between those failed efforts of the late 1920s and early 1930s and Lange's very accomplished novels, *Personas en la sala* and *Los dos retratos*, written in the 1950s. In the period in between, Lange continued her literary activity in another vein. A firm believer in the avant-garde effort to reintegrate art in the praxis of life, and an early participant, together with her husband Oliverio Girondo and members of the *Martín Fierro* group, in the "war against solemnity," she devoted herself to live art in the form of *discursos*, macaronic monuments of nonsense delivered as speeches at mock serious dinners before similarly unconventional fellow souls.[3] If the Parisian salon was Mercedes Merlin's choice form of sociability, the Dadaist banquet was that of Norah Lange.

In this same period of transition between her early fiction and the novels of the 1950s, as another type of learning experience concurrent with that of the *discursos* though different in form, Lange wrote *Cuadernos de infancia*. Coincident in time, the two ventures seem at first hard to reconcile, since they appear to point in opposite directions. Lange's *discursos* are very much creatures of circumstance, their effectiveness depending on the present of their enunciation. Conceived in a libertarian spirit, they are exercises in exhibitionism, whose meaning is to be found less in their frequently cacophonous contents than in the outrageous performance of the orator herself. Lange's childhood memoir, on the other hand, by the very nature of the genre itself, would seem to indicate a more reflexive (if no less narcissistic) attitude; an inward look turned on the past; and a need to abide by a narrative continuity at the extreme opposite of the *discursos'* arbitrary composition by aggregation. A close examination of *Cuadernos* thwarts, however, any generic expectations in the reader, revealing the unconventional slant in Lange's treatment of childhood.

Like so many childhood memoirs, *Cuadernos de infancia* focuses on the autobiographer's first years and stops short of adolescence. With only the text to rely on, the reader would be hard put to determine the precise moment covered by those years, since *Cuadernos* does not contain dates. To compound this lack of temporal moorings, *Cuadernos* never refers to events happening outside the tight family circle that would allow for the insertion of the text in a historical context. The one exception, a passing allusion to the First World War, is so incongruous that, far from supplying a concrete frame of reference, it produces an alienating effect:

During the few months that we stayed on in Mendoza after my father's death, the episodes of the 1914 War had, for us, the inconsistency of a faraway reality. When we settled down once more in Buenos Aires, we lived so far removed from what went on in the world that we even forgot its existence.[4]

The ambiguity of the last sentence – "its existence" referring indiscriminately to the war and to the world, coupling them in the same unreality – only stresses the effect of disconnection operating throughout the text. *Cuadernos* is suspended in a disquieting (and at times irritating) timelessness, as in an extended pause where temporal deictics only become meaningful within a private chronology barely made available to the reader. This is not the timeless recreation rendered prestigious by fond anachronism, the pastoral fantasy reflecting on the inadequacy of modern times, as was the case in Picón Salas: if the latter's evocation of childhood, with all its quaint references to "los tiempos de Maricastaña," cannily calculated on the attraction of the outmoded, Lange's strategy, at least in regard to time, is more straightforward. There is little yearning here for an ordered shelter no longer available to the adult. A self-sufficient world, to be sure, the childhood Lange presents is not a harmonious whole, however, but a collection of disparate bits and pieces, a dynamic reservoir of possibilities.[5]

Besides chronology, *Cuadernos de infancia* disdains other basic aspects of foundation fictions. Genealogy and patronymics, for example, suffer from distortion and are diverted from their usual purpose. As if to confirm *Cuadernos'* removal from referential reality, Lange effects a systematic renaming of characters throughout the book. While maintaining anonymity for the autobiographical self, she tampers with the names of her four sisters and one brother, applying a whimsical system of equivalents that, while not too hard to decipher,[6] thwarts direct identification. Genealogy fares no better. Presented as isolated figures, without kinsmen, without forebears, without friends, father and mother appear solely attached to each other and to their children. There is no sense of lineage, and the search for origins becomes a game of geography: "On my father's desk, I remember only a huge globe that he would turn before our eyes so that we would immediately spot Norway and Ireland" (p. 15). More than a reflection on family background, this geographical quest appears to be an exercise in the exotic, not too different from the viewing of the father's collection of Indian artifacts, the other pastime Lange remembers indulging in while in his study.

Lange also deals a death blow to the remaining, most basic component of the childhood story, place. *Cuadernos* eschews the shelter of the *hortus clausus*, does not begin by establishing – as the Condesa de Merlin did with Cuba, Cané with the Colegio Nacional or Picón Salas with Mérida – the illusion of a protected and protecting space. An eccentric text in the most literal sense, *Cuadernos* opens with displacement, not with domestication, and it is the recollection of that very uprooting that brings about the childhood story:

Disrupted and joyful, briefly interrupted by an overnight stay, the first trip we made from Buenos Aires to Mendoza comes up in my memory as if I were recovering a landscape through a clouded window.   (p. 9)

"Disrupted and joyful" is a phrase that might be applied to the entire text that follows this awakening of memory, an enumeration of childhood through haphazard succession and hiatus whose method (if not its substance) is not unlike that operating in Borges' *Evaristo Carriego*. It is within this particularly ill-defined *locus*, freed of the strictures of history, even distanced at times from the requisites of mere verisimilitude, in a space less physical than enunciative, that Lange inscribes her "I."

The clouded window that triggers this unusual memoir is emblematic of the autobiographer's activity: not so much a protagonist as an impassioned observer, the "I" of *Cuadernos de infancia* rescues those privileged moments of childhood that allow her to spy. Indeed, all the memories collected in Lange's text obey the impulse of what that other *voyeur* (and at times autobiographer), Felisberto Hernández, memorably called "the lust for looking."[7] Events, places, things, family members and the very self are subjected to this favorite activity of the child:

From a very early age on, I liked to look at people in great detail. At six, this had become a firmly established habit. I would then laugh and laugh so much that the mother had to warn visitors who came to the house that I was very *cheeky*. Even if the word in English meant *impudent*, I know it was neither impudence nor aggressivity that made me do it, for this habit was to follow me till I was much older and able to analyze it.   (p. 24)

The child's spying is, if anything, creative and leads to a highly convoluted ritual. Not only does she stare at others but, when a face catches her fancy, she imagines herself inside that face and takes pains, in an odd act of parodic contortion, to simulate its features clownishly with her body. Until one day she goes to such extremes to mimic someone's face that, frightened by her own, temporary deformity, she abandons the game. The person dies two months later and, for a long time, the child imagines her lying in her coffin, her face set forever in the posture she had mimicked.

If the game ends there, the habit of spying subsists in the very composition of *Cuadernos*. Lange refines the creative potential of voyeurism, placing it at the service of autobiography. Looks defamiliarize: the child's "I" is like a roving camera, receptive, eager to spy on oddities, subjugated and repelled by the freakish. On a second level of voyeurism, the adult who writes the text spies on those memories, as if peering at snapshots that, on closer examination, take on the value of oblique revelations. In much the same way that the child in *Cuadernos de infancia* shares her spying with her sisters, creating as it were a community of voyeurs, the text awakens in its readers the nagging sense that they too must look in. At the same time it robs them of any satisfaction, foils their attempts to explain away what they see. What the obsessive spying endeavors to unveil remains unsaid throughout *Cuadernos*; it is the uneasiness triggered by that silence that constitutes the real *événement* in what might have otherwise been a trivial chronicle of childhood in an undistinguished Argentine province.

What little subsists of family convention in *Cuadernos*, once it has been subjected to this skewed inquisitiveness, is hardly reassuring. In recounting her childhood, Lange (again, like Felisberto Hernández) has the ability to hint at the uncanny by repeatedly undermining the *regard familier*. The quotidian is a constant source of anxiety: it suffices to look at it at the right moment (or, as Felisberto would have said, to catch it unawares). On one occasion, for example, as Lange and her sisters watch their parents wander off into the woods on their daily ride, the narrator discovers there are two sides to her mother. On one side of the sidesaddle she is "luminous and whole" on the other she is shadowy and unfamiliar:

[T]hey rode off at a slow trot.

The radiant side of the mother disappeared and we were only left with the less familiar and more austere. Only when she reached the first poplars that marked the boundary of the property did we realize we had lost something. My father's reddish beard was the last thing we saw.

Now I know that the mother's other side, the luminous one, rode very close to him.   (p. 14)

A reading of this recollection as a scene of parental abandonment would not be unwarranted, but it would run counter to the book's tendency to thwart overinterpretation. *Cuadernos* refuses to elaborate on the potential for disquiet in what the child sees: it just allows that disquiet to reverberate, unhindered, throughout the text. In a chapter devoted to a photography session, memorable for the crisscrossing of looks and lines of vision, while three of the sisters pose before the camera, the child peeks into a box where the photographer's pet rabbit lies dying, eyes wide open, and instinctively turns her eyes to one of her sisters. During the hours that follow she is haunted by the thought that by encompassing the dying rabbit and her sister in one glance she may have hurt the latter. Lange records other, equally defamiliarizing, looks that, again and again, point to an uncanniness that remains unnamed. The child stares at night at "a dim line of light that troubled me" (p. 15) under the door to her father's study; she surprises her sister Marta picking at her hands till they bleed; she catches her eldest sister pretending to breast-feed their baby sister, surprises another sister naked in the moonlight; she observes an unnamed woman who comes to call with presents for her and her sisters and who, while she visits, "slowly unravelled, thread by thread, the ribbon on our gifts as if she were alone, awaiting something" (p. 67).

The "I"/eye of *Cuadernos* relishes fragmentation and hiatus and never once posits a comprehensive vision of reality or of self. It has often been asserted that women's autobiographies tend *per se* to be fragmentary.[8] While this view (which I would not extend to all women autobiographers) may apply to Lange, I would argue that *Cuadernos'* disjunctive composition is especially marked by the literary conventions – *ultraísmo* and surrealism – within which Lange chose to write. In *Cuadernos de infancia*, fragmentation is linked, very actively and from the beginning, with language and literary creation. In one of the rare chapters devoted to the child alone, unaccompanied by sisters, Lange describes her contact with words as a "typographical game of patience":

In the afternoons, while my sisters practiced their scales on the piano or learned to darn socks on those big wooden eggs practically no one uses nowadays, I would sit on the floor and amuse myself with my favorite pastime. With scissors I would cut out words from local and foreign newspapers and would stack them in little piles. Most of the time I did not know what they meant, but this did not worry me in the least. I was only attracted by their typographical aspect, the thickness or thinness of the lettering. Words in capitals such as TWILIGHT, DISCOVERY, DAGUERROTIPO, LABERINTO, THERAPEUTHIC [*sic*],[9] by themselves aroused in me an enthusiasm and a satisfaction that I would now have to call aesthetic. Their intimate qualities, their expressiveness or their mystery, the perspectives I might find behind some of them, did not interest me in the least. I just cut them out looking for the difficult resonance of unusual words, the words that always attracted me the most, those that live as if separated from the rest.   (p. 36)

An aesthetics of collage and an experimentation with forms of contiguity governs the linguistic pastimes of this "I" as it governs the actual composition of *Cuadernos de infancia*. Lange describes her mania as a child for breaking up every statement she heard into syllables, superstitiously intent on reaching a count of ten and oblivious to what the words actually said. She recalls her joyous astonishment when a new teacher had her and her sisters learn proverbs by acting out the sayings quite literally – a stitch in time saves nine, to bite off more than one can chew, etc. – in a scene anticipating Ionesco at his most ludicrous.

The child connects and disconnects according to obscure dictates. She never takes one sip out of a glass: she must take two, or four, or six. When she tidies her closet, a petticoat must be placed next to her other petticoats "lest it feel sad" but, for some arbitrary reason, petticoats must never come into contact with panties. An "emperor of quiet things," to use the expression Borges applied to Eduardo Wilde and to Ramón Gómez de la Serna,[10] Lange's child looks out for the welfare of her possessions with a benign yet implacable eye:

When I did something in an orderly way, it was not out of neatness but out of an obsessive need to provide well-being to an object and allow, if possible, that it be in contact with a similar one. My colored pencils, cut-out words and toys were never lonely because they were always close to each other, as if speaking in secret.   (p. 174)

The need to rearrange reality in private constellations, to turn trifling activities into rituals, to endow language with a life of its own, is doubtless not unusual in children. However, the insistence with which the adult recalls these breaches of convention that inaugurate a different order would signal a repossession on another level – a conscious assimilation of these childhood pastimes to the literary stance later adopted by Lange, the avant-garde writer. Lange finally found in her childhood memories the impetus for a poetics she would successfully put into practice in later works.[11] From those memories she draws attitudes distinctive of the child she was – the urge to spy, the attraction for the visually disturbing, the accumulation of disjointed images, the experimentation with language, the ritual of the quotidian – and uses them to express the writer she is. *Cuadernos de infancia* is a place for narrative experimentation, an evocation of a childhood past that allows its author to move on to the future of writing. It is a "beginning text," in Edward Said's sense of the term, the narrative of a new beginning and, at the same time, its practice.

Cuadernos de infancia was uniformly well received by critics when it appeared in 1937. The book was given immediate official recognition: soon after its publication it was awarded the prestigious Premio Municipal and, not much later, the third Premio Nacional. These were considerable honors, all the more noteworthy if one recalls the mixed reactions that had greeted Lange's previous sallies into narrative prose. Lange's earlier novels, *Voz de la vida* and *45 días y 30 marineros*, had often been judged adversely, not so much for their literary merit (which was certainly debatable) as for their purported breach of social decorum.[12] The favorable reception of *Cuadernos de infancia* may have resulted more from cultural politics than from the book's real virtues, in a not-so-subtle effort to domesticate the eccentric and somewhat scandalous Lange, nudging her into a more respectable place. At last, in *Cuadernos de infancia*, Lange had repaired to a domain better suited, in the critics' eyes, to a feminine sensibility: she was finally telling a "safe" story, that of childhood, instead of broaching the touchy issues (mainly sexual in nature) that had formerly provoked the hostility of her critics. Indeed, after what one may surmise was a very hasty reading, Oscar Bietti extolled *Cuadernos* for its "feminine candor" – a cliché, questionable in itself as a literary criterion, which only a biased *tour de force* could apply to *Cuadernos*.

Condescending readings and public honors helped critics gloss over the fact that the many-fissured *Cuadernos de infancia* did not tell a self-satisfied, nostalgic story, that the child's spying was less than candid, that the text abounded in sexual discoveries that echoed (granted, in another vein) those they themselves had condemned in Lange's previous work, and that the "feminine" element, when manifest in *Cuadernos*, invariably questioned that very cliché. The prizes that honored *Cuadernos*, besides striving to confer respectability upon Lange, in a sense isolated *Cuadernos* from the rest of her work. While tritely referring to the autobiography as *poetic*, critics never thought, for example, to refer to Lange's *ultraísmo* as a possible antecedent; never ventured to read it in the light of Lange's close association with surrealism, never once commented on the deliberately writerly slant she gives this recuperation of childhood nor on the disruptive narrative strategies and uncanny projections she inaugurated here before going on to use them, masterfully, in her fiction. The apparently reassuring terrain of childhood on which *Cuadernos* was grounded concealed the fact that it turned the recollection of life into an inquiry on literature, the house of childhood into a sometimes disquieting laboratory.

And yet, those willing to cast on *Cuadernos de infancia* a look as openly inquisitive as the one the text itself puts into practice, would see that Lange, in her own way, had inscribed scandal and not conformity, combative performance and not passivity, at the very core of her *eccentric* self-portraiture; that if avant-garde perspective had allowed her to see the by now conventional childhood plot with different eyes, her gender had allowed her in turn to contrive, within the fragmentary texture of her story, the figure of her own difference as a woman.[13] One of the final chapters of *Cuadernos* offers a memorable image of the child, defiant of her public, passionate in her verbal expenditure, shouting her message of disruption from the rooftops:

Other times I would put on a man's hat and, wrapping myself up in a poncho, would climb onto the roof of the kitchen from where I could see inside the neighboring houses. After throwing some bricks on the tin roofs to draw attention, I would begin my speech.

After yelling two or three words in different languages, I would immediately call out to all the neighbors by name with a thundering voice and, when a few distrustful heads leaned out over the fences, my voice and my gestures became so emphatic they bounced off doors, off window panes, off the tin roofs.

With a tone that was at times questioning, other times ironic, I followed my taunts with tirades in English, in French, with dislocated phrases, the name of some neighbor, the few Italian or Norwegian words I knew, collective insults, a strident peal of laughter, a sentimental verse. If some neighbor felt inclined to disapprove or to applaud, I showered him with insults, with my faulty polyglotism, with erratic gesticulation, with more banging on the tin roofs.

When I suspected that my cries were about to dry up in my mouth, I performed balancing exercises on the fence, allowing for a pause before beginning the second part of my program. Never altering my serious expression, I would let a barely audible giggle gradually become a peal of laughter that reverberated like a shot, followed so quickly by others I smile to think of them even today.

Wrapped up in my poncho, my face red, my hat well down over my eyes, I continued my work undisturbed. It lasted for over an hour, until the moment when, having lost my voice, I came down and shut myself up in my room. (p. 204)

This ritualistic performance – the child offering herself up as a spectacle, passionately chanting her cacophonous words, hurling her dissonance and her difference at the public – surely prefigures the adult Lange's nonsensical *discursos* and mock harangues. Its implications however go further. Running counter to a type of narrative that usually opts for economy and mindful husbanding – the family tale as a treasure, a wealth of recollections to be doled out carefully and shared with peers or accomplices – Lange's gesture, choosing as it does a carnivalesque setting in which to inscribe itself, breaking out from the *hortus clausus* of childhood instead of enshrining it through memory, has a wasteful elegance to it, a kind of devil-may-care dandyism that is infinitely seductive. If childhood stories such as those of Cané or Picón Salas have inscribed in their folds the image of the prominent male autobiographer as curator, as keeper of a precious past, Lange brings out into the open, proclaims from the rooftops, a different and refreshing persona: that of the autobiographer as mountebank, breaking up her childhood as she cuts up her words, and throwing the pieces, joyfully, passionately, to the winds.

PART III

Memory, lineage and representation

I analyzed these impressions, added new touches to
what I had experienced long ago, and above all,
corrected it, corrected incessantly, and this constituted my whole amusement.

Dostoyevsky, *A Writer's Diary*

Everything I live is an 'invention' from which I
could never escape. I do not know who has invented
me. Since I have never been capable of inventing,
someone is inventing in my place.

Victoria Ocampo, *Testimonios*

The image of the past cannot be superimposed on
the past itself because the past does not exist.

Georges Gusdorf, *Mémoire et personne*

8

Autobiography as history: a statue for posterity

> Monument, in the most ancient, original sense of
> the word, means a work created by human hands
> with the specific purpose of maintaining heroic feats
> or individual destinies (or a combination of the two)
> always alive and present in the consciousness of
> future generations.
>
> Aloïs Riegl, *The Modern Cult of Monuments*

Spanish America is much given to reminiscence. Borges' Funes, inexorably storing perceptions like so much refuse and condemned to a pointless lucidity, is but a nightmarish emblem of an activity much practiced in Spanish American fiction. As he lies dying, Carlos Fuentes' Artemio Cruz remembers. In order not to die, Ixtepec, the town of Elena Garro's *Recuerdos del porvenir*, remembers. Dolores Preciado remembers in Rulfo's *Pedro Páramo* and her spurious recollections lead her son to his death. For García Márquez, remembering is a way of creating; for Onetti, remembering, and usurping what others remember, is the most gratifying form of possession. Remembering is not distinctive of the most recent Spanish American literature nor is it a feature peculiar to the twentieth century. Since *Facundo*, since *María* – one might say since the Inca Garcilaso's *Comentarios reales* – Spanish American literature remembers.

All fiction is, of course, a recollection. Spanish American fiction accepts that common condition and chooses to stress it by highlighting, often within the story itself, the figure of the "recollector." Somebody, some precise individual – a narrator or a character – remembers, ruminates on the past, embellishes it, and, on occasion, writes it down. Onetti's Díaz Grey, endlessly tinkering with memories and memories of memories in *Para una tumba sin nombre*, is no different from the Dostoyevsky who, in his diary, actively reconstructs the past from bits and pieces in order to stay alive in Siberia. Memory becomes a way of life.

It is in part through these characters, whose recollections are usually doubled by a fecund commentary, explicit or tacit, on the elusiveness of their very recalling, that much of Spanish American fiction acquires its rich, reflexive texture. Yet, oddly enough, this richness so frequent in fiction is often missing from autobiography, the narrative exercise where one might expect it the most. While centered on a *memorator* who brings up a past of which he or she is (more or less) the center, Spanish American autobiography is restrained in its speculation on the act of remembering. Memory is given short shrift, its workings barely mentioned, let alone questioned. Either taken for granted, or relegated to an ancillary position, memory, as a subject, is notoriously absent from the exercise that so closely relies on it for existence. This lack of reflection is especially noticeable in nineteenth-century self-writing; it has carried over into a certain type of twentieth-century autobiography and deserves some commentary.

A consideration of the role attributed to memory in Spanish American self-writing demands that one examine the position of the autobiographer when commencing a life story. The present of writing undoubtedly conditions the salvaging of the past; it is not so much what is remembered that counts but when it is remembered and from where. By this I do not imply the personal disposition of the autobiographer, decisive though it may be, but, in a more general way, the conventions in effect at the time he or she writes. As each period rethinks genres and practices, it rethinks the means through which those genres and practices are successfully observed. In other words, and with regard to autobiography, each period has its own views on autobiographical writing and, more precisely, has its own views on memory, on the modes of remembering that will bring self-writing the closest to what the period expects autobiography to be.[1]

A look at self-writing in Spanish America in the early nineteenth century will serve to illustrate my point. As I have pointed out, autobiography, from its very inception, suffers from generic ambiguity. If its uneasy status as an in-between product is apparent to the modern-day reader, it is not forcibly evident to the author himself. The nineteenth-century male autobiographer writes a hesitant text, somewhere between history and fiction; yet he chooses to classify it unambiguously, for the benefit of his readers and his own sense of self-worth, within the more respectable limits of the former. In the nineteenth century, autobiography is usually validated as history and, as such, justified for its documentary value.

This view of autobiography, as has been noted, ignores the *petite histoire*, cuts nostalgia short (especially if there is any risk of its being interpreted as a longing for the old régime) and summarily disposes of childhood. In addition, this view affects memory, channeling recollection along precise lines and conditioning mnemonic habits. One does not remember publicly, for history, as one remembers privately. Even in those cases, rare in the early nineteenth century, when the author, untouched by the desire to vindicate himself historically, glimpses a more perplexing reality underlying the autobiographical venture, the urge to place the text within the boundaries of history, the more familiar discipline, cuts short any reflection on the complexities of memory. The brief introduction to Guridi y Alcocer's *Apuntes* is most revealing in that respect:

For days I have been troubled by [*me trae inquieto*] the thought of making notes about my life. However much I think of it and examine myself, I have not been able to ascertain the cause that moves me: such is the impenetrable character of man. At times I think I am guided by the purpose of never losing sight of my principles and my defects, so that I may meet prosperity with moderation and adversity with fortitude. At others, I fear myself moved by that spirit of idleness which draws us from our obligations and directs us to trifles we find more pleasurable than things of importance. I may be giving in to a sort of vanity that makes me delight in a few honorable traits, those one finds in even the most despicable individual, when he has had some experience of the world. Since I know myself well, I do venture to say that the first cause seems the most distant from the truth. I have not known how to cultivate the little sprouts of virtue that Nature planted in us all, I have allowed too many weeds to grow and they have smothered the precious seed. Still, whatever the cause that troubles me, it is there, and I have given in to its vigorous impulse. Perhaps my story itself, which follows, will help me understand it.[2]

Such is the introduction to *Apuntes*, refreshingly hesitant when compared with the more assertive forms of self-writing of the period. In lieu of certainties, Guridi tantalizingly announces questions, musings on the very fabric of recollection, and claims to have no "answer" prior to the composition of the text. It is the writing, the autobiographical act itself, that will perhaps cast light on his perplexity. Yet the text never does explore this unrest. Developed as a picaresque, with elegiac touches that tend to diminish as it progresses, *Apuntes* increasingly becomes a denunciation of the Church of Mexico; as such it grows monotonous, forgoing its speculative attitude and claims to introspection. In addition to this change in the narrative itself, Guridi adds a preface to his book that seriously undermines his introduction:

> It may come as a surprise to some that I have written down the events of my life [*mis sucesos*]. I could answer that this is not so rare, that Caesar composed his *Annals*, Cicero the history of his Consulate, and that many others, cited by Cicero in his letter to Lucceius, have written their own lives. I could add the excuse Cicero himself gives in his letter to vindicate himself, namely, that this is not praise but a simple narration of facts. I wish only to insist that these notes, even when speaking of me, are but a fragment in the history of Providence. Providence marks everyone's life but not everyone reflects on the fact, nor does he acknowledge it in his account. Perhaps, the discovery of Providence in my notes will move some to record its presence in their own and to submit to its dispositions.[3]

Thus, in a move that reminds the reader of Sor Juana Inés de la Cruz's defensive strategy in her *Respuesta a Sor Filotea*, Guridi validates autobiography as history; if not as history *tout court* (although touched by the Enlightenment, Guridi, writing in 1802, remains an eighteenth-century priest) as "history of Providence." Note that, in any case, the arguments set forth in this preface to validate the enterprise are similar to those adduced by other nineteenth-century autobiographers when claiming autobiography for history of man. Factual truth, usefulness and didactic value justify the telling of the personal story and guarantee its merit as a document. These self-assured protestations of the preface, then, run counter to the musings of the introduction, where Guridi speculates on his motives and on his uneasiness. It is as if, by giving his *Apuntes* two opening statements, Guridi had authored a double-headed hybrid, a text that would be *both* an assertive historical document and a self-questioning personal statement. Rather, it is as if, dubious of the reception awaiting his autobiography, Guridi had tried to ensure a worthy posterity for it by superscribing a statement that (although to a point contrary to his intentions) would beckon to the practitioners of a well-established discipline. In fact, it is interesting to note that the only existing edition of the *Apuntes*, published a full century after the book was written, followed his cue. The fourth volume in a series entitled Documentos históricos de Méjico, it appeared in 1906 with the following editor's epigraph taken from Quintana: "It is shameful that anyone with claims to some enlightenment should ignore the History of his country." Guridi's efforts at generic channeling had, in fact, paid off – to the detriment, one might add, of a more speculative reading of his text.

Towards the end of *Recuerdos de provincia*, speaking of the biographies he has written, Sarmiento declares that "biographies are the most original books South America has to offer in these times and the best material it can give to history." He then adds that *Facundo* "and these *Recuerdos de provincia* belong to the same genre."[4] Although debatable, both statements are revealing. Autobiography is taken here most literally; it is not necessarily an example of self-expression but a biography; a life, not of another, but of the self. As an example of a genre much valued at the time the world over and not only in Sarmiento's Argentina (suffice it to recall Disraeli's admonition: "Read no history: nothing but biography, for that is life without theory"),[5] autobiography seems a perfect vehicle for history and, concretely in the case of Spanish America, for the new history of the newly formed countries.

Now this generic adjudication (autobiography is biography is history), together with its specific characteristics (not only is autobiography history but new, national history), imposes a particular slant on the autobiographical text. Both autobiography and biography deal with lives in the past and imply, in whatever measure, a reassessment of those lives. However, whereas autobiography relies on memory for both its substance and its compositional thrust, biography fundamentally relies on documents. When writing the biography of the provincial strongman, Juan Facundo Quiroga, Sarmiento only sporadically *remembers* his hero. He remembers, instead, the secondhand recollections others have shared with him, the information about Facundo that has been incorporated by that sector of public opinion on which he relies and he remembers what he has read in documents. More than remembering, the biographer *records* a past in which he may be involved only tangentially. Sarmiento himself, a prodigious biographer and assiduous necrologist, wrote lives of people he knew in the past and lives of people he knew not at all. The ultimate goal of the recording, in which personal memory played, or did not play, a part, was not the pleasure of evocation but the preservation of knowledge and, one should add, the construction of a model.

Only in two of Sarmiento's biographies, and for different reasons, does this distanced approach – one that Sarmiento, quoting Villemain, would call "impartial yet not impassive"[6] – work imperfectly. These are the two biographies in which, closely knitting the life of his subject into his own, Sarmiento cannibalized two mirror images – Quiroga, his "barbaric" shadow figure, in *Facundo* and, in *Vida de Dominguito*, the son he would fashion into a copy of himself. While ostensibly biographical these texts suffer from something akin to autobiographical unrest. I shall devote some attention to *Facundo* since, besides being linked explicitly by Sarmiento himself to *Recuerdos de provincia* as another example of the "biographical" genre, it will allow me to consider the particular hybrid nature not only of *Recuerdos de provincia* but of many nineteenth- and some twentieth-century Spanish American autobiographies.

In the foreword to the 1845 edition of *Facundo*, Sarmiento, seeking to defend himself from his first critics, sought to justify his method:

It was inevitable that some inaccuracies slip into a work composed in haste, far from the scene of action and on a subject on which nothing had been written until then. Having coordinated events that took place in different and distant provinces and in different periods, consulted eye-witnesses on some issues, searched through hastily written manuscripts or called upon my own recollections, I shall not be surprised if the Argentine reader finds I have left things out or disagrees on a name, a date, that may be wrong or out of place.

Regarding the noteworthy events to which I refer and which serve as a base for the explanations I set forth, I should stress that their accuracy is irreproachable and *is corroborated by the public documents that consign them.*

Perhaps the moment will come when, free of the worries that prompted the composition of this little book, I shall recast it according to a new plan, stripping it of all accidental digressions and supporting it with *the numerous official documents* to which I refer only briefly for now. (p. 6; my emphases)

The first edition of *Facundo* in book form could well have corrected the errors found by critics when they first read the text in installments in *El Progreso*. It did not. Nor was Sarmiento ever to write the second, better composed version he announced. Sarmiento did not correct: if he returned to what he had written, it was not to revise but to write another book. *Facundo*, then, stands very much on its own from the very beginning, faithful in spirit to the Romantic tenets of inspiration and improvisation, acknowledging, even vaunting its flaws.[7] Yet Sarmiento would have it both ways. Even as he praises the book's inspired untidiness, he claims documentary status for it. The need to validate the text in a historic light certainly haunts him in this insistent foreword: he hammers away at the reader that the events he writes about are accurate, not only because others, Sarmiento's informers, have witnessed them, but because they have been recorded, set down in manuscripts, committed to "public" documents, registered in − note the authoritarian crescendo − "official" documents. If, like his models Quinet and Michelet, Sarmiento acknowledges the existence of other clues to the past besides the written word (a good portion of the second chapter of *Facundo* will be devoted, precisely, to the unwritten historical archive amassed by local bards), when it comes to establishing the legitimacy of his project, he shows himself unusually reliant on that written word, not unlike those narrow-minded "dupes de l'écriture scellée" denounced by Quinet.[8]

A purportedly well-documented text, even in its hasty form, *Facundo* immediately becomes in Sarmiento's view a *document* in its own right. Five years later, in *Recuerdos*, he declares that the book has "provided publicists in Europe with the explanation for the conflict in the Argentine Republic," and adds that "many European publications are based on the facts and on the viewpoint of *Civilización y Barbarie*" (p. 225). For all its shortcomings, the biography of Juan Facundo Quiroga, as Sarmiento sees it, fits neatly into a chain of textual reference: it takes its authority from previous documents and becomes, in turn, a document, capable of authorizing subsequent texts.

"A fable decked out as a document," wrote Alberdi of *Facundo*, drawing attention to the manner in which the purportedly "historical" nature of Sarmiento's text barely masked an exercise in personal vanity and oblique self-portraiture.[9] The expression could be applied just as aptly, if not more so, to *Recuerdos de provincia*, whose historical nature is infinitely more difficult to argue. Sarmiento claims the text belongs to the same genre as *Facundo*, that it is his own "biography." Yet this time there is no authoritative document, let alone "numerous official documents," to validate the self and attest to the accuracy of his tale. There is no previous record for that self except the unwritten text of its own memory; the only writing that supports it is the one it performs in the autobiographical text itself. As a nineteenth-century biographer, however, Sarmiento is far from what is, for the modern reader, a self-evident fact. Instead, in a deliberate effort towards consistency that is as naive as it is revealing, he will set the stage for his life story in such a way that it will allow him to deal with it *as if it were a biography*. In order to fit this preconception, and also, perhaps, to avoid charges of self-centeredness, Sarmiento will fabricate a chain of documents for his "I."[10]

To satisfy his desire for objectivity and validate his auto-biography for history, Sarmiento resorts to a ruse. Yet, there is a document on which to base the story of his self – it consists of the calumnies written about Sarmiento by his enemies. *Recuerdos de provincia* magnifies these written attacks that motivate his auto-biographical response, a magnification that cannot be entirely credited to Sarmiento's egocentricity, nor to the self-defensive strategy that guides so many autobiographies. By attributing docu-mentary value to the criticism leveled at him by the Argentine press, Sarmiento follows the pattern set in *Facundo*: he refers to a previous record to certify his project. There is, however, a disparity that even Sarmiento perceives. The documents consulted or alluded to in *Facundo* were supposedly truthful, worthy of continuation and elaboration. On the contrary, the "documents" sustaining the autobiographical project are – in the author's view – deceptive and, as such, in need of rectification. The autobiographer will not work with them but against them, striving to redress an injustice in an effort "dictated by truth and justified by need" (p. 42). The resulting autobiographical text will then be the "good" document, whose incorporation into the dossier denounces the fallacy of the other pieces therein contained.

Once the spirit of *Recuerdos* is made clear – a document in a series of documents, a text written to inform readers and redress history – then its genre is justified for the reader: it may be called a biography. Not only does Sarmiento indicate this generic attribution at the end of *Recuerdos*, as I have mentioned; he does so from the very beginning in his preface. There, besides stressing its documentary nature, Sarmiento emphasizes another feature of his text; it is an exemplary piece, quite in keeping with the principles of nineteenth-century biography, a model endowed with moral and national value:

I take delight ... in biography. It is the most suitable canvas on which to set good ideas. He who writes it exerts a sort of judicature, punishing vice triumphant, applauding overshadowed virtue. There is something of the plastic arts in biography, capable of carving a piece of rough marble into a statue bequeathed to posterity. History would not advance if one did not attend to its prominent figures; ours would be extremely rich in characters if those who can would collect information on their contemporaries, as preserved by tradition, in a timely manner. (p. 41)[11]

These views increasingly condition the life story Sarmiento has to tell. It is a public document, a text endowed with historical and moral significance, an example for posterity and a national testimony. To be sure, all of these characteristics are present, in varying degrees, in a *Bildungsbiographie*, most especially in those written in Spanish America during the period of national reorganization. In Colombia, José María Samper, with his *Galería nacional de hombres ilustres, o sea colección de bocetos biográficos* is a good example of the genre.[12] So, in Argentina, is Bartolomé Mitre, who is clearly conscious of the ideological weight such biographies can have in the consolidation of national values and plans his historiographical project accordingly. Mitre views his own "histories" of San Martín and Belgrano, together with the biographies he and others write for the *Galería de celebridades argentinas*, as integrating a textual pantheon and constituting an ideological matrix.[13] Sarmiento himself wields biography like a weapon destined to defend the memory of worthy Argentines from evil or doom the unworthy to oblivion. Eduardo Wilde tells how Sarmiento, at one point angered by an illustrious colleague, said to him, Wilde, excitedly, "I'll get my revenge, I won't write his biography."[14]

But if Sarmiento, mimicking the biographical process, "invents" documents to set autobiographical writing in motion, he very soon modifies his strategy. The very first chapter of *Recuerdos* is an eloquent evocation of his birthplace, San Juan, a city left in a state of near total decay by Spain's slothful Colonial system. In San Juan, Sarmiento takes pains to assure us, there are no written signs of the past. All that remains to keep the record are three solitary palm trees that "had caught my attention early on. Certain trees grow as slowly as centuries and, when there is no written history, serve as reminders, as monuments to memorable events" (p. 42). Besides those palm trees, Sarmiento salvages two other mementos as mute witnesses to the past – the door to a Jesuit monastery from where the embossed lead lettering has been gouged out, and a file, labeled as containing the history of San Juan, but emptied of its contents. "These, then, are the frail and deteriorated historical holdings on the first years of San Juan that I have been able to collect," writes a rueful Sarmiento of all three wordless tokens of the past. The message is eloquent: San Juan is vacant, a barren place where there are no letters, where history has become mute.[15] It is at this point that memory, personal memory – the very memory that was considered secondary to the review of records, secondary to the collation of documents – saves the day, entering the picture as a valid source for (auto)biography. Resorting to individual recollection is necessary precisely because the file is empty and the palm trees mute. The exercise of memory is not so much a privilege of the solipsistic self as a civic duty: one remembers so that a communal past is not lost.

This parallel between individual *bios* and a provincial, would-be national *ethos* is not devoid of epic overtones: Sarmiento harbors an heroic image of himself which he would gladly pass on to his readers. Yet the bond he stresses is of an even more intimate nature. It is not merely that Sarmiento pictures himself as an exemplary Argentine: he *is* Argentina, forming with his country one, inseparable body. "I was born in 1811, the ninth month after the 25th of May" (p. 160), he writes, unambiguously establishing the genetic link, having the moment of his gestation coincide with that of his newly independent country. If San Juan – a desert lost to unlettered barbarism, a blank page awaiting signs – is a synecdoche of the country, so is Sarmiento, as the remembering subject of his autobiography: he himself will be the document, the writing on the blank page.

This historical responsibility conferred on personal memory obviously imposes certain strictures on the way it is allowed to function within the text. I speak here not only of Sarmiento but of other autobiographers who have felt (or assumed) a similar obligation to recall. The short shrift given childhood, mentioned in the previous chapter, is a possible consequence of this attitude.[16] The absence of speculation on memory itself – its workings, its range, its dependability – is another. Memory is viewed as a tool, its performance as reliable as the perusal of a document, not as a subject for conjecture. A reflection on memory might indeed jeopardize the recreation of the past and its claims to veracity, opening it to doubt.

The writer might be suspected of being less a historian writing the dictates of truth, as Sarmiento fondly saw himself, and more a fanciful fabricator, filling in the gaps left by his not-so-trustworthy memory. He might be considered a fabulator, to use the term Janet would coin later, one "who adds fabrication to his story *so as to give it order*" (my emphasis).[17] Perhaps foreseeing such misgivings, which might render his whole enterprise suspect, Sarmiento takes pains to stress the accuracy of his account. Of *Mi defensa*, the autobiographical text antedating *Recuerdos* by seven years, he states that "this is not a novel, it is not a story" (*D*, p. 5). Differentiating between fact and fiction, between precise recollection (what Pichon so admirably calls "le degré sec de l'évocation")[18] and fond illusion, Sarmiento claims to be aware of the biased selectivity perpetrated by the "poetry of the heart" in the evocation of the past.[19] These signs of awareness are tenuous, however, as if Sarmiento thought any coupling of memory and imagination were better left unspoken. There are two passages that (more than the skepticism of any reader) question his claims to truth, yet he seems unaware of their corrosive potential. At the very end of *Mi defensa* (a text protesting truthfulness at every page), Sarmiento casually writes: "I have shown the man as he is, *or as he imagines himself to be*" (*D*, p. 23; my emphasis). *Recuerdos* offers another, similarly jolting passage; again presented casually, it is barely elaborated upon. Sarmiento evokes Ña Cleme, an old Indian beggar in the San Juan of his childhood who was said to be a witch. Her interest as a character, Sarmiento notes, was that she not only assumed her reputation but reinforced it, increasing her notoriety by spreading stories about herself – "trabajaba en sus conversaciones." And he adds:

Decidedly, we have a need to call attention to ourselves. It turns those who can no longer stand being old, coarse and poor into witches; those who are bold but incompetent, into cruel tyrants, and perhaps it is that very need that, God forgive me, leads me to write these pages. (p. 151)

The intuition that self-portrayal, even in the name of truth, may lead to fabulation, and that the need to call attention to oneself may be synonymous with seduction or with authoritarianism was only that – an intuition. To pursue it lay beyond Sarmiento's possibilities, intent as he was on bequeathing a national statue, a well-composed patriotic whole. It is to his merit that, perhaps unsuspectingly, he included those fissures which constitute one of the chief attractions of his texts.

Like Ña Cleme, Sarmiento "works in his conversations" to preserve a gratifying image of self that he already counts on, the very image that sustains his autobiographical act. While the auto-biographer's goal may appear to be the discovery or, even better, the construction of self, the process may be seen, at the same time, as the opposite. Self-image is an end product but it is also an initial figure, governing the unfolding of autobiography.[20] The past is recreated in order to suit the demands of the present – the demands of my own self-image, of the image I believe others expect of me, of the group to which I belong.[21] If some form of preconception invariably governs the unfolding of autobiography – that preconception that Gide called "un être factice préféré"[22] – dictating the rearrangement of the past, then one may say that Sarmiento's factitious being is the very country his text helps to found.

However, this national factitious being, in Sarmiento, has more than one face. A look at *Mi defensa* in conjunction with *Recuerdos de provincia* is once more called for. In both texts, Sarmiento presents himself as a victim of slander but the self-image that spurs his defense is different in each case. In *Mi defensa*, a text written early in his career when he has still to make a name for himself, the figuration to which the text responds is, not surprisingly, that of the self-made and self-taught hero. If autobiographical writing may be seen as an oscillation between dandyism and seduction – the desire to inscribe the unique on the one hand while, on the other, the need to attract others to the autobiographical persona – then *Mi defensa* clearly stresses the first mode (while *Recuerdos* concentrates on the second). In *Mi defensa*, isolation is stressed at all times: the word *solo* recurs obsessively in the text. Faithful to his image as an autodidact, Sarmiento forgoes all reference to lineage, devotes a brief presentation to his immediate family and then turns the focus on himself, and himself alone, as the self-taught head of the household:

From the early age of fifteen, I have been head of the family. Father, mother, sisters, servants, all have been subordinated to me and this distortion of natural relations has had a momentous influence on my character. I have never recognized any authority other than my own and this subversion has its just reasons. From that age on, I have been charged with the care of all my relatives, am charged with it even today, and never was there a burden so gladly borne.   (*D*, pp. 20–21)

This recollection – the fifteen-year-old becoming his own master and a precocious and watchful *pater familias* to boot – certainly befits the image of the self-made citizen that Sarmiento wishes to foster. Indeed, it increasingly patterns his self-writing, as one of the choice figurations representing his bond with Argentina: Sarmiento, father of the country. It is all the more surprising, therefore, that the one family tie that Sarmiento leaves unmentioned in his exemplary inventory of flattering roles and functions is, precisely, paternity – Sarmiento's own, biological paternity. When writing *Mi defensa*, Sarmiento is already the father of an eleven-year-old daughter, a fact he will never acknowledge directly in his autobiographical writings because, one suspects, it might tarnish the self-contained image he is trying to uphold. An illegitimate child, conceived during one of Sarmiento's trips to Chile and kept well out of the public eye, Ana Faustina will only be integrated positively into her father's life as an adult, when she is respectably married to the French printer Jules Belin who, let it be remembered in passing, was responsible for printing his father-in-law's *Obras completas*. For the moment, *Mi defensa* passes her over or very nearly. An oblique and none too gallant allusion, "There are in my life one or two moments of carelessness that I would gladly erase from the list of my deeds" (*D*, p. 20), might or might not refer to his daughter, indeed the product of one of those careless moments. If it does, then the desired erasure, at least textually, is achieved.

Seven years later, Sarmiento rewrites his autobiography. In the new text, *Recuerdos de provincia*, the factitious being that triggers his memory has changed. Abandoning the role of precocious family leader and solitary hero accountable to no one, he now beholds himself not alone but *en famille*, a son many times over, heir to a distinguished patriotic lineage and the product of a community: "*He querido apegarme a mi provincia*" (p. 41) – I have tried to bond myself to my province. Thus these new recollections, calculatingly dedicated "to my compatriots only,"[23] now emphasize family ties instead of short-circuiting them. In addition, far from limiting himself to the immediate family group, Sarmiento chooses to create an extended family out of prestigious figures from his native San Juan who came before him. Where he once, in *Mi defensa*, had needed to stand alone, he now must appear accompanied.

The genealogical concern at work in this new image once more bespeaks the autobiographer's need to establish himself as a historian. But it also responds to a conscious, ideological posture and to a new political plan.[24] The bellicose *Mi defensa*, written by a quite young Sarmiento, needed to sell the image of a relative newcomer to the national scene: thus the arrogant figuration of the maverick intellectual reading French books to which few had access, the self-styled young father who, singlehandedly, brought order to chaos. Seven years elapse between *Mi defensa* and *Recuerdos*, years in which Sarmiento's reputation grows through his diligent efforts and, no doubt, through the publication of *Facundo* and *Viajes*. It is a more secure Sarmiento who writes *Recuerdos*,[25] one who allows himself to widen his scope, well aware that even when he speaks of others he speaks of himself; well aware, too, that while the image of the lonely, self-made intellectual with a privileged connection to European Enlightenment might have helped project him onto the national scene, a less "original" figuration, as member of a family and, by extension, of a cultural community, might serve him better to achieve his goal, that of presidential candidate.

This new attempt at self-figuration is determined once more by what Martínez Estrada has so aptly called Sarmiento's "domestic sensibility,"[26] that is, the recasting of family romance in an ideological, precisely political mold. The approach is dexterous. Proceeding metonymically, Sarmiento works his way from remote ancestors to closer forebears to contemporary father figures to his parents (especially, his mother), to himself, their descendant. In so doing, he satisfies the biographical imperative set up for himself very successfully and many times over: each chapter, each section devoted to one of those worthy forefathers provides us with a short biography, each fashions a statue that becomes part of Sarmiento's personal gallery as well as part of a provincial, even national, pantheon.

However, these figures are linked by more than mere genealogical contiguity, as the reader finds out on reaching the striking declaration placed, quite literally, at the center of the text: "A mi progenie, me sucedo yo" (p. 159). Marking a watershed, the phrase appears to announce, finally, Sarmiento's own (auto)biography, the last in the series. Yet the phrase is unusual, its syntax aberrant. Sarmiento does not say, as one would expect, "A mi progenie *la* sucedo yo" – "I am my progenitors' successor" – but, through a grammatical sleight of hand, dramatically breaks into the genealogical line and superimposes his "I" onto the chain of ancestors: he succeeds his progenitors but he is also his own successor, his own creation. Like a two-faced Janus (a figure dear to him), Sarmiento's "A mi progenie, me sucedo yo" points at once to what precedes and to what follows. If the remaining pages of *Recuerdos* do in fact trace Sarmiento's increasingly public figuration – the visible self to the detriment of a more private one – the series of minibiographies left behind may be seen, thanks to this statement, in another light. In a recuperative rereading, it becomes apparent that what links those ancestors (like Kafka creating his precursors) is, more than family ties, a powerful process of bonding (*apego*) enunciated by a very active "I."

Sarmiento intrudes in each minibiography and compromises its illusory independence by making his presence felt in the lives of his forebears; by reminiscing, evaluating, applauding, judging, and above all taking on, in a process of deliberate affiliation, the character traits, the innermost qualities of the figures evoked. "There are young men who never knew their fathers and yet laugh, move and gesture like them" (p. 138), he writes. Giving the statement a slight twist, one might say that Sarmiento laughed, moved and gestured not merely *like* these "fathers" from the past on whom he modeled himself but, in his autobiography, quite literally *through* them. Paradoxically, Sarmiento's "I" seems much more present in those invasive appearances than in the second, more direct and univocal part of *Recuerdos*.

Sarmiento, whose claims to democracy are frequent, needs to insert himself nonetheless in a *privileged* lineage. These illustrious relatives or near relatives belong to what he terms "the nobility of patriotism and talent." The enlightened republicanism that Sarmiento has chosen previously to highlight in himself he now extends to his precursors. But these precursors also belong to what Sarmiento calls the "gente decente" – a social aristocracy to which he did not quite belong. (Sarmiento's attitude towards aristocracy is notoriously ambiguous. On the one hand, he salutes the passing of privileged castes like the Osunas and the Orléans, and welcomes the advent of democracy permitting the rise of the self-made individual. On the other hand, when tracing his maternal family back to a twelfth-century Saracen chieftain, he pointedly compares the Albarracines to the Montmorencys – not by chance one of the most distinguished families in France.) In *Recuerdos*, Sarmiento expands his "I" to incorporate others, but he artfully directs that expansion upwards. Patriotism and talent are viewed in conjunction with very real social power.

In addition, it should be stressed that most of these worthy precursors belong to the maternal side of Sarmiento's family. The series of portraits indeed culminates with an impassioned evocation of Sarmiento's mother. The emphasis on the maternal is not insignificant, ideologically speaking, if one considers the fact that the mother figure is perceived as a link to the Spanish Colony throughout *Recuerdos*; a link not to the Colonial *system*, constantly denounced by Sarmiento as the source of most Argentine evils, but to an idealized, ahistorical construct, a fantasy of origins embellished by "the poetry of the heart" and endowed with the charm of the outmoded. Thus Sarmiento's precursors on his mother's side, while models of republican virtue, also bind him to the best of Colonial tradition. Cunningly presented, these family ties make of Sarmiento, the future presidential candidate, a man for all (political) seasons.

Once again, in this second, carefully engineered recovery of the past, some things are worthier of being told than others and Sarmiento's family romance is subjected to fresh editing. A reader of *Recuerdos* who only relied on the text for information on Sarmiento – and let it be remembered that the informative function of this "biography" was highly prized by its author – would come away thinking that he had benefitted from the unique position of being the only male child in a family with four surviving daughters. Family records indicate that Paula Albarracín had fifteen children in all, several of them, male and female, dying in infancy. There was, however, one other boy who survived: Honorio, Sarmiento's senior by three years, to whom Sarmiento appears to have been quite close, lived to the age of eleven. A charming memoir written by Sarmiento's older sister, Bienvenida, refers to that brother and to the interaction between the two boys:

A child of five, he [Domingo Faustino] was sent to school to keep an eye on an older brother who was being led astray by friends and made to miss school. Things went very well between the two; the little boy spurred the older one on and they both made great progress.[27]

Even when extending the scope of his recollections to his kinsmen, Sarmiento has not renounced his claim to uniqueness; nor has the figure of the self-made hero completely disappeared. If the strategy of *Recuerdos* is to uphold the image of the worthy son, heir to the qualities of his forebears, it is clear that Sarmiento sees himself as the *only* heir: the presence of a brother (a potential rival, even at that early age) must then be sacrificed. Thus, when Sarmiento refers to his schooldays, *precisely to the same period evoked by his sister*, he edits out Honorio, presents himself as an isolated, precocious achiever, and alters the reasons why he was sent very early to school in a way that will both flatter him and fit his image:

Barely had I begun to speak when my eyes and tongue were made familiar with the alphabet, so great was the haste with which the settlers, who considered themselves citizens, hastened to educate their children in response to the decrees of the governing *junta* and of later governments of the period ... As soon as the Escuela de la patria opened, I was one of the 400 children, of all ages and all social classes, who rushed in to receive the only solid instruction that has been imparted in grammar schools in our midst ... I remained in that school for nine years, never, under any pretext, missing a single day, for my mother, with her unbending severity, was there to see that I fulfilled my duty by attending. At five I was able to read fluently out loud, with the intonations that only come with a complete understanding of the subject, and so uncommon was this early skill at that period that I was carried from house to house to display my reading, reaping a plentiful harvest of buns, hugs and praise that filled me with vanity. (pp. 160–161)

Erased from *Recuerdos*, Honorio seems also to have been deleted from Sarmiento's historical record.[28] In the guise of "the dictates of truth," the book (as its author had hoped) inaugurated the "official" version of Sarmiento's life. With few exceptions, biographers and critics have perpetuated the fiction of the unique, precocious boy surrounded by four, hazily outlined sisters. And, most remarkably, those who do mention Honorio never stop to ponder his absence from Sarmiento's life story.[29]

Now I am aware that I am venturing into dangerous territory when pointing out these presumed "gaps" (absence of a daughter, absence of a brother) in Sarmiento's life stories, gaps that only appear when the autobiography is held up to a factual account of the individual's existence. My primary purpose, in pointing out these fissures, is not to seek correspondences, or a lack thereof, between what was and what is told, thus appearing to fall back on a simplistic view of the genre's purported referentiality – a referentiality that, as de Man has suggestively argued,[30] may be a mirage of the text itself.

I find these absences striking, not merely because they occur in *Mi defensa* and in *Recuerdos de provincia* but, more specifically, because they occur precisely *there* and not elsewhere. In other texts, especially in letters, Sarmiento occasionally mentions his daughter and (infrequently, it must be said) his brother.[31] There is no wholesale condemnation of them to oblivion: these figures *do* eventually get mentioned in some part of Sarmiento's self-writing. But there is definitely a diversion, from a text where their presence could prove bothersome, to a more innocuous place in Sarmiento's work where they live on, unnoticed. If, as Gusdorf has noted, autobiographical memory is "always, to a certain degree, a revenge on history,"[32] it is also, in certain cases, a good excuse for housecleaning.

In other cases, memories connected with seemingly disaffected figures in the autobiographer's account may be put to a different purpose. This seems to be the case with women, those other phantom figures in Sarmiento's life, whom – with the exception of his mother and, to a lesser degree, his sisters – he also subjects to displacement. I use the word figure here advisedly: what Sarmiento seems to be blotting out from one text and displacing to another is not so much an individual as a symbolic configuration. I am not unaware, of course, of the psychological import of the obliterations – a female child, a male sibling, and now, quite significantly, women in general. However, viewing those deletions as part of a figurative system may provide a better understanding of Sarmiento's selective memory and of the ways in which he uses it to achieve opportune (or opportunistic) representations. In the same way that Sarmiento incorporates texts to fashion his persona, he incorporates tropes (more than persons) to add to the image he has of himself as he writes. This image is, in itself, an amalgam of symbolic representations – *el hijo, el amigo, el militar, el hombre de partido*, and so on. Adopted figures of paternity and prestigious mentors will serve Sarmiento well; as vehicles of amplification, they conveniently magnify his persona. So will the mother figure serve him; in itself, for the importance it occupies in his life, but especially as a cultural figure whose tradition goes back through Lamartine to Augustine.[33] Figures of contiguity that in some way would mirror him, even as inferior copies – the unplanned daughter, the unwanted sibling, the lover or spouse – instead of adding to his isolated monumentality detract from it. And Sarmiento, it is clear, cannot tolerate the idea of expenditure, of diminution.

In the case of women, Sarmiento is notoriously cautious, not to say miserly, as to the place he awards them in his (written) life. His sisters, never referred to by name but in a group, "mis hermanas," are murky figures. If they come to life, as they do in the chapter entitled "The Paternal Home," they do so as foils for Sarmiento's *beau rôle* in the family struggle between old ways and new. Other women receive only circumstantial mention in *Mi defensa* and *Recuerdos de provincia*, and the ones that were linked erotically to Sarmiento, none at all. Differing considerably from one of his avowed models, Benjamin Franklin, who feels he can speak freely of "the hard-to-be-governed passion of youth [that] hurried me frequently into intrigues with low women"[34] without damaging the exemplary nature of his autobiography, Sarmiento glosses over any incident that might suggest sexual impropriety. Even the proper ties go unmentioned: Sarmiento is a married man when he writes *Recuerdos de provincia* yet Benita Martínez Pastoriza, his wife since 1848, is never mentioned. The fact that there were signs of impropriety previous to the marriage might account for the silence, if only in part.[35]

Women are not entirely absent, however, from Sarmiento's self-writing. Much later, in the diary he keeps on his return trip from the United States in 1868, loosely written in the form of a letter to the woman he loves, Aurelia Vélez Sarsfield, and later published as part of his *Memorias*, Sarmiento includes a fairly long fragment entitled "Las santas mujeres," the holy women. Under this self-serving title (the expression usually referring to the Virgin Mary and the other women who ministered unto Christ), Sarmiento celebrates the women in his life, prefacing his enumeration with the following remarks:

In Paris I bought a statuette of the Venus de Milo and on its base wrote this inscription:

TO THE HAPPY MEMORY OF ALL THE WOMEN WHO LOVED ME AND HELPED ME IN THE STRUGGLE FOR LIFE

The Venus de Medici is all passion; the Venus de Milo is the woman ready to be a mother or a beloved, for she shows only her breast and is of serious mien, as if she felt the call of duty.

There are the *Women in the Bible*, the women in the works of Shakespeare, the women in Goethe. Why should there not be the *Women in Sarmiento*? Not because I have created them in my fantasy but because they have all sheltered me under their maternal wing or helped me live during long years of trial.

From the time I was born, my destiny has been woven by women, practically only women, and I can name them one by one, in a series in which, as in a chain of love, they pass the object of their affection from hand to hand.[36]

Just as he had established a formative chain of exclusively male intellectual mentors in *Recuerdos de provincia*, Sarmiento, more succinctly but no less admiringly, now rescues the links of another, no less formative chain of love made up exclusively of women. It begins with his mother, which was foreseeable, given his particular interpretation of the Venusian emblem that guides his evocation – a love not erotic but maternal, combined with a sense of duty. As in the case of Alberdi, who felt that in his letters he could rhapsodize freely about *La Nouvelle Héloïse*, even confessing to the physical attraction he felt for Rousseau as painted by Fantin-Latour, whereas in his autobiography he only "remembered" the author of *The Social Contract*, Sarmiento's recollections are tailored here to fit the image he wishes to give a precise recipient. If, in this passage from *Memorias*, a feminine "chain of love" that had no place in the more public, monumentalizing pages of *Mi defensa* or *Recuerdos* is salvaged and placed under the serene sponsorship of the Venus de Milo, it is because the text is addressed to a reader who is a woman herself and is, in addition, the woman Sarmiento loves. The purpose of the autobiographer here is not to set an example but, more subtly, to charm and to woo.[37] A small act of seduction, it posits a different persona – the author surrounded by his many Venuses, wanting to be loved: "There must be something profoundly sad in my eyes that awakens maternal solicitude in women" (p. 294). But if autobiography is indeed a vengeance on history, history, on occasion, gets its own back. Sarmiento allowed himself this portrait principally for Aurelia Vélez Sarsfield, not for posterity, to which he had already bequeathed the more solemn images of *Mi defensa* and *Recuerdos de provincia*. Posterity, in spite of Sarmiento, now reads all three pieces with an equal eye and delights in them all.

9

Shrines and labyrinths: a place to remember

> ... A kind of temporal abandonment, where
> camphor or poppy seeds, in a silent and nocturnal
> vegetal growth, prepare an oval and crystalline
> identity, and where the isolation of a group pro-
> vokes a communication that is like a universal
> mirror.
>
> José Lezama Lima, *Paradiso*[1]

That Sarmiento's memory, as an individual, should take on the form
of a reflection on genealogy – the gathering of family precursors with
whom Sarmiento identifies – is not coincidental. From the Inca
Garcilaso, who as a child eagerly heard his mother and her brothers
evoke a shared Inca past on the verge of oblivion, to Borges who, in
his inscription to his *Obras completas*, thanks his mother for "your
memory and, within it, the memory of our elders," the past, in
Spanish America, appears to be, very consciously, a family affair.
Borges himself, faced in *Evaristo Carriego* with the biographer's (and
perhaps the autobiographer's) dilemma – "that one person should
wish to awaken in another memories that only belonged to a third
person is an obvious paradox"[2] – resorts to an ingenious explanation of the workings of memory in Spanish America:

[O]nly new countries have a past; that is, an autobiographical sense of that
past, a living history. If time is succession, then we must admit that
wherever there is a greater density of events, more time flows, and that it
flows abundantly in this inconsequent part of the world. The conquest and
colonization of these domains ... was so inconsistent that, in 1872, one of
my grandfathers was to command the last major battle against the Indians,
bringing to a close, in the late nineteenth century, the conquest of the
sixteenth century. But what need is there to speak of the dead? I have not
felt the levity of time in Granada, in the shade of towers a hundred times

older than the fig trees. Instead I have felt it at the corner of Pampa and Triunvirato: what is now an insipid place full of would-be English rooftops was, three years ago, a place of smoky brick kilns and, five years ago, a place of untidy pastures. Time – a European emotion felt by men with a long past, in a sense their justification and their greatness – circulates less prudently in our republics. The young feel it in spite of themselves. Here, we are contemporaries with time, we are time's brothers.[3]

Borges' explanation, charming and suggestive though it may be, is of course fallacious. Our autobiographical memory of the past, whatever our nationality, is confined to remembering our own existence. In the aforementioned example, Borges does not remember his grandfather's battle nor, needless to say, does he remember the sixteenth century. The nineteenth-century battle is not a lived recollection but a reported fact, something he has heard an elder, probably his mother (for whom it may have been an autobiographical recollection) dredge up from the past. Borges has no *memory* of his grandfather fighting in that battle, he has a *knowledge* (albeit of a special kind) of the fact. As for setting the remote beginning of that battle in the sixteenth century, it is, as so much of Borges' writing, conjecture. All Borges really remembers is *having been told* that his grandfather fought: he has an autobiographical memory of the act of transmission itself.

However, when applied to the autobiographer, Borges' fallacy is not entirely inaccurate. There is an inordinately strong tendency to write *as if* the author's memory encompassed a past much larger in scope than that of his or her own, biological existence. Not only are the acts of transmission of memories often highlighted – Picón Salas' chatty characters telling family stories in *Viaje al amanecer* is a case in point, as is the mother's reminiscing in Vasconcelos' *Ulises criollo* – but most frequently the memories themselves are cannibalized, incorporated into an apparently unending rumination of which the autobiographer, by impressing upon the text the sign of his or her own remembering, is the origin. An extreme case, revealing in that it carries to its ultimate consequences both the act of transmission of the memories of another and the appropriation of those memories by the recipient of that transmission, is of course that most oblique of autobiographical exercises in disguise, the transcription of lives told by others. Two good examples of this type of *relato de vida*, immensely popular in recent years as a "new" genre, are Miguel Barnet's *Biografía de un cimarrón* (which the English translation submitted to an additional turn of the screw by titling it *Autobiography of a Runaway Slave*) and Elena Poniatowska's *Hasta no verte Jesús mío*.

The opening of individual memory onto the memory of others doubtlessly contributes to the nostalgic flavor of many Spanish American autobiographies even when nostalgia is not their prime goal. This linking of memories is rather a self-serving strategy, a way of enhancing the autobiographical persona: as a privileged witness, he or she is in contact with a past that has been lost to readers and can give that past the aura of lived experience. At the beginning of her autobiography, Victoria Ocampo, before speaking of herself, before speaking of her family, feels the need to evoke that past she knows through the stories of others:

I would hear people speak of the eighty years that preceded my birth, during which Argentina took on its present name, as of family affairs. The event had taken place at home, or next door, or in the house across the street, with San Martín, or Pueyrredón, Belgrano, Rosas, Urquiza, Sarmiento, Mitre, Roca, López – they were all either relatives or friends. The whole country was filled with echoes of historical dates that felt like family birthdays and with the nostalgia of the people who surrounded me and spoiled me.[4]

The *petite histoire* that nineteenth-century autobiographers dutifully excluded from their texts in the name of History works itself back, here, as History itself. In these bits of family gossip, the illustrious becomes everyday fare and the fathers of the country are spoken of in the same breath as the water-vendor and his horse-drawn barrels.[5]

By incorporating the memory of others, the autobiographer's own memory expands, becomes more powerful. It is suggestive that Ocampo should choose a metaphor of land – she for whom landowning was a natural source of wealth – to signify this growth: "Now I am flooded by memories, theirs next to mine, and these memories embrace (this is the right term) great extensions of land. They rush to the north, to the south of Argentina, they include the provinces of Córdoba, San Luis, La Rioja, the immense province of Buenos Aires"(p. 12). Recollections replace territories, memory expands to cover the surface of the country, to become that country, a new *patria* over which the autobiographer rules, a landowner turned owner of the past.

Victoria Ocampo's assertion that "it is fair to say that the History of Argentina was the history of our families"[6] – a statement that, precisely, is not fair at all – is telling in its very blindness. It draws attention to a patrician bias, not so much on history as on the conception and actual writing of history prevalent at the end of the nineteenth century (and not infrequent in the twentieth), a conception that cannot but affect the way the autobiographer thinks of him or herself.[7] Significantly, María Rosa Oliver, a member of the same class whose career would evolve along ideological lines quite opposite to those of Ocampo, having too experienced history as family gossip and heard San Martín referred to as "el tío Pepe" (and mockingly called "gallego" because he spoke Spanish with a thick Peninsular accent), remembers questioning, as a child, the accuracy of what she was told and, more importantly, of what she read. Conflicting family versions having led her to doubt that Rosas was "all bad" and his opponent, Urquiza, "all good," she recalls her reaction to one of her grandmother's stories:

I was not convinced. I mistrusted her impartiality. If Mármol's *Amalia* was true ... then the one who defeated Rosas had to be good, or at least better than Rosas. I was greatly upset at not having on one side the models of virtue and, on the other, what edifying books used to call "the prototypes of evil and vice." If this was not the case, what upset me even more was that books – for me the printed word was truth made manifest – did not say so.[8]

Expansion and wealth of memory are accompanied in most autobiographies by a no less comprehensive fear of loss. A strong testimonial stance characterizes the Spanish American autobiographer: he or she is not just a witness to this expanded past but the *only* witness to a period that is no more, a period that will be preserved solely in the telling. Given the constant changes and frequently violent upheavals that characterize Latin America as a continent, it is not surprising that the autobiographer should adopt this particular stance: seen from the present of writing, the past – one's own past – is an anachronism doomed unless one save it by giving testimony. A recurrent phrase in these autobiographies is *alcancé a ver* – "I came just in time to see." The Spanish expression implies imminent change, the idea that one manages to see something fleetingly at the very last moment, *just* as it disappears from view. "The true picture of the past flits by," writes Walter Benjamin. "The past can be seized only as an image which flashes up at the instant when it can be recognized and is never seen again ...

[E]very image of the past that is not recognized by the present as one of its own concerns threatens to disappear irretrievably."⁹

There is a passage in *Recuerdos de provincia*, one of the many in which Sarmiento quotes from his mother's memory – *cuéntame mi madre* – that aptly summarizes this gesture. Sarmiento remembers hearing his mother tell how one of her relatives, an immensely rich woman in whose mansion the most minute Colonial rituals were observed, had her servants perform once a year a task called *asoleo* – roughly, a "sunning" of the family silver – in the mansion's huge courtyard. A slave would help Sarmiento's mother, then a little girl, up a ladder that just came short of a small window looking out on that courtyard. Held firmly in the slave's arms, high enough so that she could reach the window and see out, but not so high that she could be seen, the child would watch as doña Antonia Irarrázabal's mildewed silver pesos were brought out to dry in the sun – a thick layer of metal covering the entire courtyard, stirred by two old slaves "as if they were winnowing resonant grain" (p. 67). *Alcanzar a ver*: the Spanish American autobiographer is no different from that little girl, reaching up to peek at an ancient treasure of which she is a secret and privileged beholder, and then living on to speak of it when it is lost from sight.

Examples of these "last glimpses," often endowed with the aura of terminal visions, these gazes that have seen, directly or indirectly, what is no more, abound in Spanish American autobiographies. In a sense, they undermine – with felicitous results – the factual documentary value or the narrow practice of history self-consciously claimed for the exercise. In his autobiography, *Tiempos iluminados*, the Argentine Enrique Larreta (best known for his *modernista* novel, *La gloria de don Ramiro*) describes such a moment:

I have already described in a little book what the Buenos Aires of my childhood was like. All of those who come, as I do, from the last third of the past century, have witnessed changes in our city quite prodigious and sometimes – why not say it? – unfortunate. For me, the violence of those changes is summed up in the contrast between two personal impressions that would seem not to fit in the same life. More than once, in the evening, on entering the Círculo de Armas, still dazzled by the brilliance of the shop-windows, I have seen again, as if I were still looking out from the balcony of the house we used to live in, Arias' soldiers marching down the street after the defeat of Los Corrales. I must explain that, as a child, my eyes were able to see [*alcanzaron*], from that very place, the savage spectacle

of our historical cavalries, the same hordes that appear at every page of
Lamadrid and Paz ... entering a city they were seeing for the first time ...
Here was the ancient gaucho, here was the Pampa, with all its dust, its
thorns. And all this, on the corner of Maipú and Corrientes.[10]

As a child, Larreta caught a glimpse of what can no longer be seen
at the time he writes. Looking back to it, from the threshold of the
patrician Círculo de Armas, in a modernized city that has changed
beyond recognition, he isolates it as a nostalgic fragment he can hold
on to, a mooring to his former self. This last glimpse is a constitutive
part of his "I," it is, in a manner of speaking, his personal
prehistory, comforting in times of distress. But it is also more than
that. To have seen Arias' defeated cavalry is not just a personal
recollection, it is a link with a national past. As he is quick to point
out, Larreta has *seen history*, not merely a gaggle of rowdy peasant
soldiers; he has seen the Ancient Gaucho, he has seen the Pampa,
while others can only read about them in history books. In this
context, it seems pertinent that the two authors he mentions,
Lamadrid and Paz, generals in the nineteenth-century civil wars,
were themselves autobiographical writers.[11]

Perceived as a title of glory, this link with the outdated can only be
made valid in the actual telling. If I have chosen a "last glimpse"
from Larreta to exemplify this link, it is because of the particular
nature of his text. *Tiempos iluminados* is an autobiography that was
read to a live audience before it was published. Larreta delivered it
as a (very long) lecture, on 3 May 1939, at the Jockey Club in
Buenos Aires where he had been invited by a group of fellow
members to lecture on himself. If all literature courts a community
of readers sympathetic to the text itself, if, more particularly,
autobiography courts a community of readers sympathetic to the
being in the text, then the Jockey Club lecture hall, on 3 May 1939,
was the perfect setting for this act of self-exposure. These circumstances – Larreta speaking to peers, soliciting their sympathy as one
can only do in oral delivery, all the time knowing that he had a
captive audience – were ideal. Furthermore, the circumstances were
ideally suited to ensuring the audience's understanding, even its
vicarious sharing, of the scene Larreta had witnessed and salvaged
like a treasure. As Larreta spoke, his past became the group's past,
his last glimpse, a communal vision: the fighting gaucho, spirit of
the pampa, symbol of the frontier, was bound to awaken an echo in a

conservative upper-class audience wary of change and fearful of new invasions – not Indians this time but immigrants.[12] Thus the "last glimpse" of the autobiographer, appealing to the group's defensive ideology, is recognized as a collective emblem.

The autobiographer creating a petty complicity of power and lineage in the sanctuary of the Jockey Club, holding up, in 1939, comforting symbols of Argentine nationality from the nineteenth century while ignoring signs of twentieth-century crisis – the scene is patently anachronistic, its unwitting parodic quality no less evident. Nevertheless, precisely because of its extreme character, the scene captures to perfection the communal bonding that the Spanish American autobiographer often strives for in recreating those visionary last glimpses from the past.

The urge to preserve events from the past against the passage of time, against the grain, as it were, of the present, and turn them, through telling, into shared occurrences – rituals, communal necromancies – is abetted by a canny practice of memory in the text.[13] Generally at play, in these autobiographies, are two types of memory, not necessarily simultaneous, which complement each other. On the one hand, there is individual memory, self-satisfying and at times solipsistic; it treasures choice details of personal life much like keepsakes or relics, to use Benjamin's term.[14] On the other, there is collective memory, one that would preserve the past of a community of which, as a self-appointed witness, the autobiographer is a privileged member. True rememoration (Benjamin's *Eingedenken*) is an ever renewed merging of the two memories, the communal and the individual, resulting in a "secularized relic."[15] It is such relics that the autobiographer offers up to the reader community for recognition, while not neglecting, of course, their personal, and to a point unique, value.[16] Again I resort to Ocampo who, in her *Autobiografía*, reworks her first recollection in two distinct ways according to the strategy she has chosen for each passage.[17] In one section of her text entitled "El archipiélago," where she sets forth scattered childhood memories in mock-childish tone, she presents her first recollection for its own worth:

I climbed on something to reach the well. Through the hole I looked down at the water. I shouted. The well shouted back. I was having fun. No one in the patio. The patio was mine. Suddenly, I raised my head and saw Tata Ocampo, standing in the doorway of his room. He was holding up his cane,

threateningly, I thought. He was saying something ... "Child! Child!" ...
He didn't like my having climbed onto the well. He wanted me to come
down immediately.   (I, p. 75)

The passage continues in this vein to describe a misunderstanding:
the great-grandfather comes towards the child, motioning to her
with his cane to climb down, while the frightened child, thinking
that he is about to strike her, not only climbs down but runs from
him weeping. This is a memory that Ocampo clearly sees as
fundamental in her individual retrieval of the past: "The memory of
Tata Ocampo, on the day of the well, will go first. I was five when he
died. I don't know whether the memories I list after that one came
before or afterwards" (I, p. 67). However, in an earlier section of the
Autobiografía entitled "Antecedentes" and devoted to family memories, the very same recollection has already appeared in quite
different terms. Mentioned as an incident, not as a recollection, it is
imbricated in lineage and evoked to assure a link with the past:

In 1810, Manuel José de Ocampo was appointed alderman of the Council
of the city of Buenos Aires and, as such, played a role (a cónsiderable role,
it is said) during the May revolution. That same year, in Buenos Aires, on
15 September, his son was christened with the name of Manuel José de
Ocampo y González. This was to be Tata Ocampo, Sarmiento's friend, the
great-grandfather I was to know [note again the Spanish: *alcancé a conocer*]
in his nineties, who one day became very frightened when he thought his
great-granddaughter (myself) was about to fall into the well of his house on
Florida and Viamonte, where she was taken daily.   (I, p. 20)

Here, the individual recollection is touched by collective memory
and becomes historically significant. Tata Ocampo's persona – the
family patriarch, also casually referred to, on one occasion, as "the
grandfather of the well" – takes on new attributes and is given his
full name: Manuel José de Ocampo y González. He is also placed in
a more ample setting: the family house opens onto the budding
republic. Born the year that marked the end of Colonial rule, this
Ocampo is the son of a hero and a good friend of Sarmiento, whose
fame as a politician and writer was well established. In this context,
the child's near fall into the well takes on additional meaning. It is
not merely a prank that has left an indelible mark on Victoria
Ocampo's individual memory, it is a link with the older past of the
nation. This (says Ocampo to her reader) was my physical contact –
and, as I speak, I make it yours – with "our" past.[18]

I hasten to add that this communal memory is often as illusory as the autobiographical past vaunted by Borges, for very rarely does it correspond to a shared past. If in the case of Larreta it did – an ideologically cohesive audience recognizing itself directly in the author's evocation – the very nature of the situation underscored its exceptional character. What the autobiographer relies on, of course, is the seductive power of these bonding illusions whose tropological foundations are taken from life itself. Thus, in the same way that Sarmiento seeks recognition from his readers by organizing memories according to what Martínez Estrada has called "the domestic sensibility" and Patricia Tobin, no less felicitously, "the genealogical imperative,"[19] playing up son and father figures (son of San Juan and of the independent republic, father of his family and of the country) to forge a link with his audience, other autobiographers choose to court sympathetic mirror figures, hypothetical siblings and kinsmen who will read and understand them. While the world and the community evoked by the autobiographer may not be that of the reader, the text is persuasive enough to lure that reader, an easy prey, into a much desired sense of belonging.[20]

The double vision of the past, the frequent (in the case of some autobiographers, constant) articulation of memory for the benefit of a community, real or fabricated, usually leads to a particular sense of space. There are protected places to remember and from which to remember, privileged locations chosen to inscribe these gestures of communal restoration. These locations – the sites of memory, as it were – are, of necessity, beyond the autobiographer's reach. Removed in time or in space, they are essentially *inactual*, never coinciding with the present of writing, that is, with the locus in which the autobiographical act itself originates. Distance of one kind or another is to be found at the source of all autobiographical writing, regardless of country or period. The simplest form of that distance is, of course, geographical: it is rare (though, one supposes, not impossible) to find a perfectly homebound writer, writing his autobiography in the very place where he began his days. (In that case, most probably, there would be no autobiography: Amiel, the perfect example of the nearly motionless self-writer, wrote diaries, not a life story.) But the autobiographer's distance is, above all, temporal and psychological: the sites claimed by autobiography for its ceremonies of memory are out of reach, either because they have been left forever behind or because time has eroded them beyond recognition. The first volume of Gómez Carrillo's autobiography aptly begins with a lament for his native town of Santiago de los Caballeros, in Guatemala, recently destroyed by an earthquake but indelibly fixed in his memory; "This is how I always dream of it and this is how I thought I would see it, one more time, before my death."[21]

Geographic displacement, often of a radical nature, marks many lives in Spanish America; it is not surprising that it should reinforce the abovementioned sense of distance. The autobiographer *moves away* – from the province to the capital, from his country to another country, from one continent to another. The Argentine Carlos Mastronardi, echoing perhaps Sarmiento's *Recuerdos de provincia*, calls his 1967 autobiography *Memorias de un provinciano* and makes the move from his native province of Entre Ríos to Buenos Aires, his adopted city, the focus of his narrative. The opposition of similarly contrasting spaces, provincial Mérida and present-day Caracas, kindles, as has been noted, Picón Salas' evocation in *Viaje al amanecer*. A similar progression may be observed in Baldomero Sanín Cano's *De mi vida y otras vidas* (1949), in which provincial Rionegro, in Antioquia, is abandoned for Bogotá. The autobiographer's journey usually goes beyond the move from province to capital. Darío goes from Nicaragua to Chile to Argentina to Paris; Picón Salas from Caracas to Chile to cities the world over. The Condesa de Merlin, Mansilla, Gómez Carrillo, all write their autobiographies in Paris. Darío, who lives in Paris ("I dreamed of Paris since childhood, to the point that in my prayers I would ask God not to let me die without seeing Paris"),[22] writes his autobiography during a brief trip to Buenos Aires. The idea for *Ulises criollo* comes to Vasconcelos after having left Mexico for Spain and weeks before departing for Buenos Aires. The well-worn cliché that equates life to a journey is, in Spanish American autobiography, often restored to its quite literal meaning. Gómez Carrillo, writing at the turn of the century, entitles one of his many collections of travel articles and vignettes *La vida errante* – the errant life. And, when he writes his own "errant and passionate life," he gives it the same, loose format he gives his cosmopolitan travelogues.[23]

For the Spanish American writer, globe-trotting, at the turn of the century, is the mark of modernity. As time goes by, it will become a way of life and, more often than not, a political or economic decision. Darío and Gómez Carrillo make Paris their home not only for literary reasons (the turn-of-the-century Spanish American writer makes his "journey to France" just as the French painter of the Renaissance made his "journey to Italy") but because, in Paris, as petty diplomats or foreign correspondents, they can make a living in a manner that would be difficult, if not impossible, back home.[24] In other cases, from Sarmiento to Picón Salas, political exile will serve to catalyze a wanderlust that eventually becomes second nature. And there are yet other cases where exile, though not political, becomes a personal choice: the Condesa de Merlin marrying a Frenchman and settling in Europe early in life and Mansilla choosing to end his days in Paris are good examples.

This quite literal movement away from origins, a decisive component of the Spanish American autobiographer's individual experience, should be seen in conjunction with a particular sense of history, the one leading, as I have mentioned, to privilege "last glances" of a personal past into which readers are lured. Both – distance from origins and catastrophic sense of history – seem to demand, on the part of the autobiographer, the creation of a solid *common place* for rememoration. The most frequent form of that common place of memory is of course the most obvious – the family home or *casona*. Naturally the scene of family romance – witness the frequency with which it appears in Spanish American novels, from the idyllic "El Paraíso" of Isaacs' *María* to its infernal counterimage, "La Rinconada" in Donoso's *Obscene Bird of Night* – it is also, in autobiographical writing, a shelter for memory. By a process of contagion, the *casona* often extends beyond its limits; then it is a whole town that becomes a shrine for recollection, or a city, or a region, or even a country. Picón Salas' Mérida in *Viaje al amanecer*, already referred to, is a perfect example of this amplification.

To postulate a place for commemoration is, in itself, a possessive, socially defining gesture. Putting it simply: to house the past under one's roof means that one has a roof to begin with. The autobiographer resorting most frequently to this gesture speaks from a position of social or intellectual power; the authoritarian thrust extends beyond the house itself to the tradition one would shelter in it. *Habla el algarrobo*, a text by Victoria Ocampo, while not strictly autobiographical, is singularly revealing of that attitude. A dramatic text devised for a light-and-sound spectacle in a historic site of Buenos Aires, therefore seeking some kind of communal recognition on the part of the public, it presents the voice of a carob tree "remembering" the many events witnessed in the house during 200 odd years of Argentine history. Not coincidentally, that house, the *quinta* Pueyrredón, had belonged to relatives of Ocampo's. A possessive act *par excellence*, as Blas Matamoro shrewdly points out,[25] Ocampo's text stages not merely an "I" remembering the house but the house remembering itself – that is, property remembering (engendering) property. Conversely, one look at the autobiographies of the dispossessed shows that the sanctuaries of memory are tenuous and that communal rememoration eludes them in any conventional way. The slave Juan Francisco Manzano has no place of his own to rescue from the past as a fixed space for memory: the only place in which he feels at home to meditate and daydream is, not without irony, the lavatory. A similar lack of place characterizes the testimony of Jesusa Palancares in Elena Poniatowska's *Hasta no verte Jesús mío*.

An interesting text in the way it posits a place for commemoration is the Peruvian Enrique López Albujar's *De mi casona* (1924). At first glance, this simple autobiographical chronicle appears to conform to the recuperative gesture described above. López Albújar claims the great house of the title as a repository for the *petite histoire* of his childhood and that of his native Piura: a silent witness to the past, the *casona* merits "that I speak of it, that I set down, through my own recollections, some of its history."[26] But the story López Albújar has to tell is not one of ancestral glory nor is the bonding he proposes one established through privilege. Contrary to most cases, where the home of the autobiographer is exalted as patrimony, this *casona* has not been in the family for long. It was bought by López Albújar's hard-working grandmother, a cigar-smoking storekeeper who, in less than thirty years, had risen "from poor quadroon, crowded into a back street, to respectable lady, mistress of a great and luxurious bustling provincial house" (p. 25). Yet another Spanish American *mamá grande*, this enterprising "mamá señora," continues to work despite her newly-gained status, turning part of the *casona* not used by the family into a hotel. The mansion has been invaded; inherited glory has been replaced by active commerce.

The history of López Albújar's family house is narrated in conjunction with the child's family story, in itself unconventional. An illegitimate child, López Albújar was separated from his mother and brought up by his grandmother; his parents only married after the *mamá señora*'s death. But the text does not dwell for long on the individual, clearly subordinating him to the story of the *casona*, rich in picturesque anecdotes and possibly less disturbing to narrate. *De mi casona* reads like a series of vignettes, benevolent and mildly humorous in tone, at times marred by the sentimental pathos that so often accompanies populist zeal. Bypassing these shortcomings, I am interested in the text for the way it plays with the notion of place, subverting the habitual model and questioning (albeit naively) the notion of a culturally privileged sanctuary. The chapter "Mi blasón" [My Coat of Arms], for example, distancing itself ironically from its title, is precisely a disavowal of lineage:

Unfortunately for those who have heard my name mentioned and for those who occasionally read me, as also for those *criollos* who never stop improvising illustrious ancestries while shaking off the mud gathered by their elders as they plodded untidily through life, I do not know where my lineage begins. Perhaps in the tail of some unlettered *conquistador*'s horse, or in some petty magistrate's ruff... What do I know! (p. 53)

In the same way, the notion of family bonding through shared memories, that *entre nous* attitude towards a national past that Ocampo so aptly exemplified, is ridiculed and emphatically debunked through the calculated celebration of the present:

Our evenings at home were always simple and devoid of historical atmosphere. One always spoke of the present, the state of business, the next family anniversary ... whatever had happened in the *casona*, street gossip ... Emphatic and tendentious statements like "When my grandfather, the general" or "At the time when father was Minister" or "One night when grandfather had the Viceroy for dinner" or "Our cousins, the Osunas," and others of the type were never heard in the *casona*. (p. 54)

From the little world of Piura, with its petty aristocrats and old-world pretensions, López Albújar rescues a venerable Colonial house and recycles it for the present, turning it into a democratic abode. Not eminence but popularity accounts for its historicity: "if my big house is not the most glorious in Piura, it is the most popular, the best known, the most historic" (p. 9). To him it is a monument not to lineage but to personal effort, housing the racially mixed instead of the pure of blood. Thus, if there is a call to communal recollection,[27] it is one founded less on the grouping of an élite than on a somewhat ingenuous call to a nationalist, basically populist bonding.

And yet, in an odd way, López Albújar's text gives in to the attraction of the very model it spurns. It mimics, not too consciously perhaps, the same defensive clichés and figures of stasis typical of an ideology it otherwise disdains. For it too condemns the *casona* to timeless immobility:

[I]n the midst of gasping cars and twinkling electric lights, of shrill factory sirens, of whistling locomotives, of thundering trams, my house, like a symbol, will continue to be the glorious grandmother of the town. (p. 13)

López Albújar's urge to preserve the *casona* from change by with-drawing it from historical circulation, all the while celebrating the fact that, thanks to change itself, he and the new generations he represents now dwell in that *casona* and will make new history, may appear contradictory. "In every era the attempt must be made anew to wrest tradition away from a conformism that is about to over-power it," writes Benjamin.[28] If López Albújar succeeds in wresting tradition away from the conformism dictated by an élite – his text might be seen, in this respect, as the exact opposite of Ricardo Palma's *Tradiciones peruanas* – his means of storing that "recycled" tradition powerfully resemble those of that élite. The need for conservative spatial icons, in autobiographical writing, would seem to override, at times, ideological coherence.

> Buenos Aires is also a house, a great house that has undergone changes as generation after generation has adapted it to its taste. Ever since its birth, by the river, its inhabitants have delighted in erecting and tearing down its walls, in moving its furniture around, in changing its decoration.
> Manuel Mujica Láinez, *Estampas de Buenos Aires*

When Lucio V. Mansilla wrote his autobiography (if such a word applies to one of the most undulating forms of self-writing in Spanish American literature) his place of origin was far behind him. Time and travel were of course responsible for that distance: although *Mis memorias* had presumably existed in book form for some time, Mansilla only decided to publish it in 1904 when he was seventy-four and living in Paris as an expatriate. Long before that, however, political change in Argentina, and a restructuring of power that had made Mansilla if not an outcast a definite misfit, had contributed no less effectively to his disconnection from home. As

Juan Manuel de Rosas' nephew, Mansilla never quite succeeded in claiming a meaningful place for himself in the public and specifically political scene of the new Argentina of the 1860s and 1870s, where any connection to the deposed dictator was more than suspect.[29] Reduced to an isolation which he took good care to make splendid, Mansilla chose his persona wisely, cultivating the role of the prankster; by constantly calling attention to his outrageous escapades, he earned the dubious distinction of being "together with Sarmiento, the man who has talked most about himself in this country."[30] Indeed, two portraits of Mansilla, who eagerly acquiesced to any form of self-promotion, are eloquent proof of this involvement with his person: special-effects photographs using mirrors, they show him multiplied into many, engaged in amiable conversation with replicas of himself. A histrionic gesture, the gimmick is an apt emblem of Mansilla's writing, an endless exercise in self-reflection and self-dispersion.

Mansilla's autobiographical writing is, at its best, richly multifaceted, at its worst, annoyingly untidy. Its compelling founding gesture – a perpetual digression from a center that exists only through its absence – can also prove its own undoing: textual roaming, if not curbed, can result in tiresome rambles, "unbearable dishevelled prattle," to quote Paul Groussac.[31] Four basic texts set the scene for Mansilla's self: *Una excursión a los indios ranqueles* (1870); *Entre-Nos. Causeries del jueves* (1889–1890); *Estudios morales o sea el Diario de mi vida* (1896); *Mis memorias* (1904). Two of these texts, *Una excursión* and *Entre-Nos*, appeared in installments, in *La Tribuna* and *Sud América* respectively, before becoming books. The first was a travelogue in the form of letters, describing an expedition to Indian territory; the second, a series of informal chats, weekly performances at which this Proteus excelled.

Given Mansilla's penchant for fragmentation, the fact that he often published in installments is not without importance; indeed, installments furnished him with an ideal mold for his scattered bits and pieces, for the unending, chatty recreation of an "I" anxious to put himself into words. "Quand on est pressé d'être lu, il faut écrire des feuilletons," is the anonymous epigraph that Mansilla gives one of his *causeries*.[32] However, quite often in his chats, Mansilla tantalizes his readers with the promise of a more cohesive body of self-writing, the publication of which he keeps announcing, then delaying.[33] In fact, the actual writing of *Mis memorias* (always referred to by Mansilla as a *book*) took place simultaneously with the loosely wrought, circumstantial *causeries*. It is not surprising then that when the *Memorias* were finally published, they should greatly resemble the *causeries* themselves; that they should appear to be one more protracted chat to be read in combination with, and as a culmination of the preceding *causeries*. In a sense, the *causeries* had infiltrated the *memorias* while the *memorias* proposed a retrospective, more tightly autobiographical reading of the *causeries*. The reader curious to trace the way in which Mansilla recaptured the past and fashioned his persona could follow this meandering "I" from one text to the other, indeed was encouraged to do so by the author. Yet in spite of their common tone, Mansilla clearly felt a need to keep the two texts somewhat apart. While the *causeries* were open-ended installments to be consumed immediately, the *memorias* were a *book* whose publication he delayed until 1904.

Even if *Mis memorias* would turn out to be, in substance, one more chat, Mansilla, because he considered it a book, needed to frame it as he had never framed a text before. Given the digressive nature of his writing this framing would be tenuous; it was nonetheless there. Instead of commencing *in medias res* as in his weekly chats, bringing up the topic that first came to mind, or instead of having the narrative coincide with a distinct portion of his life (like the expedition to the Ranquel Indians), he had to begin this time at the beginning of his life or rather, had to choose a beginning for the life he was about to tell. *Mis memorias* opens precisely on the question of how to begin, offsetting the autobiographical exercise with an inquiry into its origins and devoting part of its opening pages to an extended reflection on the pitfalls of memory. This was atypical, to say the least, in a Spanish American autobiography of the nineteenth century; such musings, as has been noted, were in general avoided since memory was considered, above all, a trustworthy historical tool. (Even in twentieth-century self-writing, resort to considerations on memory, in Spanish America, would not be the most usual opening move.) Mansilla's first pages run counter to the blind acceptance of memory that characterized nineteenth-century self-writing before him. Questioning the reliability of memory, denouncing its accuracy when subservient to vanity, Mansilla, in his opening pages, recalls the answer given by Domingo de Oro (one of the Oros whom Sarmiento had chosen for an "ancestor" in *Recuerdos de provincia*) when asked why he did not write his memoirs: "I have seen such filth. Why bequeath more sh... to history?"[34]

The musings that open *Mis memorias*, calling attention as they do to an autobiographical quandary, initiate a fertile reflection. Not only does the autobiographer ask himself how to start (and, as Domingo de Oro, whether to start at all), he also ponders on what he remembers, on how he remembers, on what he should tell and, ever conscious of his audience, on whether he will be believed. The path he finally opts for, a calculated challenge to his reader, is deliberate evasiveness. A method of "fluid insinuations, of *à peu près*," it will evolve as he writes: "In this way I shall meditate at the same time I evoke my memories and write them down. Gradually I shall develop my criteria for telling what I think I should not leave out" (p. 64). Foreseeing his readers' attempt to piece together these fragmentary memories, Mansilla resorts to metaphor:

He who is capable of reconstructing will reconstruct the situation, the event as it was, in the manner of Cuvier who with a molar reconstructed a megathere, guided (as those who followed him) by the uniformity of natural laws; or, in the manner of archeologists, who, trace by trace, little by little, bit by bit, going about their work like ants, restore and reconstruct precious mosaics that were shattered, monuments, entire cities that lay buried under the dust and lava accumulated from the quakes of this our planet. (p. 64)

This curious scientific analogy appears more than once in Mansilla's writing in connection with the autobiographical venture. In a posthumously published *causerie*, "A Confidence and a Piece of Advice," the very thrust of which is to make the reader doubt the autobiographer's veracity, reference to Cuvier is made in the epigraph, not as an encouragement this time but as a deterrent to the reader: "Cuvier was able to reconstruct an entire world of fossils from a few bones and teeth. With a few ideas and phrases one can but imperfectly sketch a character."[35] Thus the idea of reconstruction of the past, based on either the paleontological or the archeological model, is ambiguous in Mansilla: all attempts at restoration are thwarted, flawed from the start.[36] Mansilla challenges the reader (as he challenges himself) to piece together a past which is actively being dispersed in the present, in the digressive rambling that informs his writing. "It is my intention to dislocate myself," he tells us: Cuvier's fragment becomes Mansilla's figment.

Yet the hankering for reconstruction lingers in the text, like a mechanism that no longer works efficiently but is never totally discarded. In the context of Mansilla's life, the terms *restoration* and *reconstruction* are not to be taken lightly. The first term was the key word of his uncle's government; indeed one of the titles given Rosas was that of *Restaurador de las leyes* – the Restorer of the Laws. The second word, reconstruction, permeated the official rhetoric of the 1860s and 1870s after Rosas' defeat, at a time when politicians and intellectuals were advocating, and busily participating in, national reorganization. In a sense Mansilla is caught in the no-man's-land between the two, restoration and reconstruction, ill at ease with his story. His resort to scientific imagery to illustrate his preoccupation with reconstruction and reorganization highlights his no less critical discomfort with origins. In this respect, he is of course very much in tune with the quest for origins-as-truth that, from archeology to philology, characterized so much of nineteenth-century science. Specifically, the questions so playfully asked by the "I" in the opening pages (how to begin, where to begin, and if to begin), while referring to the text itself, parallel a more basic, genealogical preoccupation of Mansilla: where do I, who am asking these questions, begin?

Mansilla's family story appears marked by some form or other of displacement and dislocation. On both sides there are signs of genealogical unrest. Mansilla's father, Lucio Norberto, whose action against the British and French blockade of the port of Buenos Aires, in the combat of Vuelta de Obligado of 1845, had given him heroic stature, came from a family with two distinct branches: "one, legitimate, was that of Dr. Manuel Mansilla and his lineage; the other, to which my father belonged, was spurious." (p. 94) While Mansilla does not elaborate on the nature of this genealogical impurity that affects him, proclaiming, moreover, the supremacy of personal merit over lineage,[37] he does allow familial disquiet to reverberate throughout his text. For example, he calls into question generational divisions by highlighting the fact that his father was fifty when he married the fifteen-year-old Agustina Rozas and already had children even grand-children, from a previous marriage. This leads to family confusion and, not infrequently, to the blurring of roles, unforgettably illustrated in a passage of *Mis memorias*:

Besides being very young, my mother was very childish when she married my father, General Mansilla ... This to such an extent that, one day, when he was scolding black María Antonia, my wet-nurse who had stayed on as my nanny, for all my wailing which he usually heard as he walked in the door, he discovered that my tears and sobs were caused by my mother, who stole my dolls and my toys in order to play with them herself.   (p. 114)

On other occasions, Mansilla gives the notion of legitimacy an additional twist by actively fantasizing. At the beginning of *Mis memorias* he devotes a lengthy footnote to imagining who he might have been had his mother married Carlos Pellegrini, the young engineer who was in love with her (and whose son would be the president of the Republic), instead of Lucio Mansilla senior. Adolfo Prieto has accurately pointed out that General Mansilla (as other distinguished fathers whose reputation overwhelmed their sons) was a permanent source of conflict for Lucio.[38] The assertion, which Prieto sees borne out mainly in the political arena – Mansilla senior's active participation in the Rosas régime definitively closed doors on his son after Rosas' fall – has other, equally important effects on the way Mansilla structures his family romance and on his choice of mnemonic strategies. If General Mansilla, the father, has indeed eclipsed his son and thwarted his political ambitions, he also, most importantly, seems to have robbed him of a name:

There are many who believe that General Mansilla Street was named after me. They should be corrected in their error. I have given my name to nothing. I have no homonym, I am something like the last of the Mohicans. If I have children, they do not bear my name.   (p. 71)

This namelessness arises from what might be seen as a nominal excess. The heroic General Mansilla valued his own name sufficiently to pass it on to his two oldest sons: both of them were called Lucio. Somewhat surprisingly, however, the father's complete name, Lucio Norberto, was not given to the firstborn – the writer, Lucio Victorio – but to the second son, Lucio Norberto, "who resembled me like a twin" (p. 125); "we were identical" (p. 117). Mansilla speaks sparingly of this shadow figure, the sibling who, at age twenty-one, committed suicide rather flamboyantly by shooting himself for a woman in a busy Cádiz square. In the economy governing the use of the name, however, this mirror figure is important. The father's name is passed on to a second son, with whom it dies, and to a street, where it lives on as a monument. Lucio V. Mansilla is left, in a sense, with an emptied out name, a vacancy.

If the father's complete name bypasses the son, the son will nonetheless endeavor to vindicate it, rewriting the father's role in Argentine history in a more favorable light. For the benefit of a public that had turned against Rosas and was critical of his erstwhile allies, Mansilla recasts his father as a reticent *rosista*, a *unitario* at heart, whose loyalty Rosas himself presumably doubted. The contention barely holds up under scrutiny, as Adolfo Prieto justly points out;[39] however, it does serve to illustrate the auto-biographer's need to give the father a new and better name, to endow him – quite literally – with a worthy *renombre*. This positive rewriting of family romance, so evident in *Mis memorias*, has its negative counterpart in *Rozas. Ensayo histórico-psicológico* (1898), a critique of Rosas. In spite of its claim at objectivity, this "study" does for Rosas (whose name it spells with the traditional *z* and not with the subversive *s* the dictator chose to distinguish himself) the obverse of what *Memorias* does for the father. It questions the name of authority instead of redeeming it.

I do not bring up Rosas idly. His presence in *Mis memorias* as the *other* father ("a semi-God, the kindest man of earth" [*EN*, p. 55]) in the eyes of the very young Mansilla is decisive, generating affection, anxiety, reticence, and mixed reactions. The fact that Rosas was Mansilla's mother's older brother and she his favorite sister, that Agustina Rozas called her brother *Tatita* (Daddy), and, most remarkably, the fact that Mansilla records, in a "near luminous vision" (p. 118), a primal scene in which, as a child, he shares the bed with Rosas and his wife instead of his parents, all contribute to muddle familial hierarchy. Another episode will prove my point. Mansilla recalls the aftermath of the battle of Caseros, when the troops under Urquiza, having defeated Rosas, make their entrance into Buenos Aires three days later. The order had been given to put out flags in celebration of the winning troops. Complying with the order in spite of herself, Agustina Rozas, Mansilla's mother, dis-played on her balcony the only flags her son claims she had – not the traditional blue-and-whites but the modified, *rosista* versions with red in them. When the parade went past her balcony, Sarmiento, who was with the troops, noticed the offending flags. Observing a hole in the very center of one of them, he put his sword through it and "destroyed the rag" (p. 128). A relic of what had been, at least for the Mansillas, a better time, the torn flag was thereafter kept in the most important room in the house – the mother's *costurero*, a sewing-room *cum* parlor where she received company and held an informal *salon*.

Mansilla's account of this episode is, one suspects, somewhat tendentious. He reads his mother's gesture as an "innocent" compliance with orders, never once interpreting it as the act of defiance it doubtless was. He equally strips Sarmiento's response of all intentionality, claiming that Sarmiento, unaware of the fact that he was passing the home of Rosas' sister, merely responded "mechanically" to the "magnetic impression" on his "retina" caused by the hole in the flag.[40] Deleting the violation the incident so clearly, and so sexually, implies, Mansilla reproduces a scene markedly lacking in passion: if one is to believe Mansilla, no one – not his mother, representing the old restoration; nor Sarmiento, representing the new reconstruction – seems to have acted with any emotion or forethought. Indeed, the only passion made explicit in this passage is the autobiographer's desire to reconcile opposites, to defuse aggression on either side, to obliterate *rosismo*. Rosas cleaves his nephew's world in two and his figure stands in the way of Mansilla's felicitous restoration of the past: to restore that past as a harmonious whole might be judged ideologically equivocal, while to retrieve it in a negative vein, as a devalued ruin, would betray the spirit in which that past is remembered. "As in an anguishing nightmare – writes Mansilla referring to the reactions Rosas' memories arouse in him – I nearly feel within me a chimeric entity, with two faces, one of which I perceive as peaceful while the other disturbs me" (p. 104).

Mansilla's description of the scene between Sarmiento and his mother reveals a choice on his part: he calls the *rosista* flag a "rag" while the flag brought back by Rosas' enemies is called the "real" flag (*la verdadera bandera nacional*). Despite this choice, *Mis memorias* may be read as an attempt to patch the hole in that flag, to mend the tear perpetrated by the new order, to hold together, in the short-lived scene of writing, the two faces of the chimera. Most importantly, *Mis memorias* is fixated on the very place where the incident occurred – the family house – and in the very room – the mother's *costurero* – where the pieces of the flag, which remained forever unmended, were later kept.

Agustina Rozas is a key figure both in *Mis memorias* and in *Entre-Nos*. Like Sarmiento before him, Mansilla's autobiography resorts to the mother to filter the past. Yet while Sarmiento, through his mother, delves into the past to expand the scope of his memory, dilating chronology and establishing lineage, Mansilla, through Agustina Rozas, attempts to retrieve a *space*. It is not so much her memory that the son incorporates as her territory, and more precisely, her home, her interior: "[I]n my mother's house I feel at home, I come and go, my movements do not disturb or call atention. I am in the habit of always sitting in the same place, so much so that at times I am surprised to feel like an automaton" (*EN*, p. 670). Mansilla's attempt to remember his mother's space ends up, however, dismantling that space, verifying that it cannot be reassembled into a whole.

Space allied with memory, space as memory, is of primary importance in Mansilla's text. Mansilla is, essentially, visual; when referring to his recollective abilities (which, he claims, are excellent), he speaks of his "topographic memory" (p. 119) which closely connects space with signs. This visualization of the past reaches, he tells us, quirky proportions. His memory associates words with the specific places where he first heard them pronounced; "For example, when I was very young, on the corner of Corrientes street, a North American taught me the word *cosmos*, Santiago Arcos the word *archetype* and an old man from San Luis, who at that time was living in Achiras (Córdoba), the word *cliff*" (p. 119). Not only does Mansilla remember the exact location where the words (two of which indicate space) were first heard but also the geographical origins of two of the informers and, in one case, besides the place of origin the place of residence at the time when the information was provided. "However, what I cannot do" – concludes this passage celebrating topographic memory – "is to memorize myself [*aprenderme a mí mismo de memoria*]" (p. 119). By this Mansilla means something quite simple: he cannot learn what he has written by heart. Nevertheless, the declaration is sufficiently suggestive for it to be allowed to reverberate beyond that first, explicit, meaning. Mansilla cannot visualize himself in one distinct space of memory that would be his, or more precisely, that would be himself. He can, however, visualize the space of others, and, most concretely, the space of his mother.

This space, the locus of Mansilla's autobiographical "I," though difficult to circumscribe physically, never loses its essentially topographical nature. In other words, it never becomes a token for lyrical evocation: a memorator, no doubt, Mansilla is also an explorer. Inasmuch as it may be said to rely on other genres for support, *Mis memorias* refers back to travelogues more than it does to (auto)biography, whether historical or mythical in nature.[41] With

the same attitude as when he set out to discover Indian territory in
Una excursión a los indios ranqueles, Mansilla, in *Mis memorias*, sets out
on a *flânerie* through the streets of the Buenos Aires he remembers, in
order to chart a (rhetorical) space.[42]

A first figuration of this space would suggest a series of widening,
concentric circles, with Agustina Rozas' *costurero* at their core.
Surrounding the mother's sewing-room is the big family house, one
of the oldest buildings in Buenos Aires better known as the *presidio
viejo*; surrounding that house is a sort of clan compound belonging to
the Ortiz de Rozas family and occupying a whole city block;
surrounding the block are more blocks alive with more family and
friends and constituting the old center of Buenos Aires; surrounding
the old center are summer dwellings, *quintas*, and, on the periphery,
Rosas' estate in Palermo. This neat concentric arrangement might
give the impression of protection, of a progressive system of enclos-
ures and fortifications with a maternal *sanctum sanctorum* (as Mansilla
calls it) at its heart. This, however, is not the case. If those spaces do
exist and are carefully described, they are recalled only to be merged
dynamically, through the crisscrossings and meanderings of a
tireless wanderer. Thus the place of origin gradually loses its
deceptive orderliness; the divisions become blurred, the circles turn
into a maze – a "mnemonic labyrinth" (p. 67) to which Mansilla
holds the guiding thread.

There is a great deal of coming and going in this text, a perpetual
need to be on the move. Immediately after the first mention of the
family home, the narrator strays, in a sort of centrifugal frenzy, to
the houses adjoining it and from there, house-hopping more or less
at random, goes on to speak of the rest of the city before returning
home once again. Family members fare no differently: mention of
the father, for example, brings on comments about the father's first
wife, the children they had together, those children's children, their
neighbors, and so on. Contiguity and communication are the main
resources of this apparently aimless drift. I use the words quite
literally; more than one passage is devoted to doors that are always
left open, to passage-ways leading from one house to another, to
windows that allow one to see into other windows across from them;
the figure of the labyrinth is given topographical reality.[43] Spatial
contiguity is reinforced by consanguinity. As houses connect, so do
families. Cousins marry cousins (this will be the case for Mansilla
himself), family members play dual roles (Rosas, brother and

Tatita), relatives intermingle; the *flânerie* through families is no different from the one through the city.

The Buenos Aires retrieved by Mansilla is that of his childhood since *Mis memorias* is the first volume in a series that was never completed.[44] It is the city of the old order, the *gran aldea* or sprawling village of Rosas' period, "that court in a manner of speaking [where my mother] played the role of a princess of the blood" (p. 223), and where coexistence between *federales* and *unitarios* was less conflictive than historians contend. The city may appear to be a lost realm but there is little sense, in *Mis memorias*, of the irreparable loss that marks so many autobiographical texts. Either from a sense of fatalism or from plain insouciance, Mansilla regards the present with equanimity: old times were no better and no worse than new times – they were just different (p. 107). If there are some complaints that betray a momentary loss of *place* – "they have so changed my Buenos Aires that it is easier to remember the names of the stores than their exact location" (p. 191) – what prevails is a general feeling of composure in the face of urban change. Nothing is more revealing, in this respect, than the ease with which Mansilla goes from one street system to another,[45] combining improbable intersections between streets which he calls by their old names and others he calls by their new name: "Now that I am back from my outing, as it were, to the Lezama country house, I take up where I had left off: on Tacuarí Street, between Alsina and Moreno (I use old names and new indiscriminately) ..." (p. 181), he ingenuously tells his reader. Mansilla concocts a phantasmagoric map for his *flânerie* where the old city of his childhood and the new city of his writing come together.

If there is no momentous sense of bereavement in Mansilla, there is, nonetheless, the need to enumerate the Buenos Aires of the past in detail, as much for documentary purposes – "to help keep national tradition in some way alive" (p. 65) – as for the purpose of telling oneself that that space once existed. Prieto notes that *Mis memorias* often resembles a catalogue or a social register, that Mansilla accumulates names of neighbors, gives us detailed lists of visitors that came to his house. He interprets that inventorial penchant as a class reaction to immigration, a bonding gesture to ward off an alien threat.[46] There is doubtless truth in this, although of all the members of his generation, Mansilla was certainly the least vociferous (and Cané the most virulent) in his dealings with the alien Other – be he Indian or poor Southern European.[47] Further-more, Mansilla catalogues with equal gusto streets, places, customs, foods, smells, because "the same thing occurs with details as with coin collections, some coins have an intrinsic value whereas others are worth little, but this does not mean that they do not all have real merit" (p. 65). Mansilla's maternal space, the old city of his childhood, turns from mnemonic labyrinth into mnemonic bric-à-brac.

Where is the "I" in this space so pressingly evoked? The figuration of self amongst the bric-à-brac is curiously complicated.[48] Nothing is further from Mansilla's mind than the desire to monu-mentalize the "I" or to endow it with a representative role – teacher, curator, prophet – for posterity. In this scattered enumeration of the old city there are, of course, memories that refer concretely to the individual, allow the reader an entry into the family tale, give an idea of the man. Amongst these, perhaps the most striking are those that record fear – fear of the dark, fear of spirits, kindled by the servants' stories, fear of dogs, fear, especially, of the effects of Rosas' politics.[49] The zeal with which Mansilla lists these childhood fears, returning to them frequently in the text, insisting that he still experiences them as an adult, seems suspiciously disingenuous for the son of the hero of Obligado – a deflating strategy, perhaps, not unlike the irony and comic effects that constantly undercut the "heroic" stance of the explorer in *Una excursión a los indios ranqueles*. In spite of these snippets of personal anecdote, dispersed throughout the text, *Mis memorias* does not trace, as do most autobiographies, the progress of an "I" in any consistent way. And yet the book is not the chronicle of the old Buenos Aires either, as in the case of some Spanish American autobiographical texts in which space (house, city, country) supersedes the self-effacing "I" who sets it forth. There is nothing self-effacing about Mansilla's "I"; of all possible adjectives that might apply to him, this surely must be the most inadequate. While not always the subject matter of *Mis memorias*, in any conventional way, Mansilla's "I" unremittingly commands attention; the substance of his story, while certainly not meaning-less, pales before the display of the storyteller.

I would call this "I" a gossip, as he establishes chatty connections in a city turned bric-à-brac, had I not used the notion – auto-biographer as gossip – when discussing Mariano Picón Salas' *Viaje al amanecer*.[50] This was done in a somewhat unfavorable context, as a means of qualifying Picón's smug delight in small-town tattle and his penchant for endowing quaintness with eternal values. This is hardly Mansilla's case: quaintness and self-righteous complacency in things past are alien to his text. Even nostalgia, although by no means absent, is more often than not averted through humor. Mansilla never stops for long in one place, never pauses to embellish this or that episode. Perhaps the best way to describe the figuration of this "I" is indeed to refer to the term he himself uses at every turn, that of the conversationalist, the *causeur*.[51]

Mansilla's chats in *Entre-Nos*, dramatizing the struggle between self and digression, had already established the parallel between *causerie* and *flânerie*:

After all, doesn't Anatole France, whom you consider a better writer than I, defend himself from certain incoherences ... by saying: "I would like these *causeries* to resemble a stroll, I would like these little black lines to give the idea of a conversation capriciously maintained along a meandering road?" And doesn't he, a most popular writer, a keen observer, both benevolent and learned, conclude by saying: "This is where our stroll ends. I admit to having roamed more than was necessary. I was in a wandering mood today"? (*EN*, p. 648)

In *Mis memorias*, Mansilla's digressive loquaciousness finds its ideal form: the fiction of displacement and the fiction of orality are one. If contiguity and communication, as I have pointed out, are emphasized in the text, it is not only because rooms and houses intercommunicate or because families intermarry. It is because the "I," in his *sideration* (to use Barthes's term), applies the very same terms to speech and to space. Formulas highlighting the narrative act and emphasizing its immediacy – "let me now go," or "we must return to" – take on topographical reality. Thus, for example, Mansilla writes: "Now we must go back." And he continues: "In doing so, let's stop at Rivadavia street. We'll find unexpected contacts there" (p. 164). On occasion, the confusion affects not only speech and space but time. When Mansilla writes: "We shall not return to the property on the long street in Barracas, near Santa Lucía" (p. 225), the reader, feeling incorporated by now in the "we," is deceived into accepting the declaration as a marker of the narrative "I" ("he will not speak again of Barracas"), when Mansilla is employing a form of future-in-the-past to state a fact in his story: he and his siblings (the "we" within the story) would never again return to Barracas. The mnemonic maze of the old

Buenos Aires, the space of Agustina Rozas, becomes, in the telling, the linguistic maze of the text – the space of a conversing "I" best characterized in his own words: "a man writing, following a random course ... like a traveler who does not know where he is going but who will arrive somewhere" (*EN*, 293).

Paradoxically, Mansilla's autobiography, even while relying strongly on family space and on author–reader ties (the "I/you" constantly put into play in the text, the *entre-nos* chumminess), in fact discourages the recognition of a communal memory. It precludes the illusion of fond reminiscence sustained by group bonding, the fiction of "remembering" a past through the reminiscing of another. The fact that Mansilla's past was a *rosista* past, a world cast off to the margins or repressed by general opinion in his day, and the fact that Mansilla himself felt uncomfortable with the ideological implications of that past, may well hamper that communal recognition; it is not enough, however, to stifle it. Communal longing has been known to have more unsavory foundations that the régime of Rosas and questionable periods can always be retrieved as "good old days." If *Mis memorias* constantly undercuts identification with a memorator, it does so less by the nature of the past evoked than by the strategies adopted to re-present that past. *Mis memorias* avoids a cohesive representation of the "I" that might invite the reader to complicitous commemoration; it continually shatters the possibility of nostalgic illusion by abruptly shifting to the critical present of enunciation. The *causeur*, the "I" who chats to the reader, addressing him directly, pausing to share his thoughts with him on aspects of the past, is, in a way, the greatest obstacle to commemoration. For it is essentially at that level, in that present of writing, in the narrative give-and-take itself, that Mansilla's "I" functions; it is there that the "I" *makes sense*.

10

First memories, first myths: Vasconcelos'
Ulises criollo

The history of Mexico is that of man in search of his
filiation, his origin.

Octavio Paz, *The Labyrinth of Solitude*

At first glance, José Vasconcelos appears to be a throwback to the
figure of the heroic nineteenth-century writer-statesman, striving to
combine intellectual reflection with direct political action and
believing himself destined to play a leading role in the development
of his country. In many aspects (the sense of a quasi-messianic
calling not being the least of them) he reminds the reader of
Sarmiento. Both men are educators, self-appointed "civilizers" of
their barbarian compatriots (Vasconcelos espouses Sarmiento's
simplistic yet effective formula, *civilización y barbarie*, which he
translates into Mexican terms – Quetzalcóatl vs. Huichilobos), both
perceive themselves as greater than nature and are eager to have
others see them with the same generous eye. If Adolfo Prieto,
borrowing from Karl Mannheim, found a matchless description for
Sarmiento's overbearing, chaotic personality – "the gesticulating
adult"[1] – Francisco Madero himself, during the first days of the
Mexican Revolution, echoed Nietzsche in his own, perfect char-
acterization of Vasconcelos – "el supermuchacho," *Superboy*.[2] As in
Sarmiento, there is indeed in Vasconcelos an element of near-
adolescent instability coupled with a constant need for recognition;
a fervent desire to *do* rivaled only by the desire to *show* himself doing;
finally, a tendency to tantrums and overreactions that make him
(again like Sarmiento) all the more vulnerable to criticism and jibes.
Excess seems to mark everything Vasconcelos touches: "actuar en
grande," to act on a grand scale, was one of his favorite phrases.[3]
His choice of a book-plate is equally revealing; it pictures a crusader

186

on a horse, a banner held aloft with the motto, "I exasperate the wicked and gratify the good." No less grandiose is the motto he devised for the University of Mexico when he was President of that institution in the 1920s: "por mi raza hablará el espíritu" – through my race, the spirit will speak. (A journalist, weary of Vasconcelos' bombast, had another, less dignified motto to suggest for Vasconcelos himself: "por mi raza hablará Cantinflas."[4])

With a considerable portion of his work already published – two of his best-known books, *La raza cósmica* (1925) and *Indología* (1926), had been greeted by critical acclaim – and, more particularly, with most of his political activity behind him, Vasconcelos set out to write his autobiography in exile, two years after what was probably the greatest defeat of his life. The year 1929 marked a turning point in his public career. Running for president of Mexico on a vaguely formulated liberal platform destined to oppose the chaotic *caudillo* power of Plutarco Elías Calles, Vasconcelos was defeated at the polls in fraudulent elections and, after a half-hearted promise to fight back, left the country and went into exile for the next seven years. From that defeat on, Vasconcelos would channel most of the verve formerly devoted to upholding the Revolution's achievements – some of which, like the massive reform of the education system, were due to his efforts as Secretary of Education – to denouncing its flaws. José Joaquín Blanco summarizes the process:

An intellectual of Porfirio Díaz's middle class, exceptionally vigorous and bold, he takes part in the Mexican Revolution, establishes the cultural and educational policies of the post-revolutionary state, has a noisy falling out with the *caudillos* and tries to defeat them in a democratic confrontation. When he fails, he turns into a critic of the Mexican government with such fury that he soon becomes a critic of the country, of its history, and even endorses the worst causes (such as Nazism) throughout thirty years in which he shows himself extremely deft at invective and insult, both in his texts and in his attitudes.[5]

It is not coincidental that in the years immediately following his final political debacle, at the very juncture of two apparently conflicting periods (though there is less contradiction than meets the eye between the "good," reformist Vasconcelos of before 1929, and the "bad," reactionary one that came after), Vasconcelos would write his autobiography. If Sarmiento, on the threshold of the most important period of his political career, had used the image projected in *Recuerdos de provincia* in a prophetic manner, not only to present the man he had been in the past but the politician he would be, if given a chance, in the near future, Vasconcelos used his *Ulises criollo* retrogressively, to voice a lament: he presented an image not of a man who might one day be president but of one who, had his country been wiser, would have attained that office. The autobiographical venture allows, then, for a respite and a settling of accounts. It marks a time between Vasconcelos' failure as a political hero and his subsequent return to the public scene, in the decidedly bellicose guise of the pamphleteer, armed with less than generous reflections on Mexican politics. As Vasconcelos himself states, the writing of his autobiography affords him "a rest ... to see the whole affair from a better perspective."[6] What my commentary will try to elucidate here is the precise nature of that "whole affair."

Vasconcelos' autobiography is divided into four volumes, written between 1931 and 1938. The first book, *Ulises criollo*, goes from childhood to young adulthood and ends with the assassination of Francisco Madero, whose cause Vasconcelos had joined. The second, *La tormenta*, goes up to 1920, covers the chaotic régimes of Huerta and Carranza, Vasconcelos' frequent flights and exiles and his growing erotic obsessions; it also "chronicles the terror with which Mexican liberals saw the masses take over the Revolution and occupy the country, and the violence and infamy of those manipulating the masses."[7] The third volume, *El desastre*, going from 1920 to 1928, relates Vasconcelos' tenure as Secretary of Public Education under Obregón, his launching of the huge collective effort to develop a national culture, the deterioration of the project, then his growing disenchantment with a régime that, under the influence of Calles, compromised more and more with the *caudillos*. Finally, *El proconsulado*, whose title refers sarcastically to the interference of the United States government in Mexican affairs through its ambassador, loosely chronicles Vasconcelos' political defeat, his disastrous relationship with Antonieta Rivas Mercado ending in the latter's spectacular suicide, in Notre-Dame cathedral in Paris, and the first years of his exile. Coming round full circle, the life story ends, appropriately enough, where it began, with Vasconcelos writing the first volume of his autobiography.

A chronological summary such as the one I have attempted necessarily betrays the spirit of Vasconcelos' autobiography. I have made it sound like a history of the Mexico of those years, a huge mural, such as the ones Vasconcelos himself commissioned, that includes him as narrator, participant, and even protagonist, but inevitably dwarfs him. This is far from the case. It would be more accurate to say, since I have resorted to the perhaps facile but tempting metaphor, that in the same way that he turns Mexico into a mural,[8] Vasconcelos "muralizes" himself, presenting a gigantic self-image that overshadows that of Mexico while feeding off it, an image that finally becomes, through a sleight of hand, Mexico itself.[9] Again I resort to the comparison with Sarmiento, the politician, the better to distinguish Vasconcelos' particular traits. Sarmiento's willful conflation of self and country was a political card that, in the context of the Argentine nineteenth century, fully retained its efficacy. Years later, as a presidential candidate in a different political arena, Vasconcelos tried to play the same card:

It was History as representation: Calles would be Caliban, Doña Bárbara, the ferocity and the primitive nature of an unredeemed people; Vasconcelos would be Ariel, Santos Luzardo, the culture of the West reduced to a mirage: the Spirit would defeat the Sword.[10]

But the Spirit did not and Vasconcelos lost the presidency. This ineffectual representation which in real life had failed, this exaggerated national icon that he held on to – much like the empty title of *Presidente Electo de México* which, after his defeat, he insisted on keeping – would become, in the autobiographical project, a compensatory spectacle of monumental proportions. *Ulises criollo* (the title speaks for itself) and the other three autobiographical volumes were an attempt to infuse a dead rhetoric of messianic nationalism with new life, recycling it on the level of personal myth. The opportunity for reconstruction that Vasconcelos felt had been denied him in the presidential elections would now constitute the basis for his self-writing: what had not worked for Mexico would work for him. And curiously enough, for all the shrillness of the representation he left behind, work, in a way, it did.

In spite of his historical pretensions (he wrote a few, tendentious biographies, one of them on Cortés as a Mexican founding father, and an equally controversial *Breve historia de México*), Vasconcelos does not claim, or at least does not primarily claim, historical status for his autobiography. When referring to the conception of *Ulises criollo*, he describes it as "a book I had wanted to write for a long time. A novel, and what better novel than one dealing with one's own adventures and passions?" (*PR*, p. 1141). Now it is obvious that *Ulises criollo* is not a novel, although critics have more than once loosely characterized it as such. (And then have promptly dismissed it as a "bad novel.") Vasconcelos' use of the work *novel*, although in appearance inadequate, is not, I venture, frivolous. It seems to indicate not so much what the book is as what the book is not: in an exact reversal of Sarmiento, who wrote "this is not a novel" thereby implying that his autobiography was history, Vasconcelos implies that *Ulises criollo* is not exactly history by calling it, precisely, a novel. But if it then turns out not to be a novel, what is it? The foreword to the first edition indicates that Vasconcelos is conscious of the work's hybrid nature. On the one hand, he points to the book's autobiographical, even confessional, nature: "It contains the experience of one man and it aspires not to exemplarity but to awareness" (I, p. 8). On the other, however, when explaining the choice of the title, *Ulises criollo*, he proposes a less personal reading and points to loftier designs:

The title I have given the whole work [i.e. *Ulises criollo*; he refers to all four volumes] is explained by the contents. A destiny rising like a comet, suddenly blazing into life, then extinguishing itself during long periods of darkness, and the turbulent atmosphere of present-day Mexico, justify the analogy with the *Odyssey*. As for the adjective *criollo*, I chose it as a symbol of the defeated ideal of our country. . . . *Criollismo*, that is to say, a culture of a Hispanic type, in its ardent, unequal struggle against a spurious *Indigenismo* and an "Anglo-Saxonism" disguised in the trappings [*que se disfraza con el colorete*] of the most deficient civilization known to history: those are the elements that have battled in the soul of this *Creole Ulysses* as in that of each of his compatriots.   (I, p. 8)

There appears to be some contradiction here. Is this autobiography about personal awareness and the individual man or is it about exemplarity and a mythical hero embodying virtues his national community holds dear? It is, in a way, both. Vasconcelos, in the twentieth century (unlike Sarmiento, in the nineteenth), works with two diverging, even conflicting modes of self-representation. Without forgoing his confessional personal story – one that clearly *needs* to be told – Vasconcelos would elevate his life story to the realm of myth, a myth in which one man's recollections will be translated and reformulated with a communal reading in view. In choosing to identify with Ulysses, Vasconcelos stresses the heroic quest, and in assigning a national identity to his mythical persona, he is also presenting himself within a group and within a tradition. That mythical conception of self – of a compensatory nature in the case of Vasconcelos – channels the retrieval of the past.[11] Thus, as the autobiographical venture progresses, personal memory will gradually strive to merge with collective memory. The impression the work seeks to give is that here is not only an "I" but all of Mexico recalling.

A look at the structure of the work would confirm that Vasconcelos saw his autobiography as more than a pause devoted to reminiscence between two politically active moments in his career. For all of its busy narration and constant reference to public events that seem to stress its historical nature, Vasconcelos' four-volume autobiography is framed in a way to stress atemporality, prompting the reader to see the project as a timeless construct. The text begins with a striking first recollection of origins, taken from earliest childhood. It is an ecstatic image of pleasurable, symbiotic contact with the mother; "My first recollections arise from a feeling that is both caressing and melodious. I frolicked in my mother's lap, feeling myself a physical extension, a section barely severed from a warm, protecting, nearly divine presence" (*U*, p. 7). Four volumes later, when Vasconcelos' story comes round full circle, narration ends at the very point when the autobiographer's activity begins: Vasconcelos starts writing *Ulises criollo*. And, as he takes leave of the reader, faithful to the circular structure he has adopted for his account, he closes on an image that neatly refers back to the one that had opened the first volume. Vasconcelos is on board the ship that will take him, his daughter, her husband and their child to Buenos Aires where he will continue his exile. Alone on deck with his granddaughter, he falls to musing as he looks at the frightened little girl:

Plunged in deep meditation, I imagined we went back in time to the last century [*que desvivíamos un siglo*]. In my granddaughter I saw my paternal grandmother as a child, leaving Spain in her ancient ship, finally able to return to her native Oaxaca with her family after the order expelling certain Spaniards from Mexico had been lifted. The bond between generations then gripped my conscience so tightly that, for a moment, I could not tell whether the small being now travelling at my side, whom I so deeply cherished, was in truth my granddaughter or my grandmother, wrested from the past. Perhaps she was, I concluded, another, future grandmother, who would create another chain of destinies in the young yet already corrupt regions of our unfortunate Spanish America.

(*PR*, p. 1178)

Time has gone by, since the beginning of Vasconcelos' autobiography, but it is as if it had not. The autobiographical exercise begins and ends with an emblem of family bonding that transcends chronological limits, a family bonding perpetuated – and this is of utmost importance – through maternal presence. The symbiotic, regressive union with the mother, in the beginning, is mirrored, at the end, by a tie back to motherhood; a new, timeless motherhood that looks to the past (the grandmother, the maternal places of Oaxaca and Spain) and to the future (Vasconcelos' granddaughter, future mother and grandmother). In fact, the figure of the mother dominates Vasconcelos' autobiography quite explicitly in the first volume of *Ulises criollo*: in addition to being an important presence, she most clearly has a decisive function as purveyor of vitality, of identity, of culture and, most particularly, of memory. Of all Spanish American autobiographers by far – and I am not forgetting Sarmiento's exalted evocation of Paula Albarracín, Mansilla's privileged recollection of Agustina Rozas nor González Martínez's fascination with his own mother – none has devoted more impassioned, and at times more disturbingly intimate pages to the memory of his mother.[12]

In the same way that Vasconcelos does not claim that his book is history, he does not profess to be using memory as a historical tool, going so far as to declare himself unqualified for objective evocation (I, p. 8). This limitation, or rather, this particular bent of memory that only rescues the emotionally striking and neglects the rest, is often referred to in the text. When questioning himself on the persistence of apparently stray memories, for example, Vasconcelos comes close to vindicating the workings of an affective memory not unlike that of Proust – an author he denigrates elsewhere with unmitigated scorn. (*U*, p. 271). Availing himself of a cinematic metaphor, he writes:

The flow of memory is not precisely a reel of film that unwinds rapidly or slowly, it is rather a multitude of arbitrary surges, similar to the explosion of fireworks that sometimes burst into a spray of light and at others fail to function, leaving only smoke. Thus the images in the game of memory arise or are lost for reasons that escape us and the importance of the occasion is not decisive for its conservation.   (*U*, p. 89)

This alternately bright and blurry film is set in motion by a first, distinct, recollection that Vasconcelos takes pains to highlight, calling attention to its importance within his text. Precisely because Vasconcelos calls attention to this gambit, I will briefly consider the implications of "first" memories in general before going on to deal with his specifically.

Not all autobiographies start, of course, with recollections. A comparative study of openings would show that many, indeed, prefer to begin with facts, having the initial pages coincide not with the beginning of awareness – an occurrence that they would remember – but with an event they cannot remember, their birth.[13] One might be tempted to attribute such factual beginnings, so observant of sequential time, to the pull of nineteenth-century biography and to the never quite forgotten documentary pretensions of self-writing, yet this explanation does not prove entirely satisfactory. Sarmiento, whose claims to historicity are well known, chose to link events according to an idiosyncratic logic of cause and effect that bent chronological order to serve its own purposes, and did not start out *Recuerdos* with his birth (in the same way that he had not begun *Facundo* with the birth of his hero). Macedonio Fernández, whose pretensions to historicity, as one can imagine, were nil, fell back, instead, on chronology and began his autobiography (albeit parodically) with his birth: "The Universe, that is to say, Reality, and I were born in June 1874 and it is fair to add that both births occurred close by, in a city of the province of Buenos Aires."[14]

It is true, nonetheless, that autobiographies that resist the blind plunge into chronology, casting about for alternative entries into their life matter, are more frequent in the twentieth century. After times when memory was taken for granted, the moment is ripe for reflection. This is obviously the case for autobiography in general, and for Spanish American autobiography in particular, once the autobiographer commences to feel – as did Mansilla, for example – that the "I" need not be as rigidly "historical" as that of one's predecessors; in other words, once one begins to feel that there are other, acceptable literary channels for self-writing. The autobiographer, if hesitating ever so slightly before giving in to chronological order, is faced with a series of questions, the most disturbing of which concerns the very nature of the exercise.[15] From the chatty musings of a Mansilla in *Mis memorias*, to the ironic reflections of the Chilean Augusto d'Halmar in *Recuerdos olvidados*, to the earnest questions of Victoria Ocampo in her *Autobiografía*, many twentieth-century Spanish American autobiographers, endowed with a new awareness of their enterprise, resort self-consciously to reflections on (and often justifications of) the mechanisms and selective criteria of their memory. More than others, they look back to that "first" recollection to begin their stories.[16]

Placed at the very beginning, or close to the beginning of the narrative (this is usually the case: Vasconcelos, Eduardo Wilde, Darío, Subercaseaux, Neruda, to give but a few examples), the first recollection serves as a sort of epigraph, a self-quotation that, if not summarizing the gist of the text that follows, will nudge it in the right direction. If, as on occasion happens, that first recollection appears tucked away in the middle of the text (such is the case of Victoria Ocampo), it will not be any less insignificant, although it may drastically redistribute for the reader, in a process not unlike that of psychoanalysis, what has been previously narrated. At any rate, one must believe that, in the same way that no memory is innocent, no use of memory will be innocent. In rescuing a "first" recollection from the many that memory has stored, the auto-biographer is recognizing a beginning in some way attuned to the image the adult, writing in the present, holds of him or herself.[17] One could liken its function to that of a charge of energy, a nucleus of intensity (at times brutal: think of the first recollection in Elias Canetti's autobiography) that sets the text in motion and marks the deliberate irruption of, to borrow an expression, "being in the text."[18]

A look at first recollections in Spanish American autobiographies will indeed confirm the emotional intensity that seems to char-acterize them. Most of them speak of violence: Eduardo Wilde and Victoria Ocampo recall misunderstanding and injustice; Darío and Chocano, abandonment; López Albújar, shame; María Rosa Oliver, shock at the birth of a sibling; Subercaseaux, violent sickness; Torres Bodet, death; González Martínez, a memory so troublesome that, years later, it still cannot be named – "a tragic and penetrating mystery that even now pierces my heart."[19] The only one, quite remarkably, who settles on a positive first recollec-tion is Vasconcelos.

This first recollection is multilayered. I shall devote some atten-tion to it and follow its unfolding, its "spray of light," to borrow Vasconcelos' expression, throughout *Ulises criollo* since it illuminates important aspects of the mythological persona he created for himself. Furthermore, it helps one understand the particular ideological quality that his practice of memory takes on, one that affects both his self-presentation and his reading of Mexican history. I return to the first paragraph of *Ulises criollo* which I quote in its entirety:

My first recollections arise from a feeling that is both caressing and melodious. I frolicked in my mother's lap, feeling myself a physical extension, a section barely severed from a warm, protecting, nearly divine presence. The beloved [*entrañable*] voice of my mother guided my thought, determined my every move. It was as if an invisible umbilical cord tied my will to hers, many years after the physiological tie was cut. Without a firm will of my own, I invariably returned to the shelter of her protective arms. I remember the provisional world of the mother–child composite with effusive delight: we were one sensibility, endowed with five experienced senses and five new and avid ones, penetrating together the mystery of each day. (*U*, p. 7)

It is of interest to consider this first recollection of Vasconcelos in context (as an analyst might when considering not one dream but a sequence of dreams in one night), to read it in conjunction with the surrounding text that might illuminate it.[20] Vasconcelos himself is not unaware of that polyphonic composition, calling attention to the diversity of elements in this first recollection. Far from seeing these elements as products of arbitrary memory, he carefully points to their ulterior significance as a patterning mechanism: "and so the pieces gradually come together into the structure that finally gives us shape" (*U*, p. 7).

The first image stresses physical union; also, as a molding factor of personality, the mother's voice. A second image appears immediately to supplement that first recollection giving that voice substance:

The deteriorated reel of memory spins on, clouded sections go by and, suddenly, there is an indelible vision. My mother holds the Old Testament on her lap. She discusses her reading, tells how the Lord created the world from nothing, first creating Light, then immediately Earth with fish, and birds, and man. One God and the first couple in Paradise. (*U*, p. 9)

These foundational images are reassuring, their solipsistic, self-referential nature, protective: the mother with the book on her lap and the child so tightly bound to her are mirrored in the first couple of the fable. But the soothing quality of this first recollection is seriously compromised by what the mother goes on to read – a

contradiction bringing to mind those lullabies whose melodies
pacify while their words threaten. This mother, from whom Scrip-
ture stories effortlessly flow, repeatedly tells her son "the adventure
of the lost child" – the story of Moses abandoned in the rushes – as
a foretaste of the fate that may await him. Biblical exodus is reread
in the light of the family's present-day exile. Banished (or so they
like to feel) to an outpost of the Mexican border where the father, a
customs officer, must watch out for possible "Yankee" infringe-
ment, the Vasconcelos live in constant dread of Apache invasions.
Thus the age-old fear of separation is fostered in the child through
the biblical story and further elaborated upon with elements from
everyday reality: "If [the Apaches] do come (my mother would
instruct me), don't worry. They'll kill us but will dress you in skins
and feathers, give you a horse, teach you how to fight and, one day,
you will escape to freedom" (U, p. 8). In this way, fear of separation is definitely integrated into Vasconcelos' first recollection, omi-
nously coloring what was initially pleasurable and good. Incidents
are remembered that feed into that fear: a flickering light seen
outside in the dark; the family barricaded inside the house praying
for protection; the father and his aides on the roof with guns. The
first image Vasconcelos retains of his father refers in fact to that
fear: he remembers a strong man with a black beard jovially prac-
ticing his marksmanship during the family's Sunday afternoon
picnics.

The mythical overtones established by the mother's story cannot
of course be overlooked in this composite first recollection. They
are further defined as the mother continues to embellish this fiction
of exile and death that she holds (as does the adult Vasconcelos,
when evoking it) so close to her heart. The child survivor pictured
in the mother's forebodings is entrusted with a mission of both familial and cultural import:

If the Apaches do come and take you with them, do not be afraid. Live
with them and serve them, learn their language and speak to them of Our
Lord Jesus Christ who died for us and for them, for all men. It is important that you do not forget: there is an Almighty God and Jesus Christ, his
only Son. Everything else will take care of itself. Then, when you are older
and learn to tell the roads apart, go South, make your way to Mexico City,
ask after your grandfather, his name is Esteban ... Yes, Esteban Calderón, from Oaxaca, they know him in Mexico City. Go find him, he will
be pleased to see you, and you will tell him how you escaped death when

they killed us ... And if you cannot escape, or prefer to remain with the Indians, you may do so, just never forget there is only one God, the Father, and Jesus Christ, his only Son. This very thing you will tell the Indians.

(*U*, p. 10)

Vasconcelos dates this first recollection back to 1885, when he was about three. Needless to say the highly articulated maternal admonition he reproduces so eloquently has been the object of many revisitations on the part of the autobiographer, and, one suspects, of considerable polishing.[21] There is a ceremonial tone to this scene that clearly distinguishes it as a set piece and removes it from the realm of "spontaneous" recollection. It forcibly reminds the reader of a later, equally momentous scene in Mexican literature, the one opening Juan Rulfo's *Pedro Páramo*, in which a dying mother extracts from her son the promise to return to the place of their roots and seek recognition.[22] But the "original" form of Vasconcelos' recollection is of no importance since it cannot be determined anyway. As he himself tells us, "objective memory" pales before "emotional memory," and it is surely the latter that has stored these scenes in the mind. It is not emotional memory, however, but a clear sense of purpose that accounts for the sagacious placing of these scenes at the beginning of the autobiography, disposed in such a way as to suggest an immediate pattern of interpretation for the rest of the work. Out of memorable bits and pieces of his earliest childhood, Vasconcelos fashions an image of heroic proportions to suit his present stance, justifying the national mission he feels fated to accomplish in terms of his family romance. In a sense, Vasconcelos will twice attempt to carry out that mission assigned by his mother: once, if imperfectly, in his political and cultural pursuits, and then again, and perhaps more successfully, in the writing of *Ulises criollo*.

In the pages that follow that first recollection, indeed throughout the first half of *Ulises criollo*, the mother will be pictured as a cultural guide, and even more than that: as a figure representing the "civilization" left behind, a key to a fundamental (and highly idealized) Mexican past. In a frontier world doubly exposed to invasion from the barbarians – Indians or "Yankees" – the mother plays the role of chief *memorator* in a family much given to dwelling on past glories. She may be a harbinger of woe, but she also instructs her son in his Mexican heritage, "cosas de mi nación" (*U*, p. 42) as he calls them, the things of his country. This is a much needed source of pride at a time when the child's cultural identity is threatened at school and when he has to stand up and even fight for his country:

The independence of Texas and the war of 1847 divided the class in rival factions ... [W]hen someone said in class that a hundred Yankees could make a thousand Mexicans flee I would get up and say:
"That is not true."
I was even more irritated when, in comparing the customs of Mexicans with those of Eskimos, some student would say:
"Mexicans are a semi-civilized people."
At home I heard the contrary, that Yankees were the newcomers to culture. So I would get up again and repeat what I had been told:
"We had printing presses before you did."
The teacher would then intervene to bring peace ... but it only lasted until the next lesson when statements were made and opinions voiced that forced me to speak up and refute them.   (U, pp. 31–32)

The adult who recollects these memories is fully aware of the "patriotic prejudice" that blinded his family, a prejudice that leads to oversimplifications as trite as those he heard from his schoolmates. His mother's position, he realizes after her death, as he leafs through her yellowing copybooks from childhood, had remained unchanged since she wrote in a composition: "To the South of Mexico is Guatemala, a country once part of ours. To the North there are rough and redhaired men who put their feet on the table when they sit down to talk and who all practice the Protestant heresy" (U, p. 44). Yet for all the understanding that time and distance would bring, it is evident that Vasconcelos singles out this family attitude embodied in the mother, simplistic though it may be, as the vital source of his anti-imperialism, an attitude he will uphold again and again, regardless of the political cause he has espoused.[23] Indeed, if one looks at the Vasconcelos of the end, the rabid right-winger casting aspersions on the infidel, condemning all that lay beyond the confines of *Hispanidad* and Catholicism and reducing the notion of goodness to what was white, middle-class *criollo*, Catholic and "civilized," one will see that there was every reason for him to recognize himself in his mother's lesson.

A provider of national culture, religious faith and radical zealotry, the mother is given yet another role in *Ulises criollo* that corroborates Vasconcelos' self-image. As other illustrious mothers of predestined men, conscious of the greatness that awaits their sons, she is portrayed by Vasconcelos as aware and supportive of his singularity. Fashioning personas for him out of her readings, she casts her son in the mythical roles to which he will become accustomed, and, indeed, will expect others to see him in. She beholds him as hero: in the role of Moses, destined to lead a nation, to set down its law; in the role of Jesus amidst the doctors, astonishing the world with his wisdom. Finally, she sees him playing Augustine to her Monica: "imitating St Monica she carried the fervor of her prayers to an extreme to sustain me in my trials. Enraptured, at times she saw me like a new Augustine who must experience evil the better to conquer it" (*U*, pp. 124–125). The hero, in the eyes of the mother and, increasingly, in the eyes of the son himself, is also saint and savior. As in Rousseau, so perceptively analyzed by Starobinski, there is in Vasconcelos "a strange hybridization of the scriptures and personal fable. The great biblical 'moments' not only become contemporary with [his] life, they merge with it."[24]

If, as I have tried to argue, Spanish American autobiographers fashion themselves according to an image gleaned from other texts, in the case of Vasconcelos, one could contend that the mother – specifically recalled, in the unforgettable primal "vision," holding a book in her lap – is the pre-text to which Vasconcelos conforms. In other words, texts do precede Vasconcelos' image of self, but they are texts invariably mediated by the mother's reading:

My reading was governed by casual discoveries in the Library but was also guided by the dialogues, on all kinds of subjects, that I had with my mother ... [A]t her side, I maintained a level of high and assiduous reading. It was she who put in my hands what was to be the intellectual event of that whole period in my life, Chateaubriand's *Génie du Christianisme*." (*U*, 97)

Years later, when Vasconcelos discovers Dante after his mother's death, the process of reading through her eyes is echoed and meaningfully reversed: "An early reader of the *Civitas Dei* and the *Confessions*, I do not understand why my mother did not also read Dante as guide. It was what she would have liked most and now, as I read, I imagined I was also reading in her place" (*U*, p.186).

A purveyor and interpreter of texts, the mother becomes one with those texts, and eventually, in the son's perception, she obscures and replaces them. Vasconcelos perceives the mother figure, quite literally, as a textual and ideological matrix. The implications of the word do not stop short, however, at ideology: all of Vasconcelos' journey is a representation, literally an acting out, of perpetual separation from and return to the mother in which the textual, the ideological, the physical, and the erotic are inextricably mingled.

The connection between mother, text and son, consolidated in the first recollection, casts on Vasconcelos' self-writing a particularly illuminating light. As the boundary between mother and text is blurry, so is the line between mother and son. If Vasconcelos rescues that precise image – the infant as one with the mother – as his opening image, he is fully aware of its import. Time and time again, in *Ulises criollo* , that image will be reiterated as additional confirmation of the initial bond in which Vasconcelos recognizes the origin of self. The first confirmation occurs at Eagle Pass when the child is about ten. It is a time of family problems, marital difficulties between father and mother, and a general feeling of confusion on the part of the child. That situation of emotional turmoil and insecurity is followed by a short chapter entitled "Who Am I?" in which Vasconcelos reports an incident that, like the earlier passage containing the mother's injunctions to the child, has obviously been the object of much elaboration on the part of the autobiographer:

One day, when I was buying sweets at Eagle Pass, I saw my face reflected in one of those convex glass cases that protect cakes from dust. I had seen myself before in mirrors, absentmindedly, but on that occasion, seeing myself by accident took me by surprise and perplexed me. The dim reflection of my own face prompted disturbing questions: "Is that what I am? What is that? What is a human being? What am I? And what is my mother? Why is my face no longer my mother's? Why must she have one face and I another? ... In sum, I did not want to be myself. And when I returned to my mother, I hugged her and pressed myself against her in despair. Is there a moral womb one must forcibly leave, as one does the other?   (*U*, p. 29)

Ulises criollo would seem proof that the question can be answered in the negative. The book is obsessed with the mirroring of the son in the mother, with the merging of the son and the mother, in a process of constant *replication*.[25] References to this bonding appear at key moments of the narrative, on occasions when the autobiographer questions his identity in view of a vital change experienced in his life. "It is easier for me to remember what my mother was like then than what I was myself" (*U*, p. 68), he writes of one such occasion. I shall examine two of those moments which I find especially revealing: Vasconcelos' separation from his mother in Mexico City, a move that coincides with the beginning of adulthood; and his first visit to Oaxaca after his mother's death, a ceremonial return that is both a compliance with his mother's injunctions to him in childhood and a necromantic celebration. These moments (and there are others) mark another, more private itinerary than the one announced in the book's title and confirmed in the foreword: they outline less the wanderings of a Ulysses than the journey of a present-day Telemachus, companion to a mother to whom he is tightly bound; a myth (says Vasconcelos of Telemachus) "on the sense and details of which I never tired of pondering" (*U*, p. 96).[26]

Accompanied by his mother and his younger brothers, Vasconcelos moves to Mexico City in his adolescence to complete his secondary studies. The most impressive fusion of mother and son occurs on the eve of the mother's departure from the city, leaving the son for the first time on his own – a separation Vasconcelos singles out as the most difficult of his whole autobiographical endeavor: "Everything I have told until now has been objectified by my attention and is nearly indifferent to me. Only the memories of this separation from her are a wound that will never heal, they rekindle a pain that once more grips my throat" (*U*, p. 126). The text arrestingly describes the closeness between mother and son and their harrowing last moments together prior to separation. The fact that this separation was to be definitive – the mother's death, away from her son, was to follow soon after – unquestionably tinges this evocation. At no other moment in his self-writing does Vasconcelos (who was not loath to celebrate his erotic adventures) reach the heights of passion or the scope of revelation that he does in this sequence. The agony of two lovers crossed by fate, torn between desire and duty, could not be better described:

We tried not to speak of a pain and anxiety that we transformed into bursts of prayer and hope for the future. The church of Jesús María or the Sagrario often saw us on our knees before the altar, asking the Almighty to comfort a sorrow as heartrending as it was inevitable. Often, having gone to confession the day before, we would take communion at early mass before the altar of Pardon.   (*U*, p. 124)

As the description of these last shared moments progresses, so do the signs of closeness, a closeness of a pronounced physical nature. The text highlights the relationship to the exclusion of all other members of the household, indeed of all other human beings. There are but two actors, Vasconcelos and his mother, the "first couple"; there are but two spaces for their farewells, the church and the mother's bedroom. Resorting to a particularly intimate use of the first person plural, the text describes mother and son, both sick with malaria, taking care of each other ("nos administrábamos la quinina") and finally, the thought of separation becoming intolerable, sharing a bedroom: "During the last weeks, so as to talk more comfortably late into the night, I moved my bed into my mother's room. As one suffused with sacred music, I listened to recommendations, advice, and words I did not know would be her last to me" (*U*, p. 125). One of the most touching moments of Vasconcelos' autobiography, worthy in its muted poignancy of the Flaubert of *L'Education sentimentale*, is, precisely, the end of this chapter. In order to avoid the final farewell, the son spends an afternoon wandering aimlessly through Mexico City, his yearning for his mother rekindled with every trivial detail – a little cake seen in a shop window, a street corner, a familiar store – that brings back memories of a shared past. Then, as the hour of the departure nears, he is irresistibly drawn to the train station to see his mother's face once more. Purposefully avoiding a direct encounter, he gazes at her from afar, through the waiting-room window: "as one quenching a burning thirst, I drank her image" (*U*, p. 128). Then, overcome by loss, he rushes off into the night.

For Vasconcelos, the mother's presence operates not only as a textual but also, clearly, as a sexual mediation. The previous passages of *Ulises criollo* may begin to give an idea of the peculiar candor that marks this text, a candor quite out of keeping with the usual caution of the Spanish American autobiographer. Giving the lie to Juan Carlos Ghiano, who sees in most autobiographies written in Spanish "a desire for concealment or discretion ... based on a Catholic conception of life"[27] (a judgment that would seem more relevant were the word "prejudice" to replace "conception of life"), Vasconcelos feels the need to join the tradition of the great confessors, or, perhaps more accurately, that of the great exhibitionists. This need is all the more easily satisfied since the urge to "tell all" does not really tarnish Vasconcelos' image but, on the contrary, as one more excessive trait of his overpowering persona, serves to exalt him. Submitting his contradictions to a prestigious, Manichaean twist, Vasconcelos pictures himself grandiosely as a hero torn by opposing forces and, as Monsiváis pertinently points out, "turns the idea of 'living intensely' into a fetish."[28]

Vasconcelos' sexual exploits, what Blanco calls his pursuit of "el Gran Erotismo Promiscuo,"[29] are certainly an important part of this attempt at total confession and appear, early on in the text, more or less innocently linked to the mother.[30] A seemingly disconnected series of casual phrases suggests a pattern that alerts the reader to this connection. When Vasconcelos, his mother and brothers, leave Piedras Negras for Mexico City, the adolescent meets other relatives but never quite feels a member of this extended new family. He justifies his tendency to isolation in a curious fashion: "In my family, perhaps on account of the frequent traveling, the clan spirit had weakened ... Besides, in kinship, there is a certain rejection of sameness, what a Freudian would call a defense against incest. The truth is that although excessive in my affection, I never felt a strong attraction for any relative" (*U*, p. 72). Incest seems an excessive word when referred to these new, barely familiar relatives. It is not excessive, however, if one considers the actual context in which it appears – a chapter stressing sameness with the mother through the very intimate sharing of religious experience and physical penance – and if one sees it as an unconsciously displaced reference. Vasconcelos safely projects the threat of incest onto his relatives to safeguard the relationship with his mother.

A reference to sexual fantasizing and masturbation, again linked with the mother, furthers the configuration of this pattern of displacement and substitution, one that will be recurrent throughout the text up to his mother's death: "Helpless, I waged the only battle in which my mother could not come to my aid. And yet even in this she gave me a remedy that was relatively effective – penance, which for her was not a word but a practice ... She accustomed us from childhood to mortify our bodies as a discipline that was good for the soul" (*U*, 101–102). Finally, when the adolescent finds a recipient for his sensuality in someone clearly differentiated from the mother, a young girl with whom he reads Isaacs' *María*, the displacement and substitution are spelled out:

Accustomed from childhood to the pleasure of adoration, I practiced it on my mother and elevated it in prayer. But now, in this new love I dared not name, a need for physical proximity added itself to the usual state of ecstatic admiration. I quivered at the mere thought of brushing against those rounded arms ... (*U*, p. 114)

The actual substitution of the mother by another woman will only be fulfilled after the mother's death; it will bear a negative sign, like a grotesque parody of the sublime. It is indeed striking to observe how forthrightly (and how simplistically) Vasconcelos overstates his case: "Accustomed to fight desire, I had avoided till then all opportunities for temptation. Now, on the contrary, I sought them, relishing them with cynical abandon" (*U*, p. 139). The mother's death, the death of the "portion of myself [that] had disappeared forever" (*U*, p. 138), does in fact unleash in *Ulises criollo* a celebration of the flesh at its most abject, as well as an unconcealed contempt for woman.[31] The descriptions of Vasconcelos' insatiable philandering, his attraction to the bawdiest versions of lovemaking, intermingle with visits to hospital wards where prostitutes are treated for venereal disease, or to mental institutions where nymphomaniacs lewdly call out to him. His portrayal of his future wife is a model of indifference, his description of their life together, brimming with distaste, his reflections on family life in general – and his own paternity in particular – significantly negative. Vasconcelos describes in detail how, while his wife was in labor giving birth to their first son, he sat in an adjoining room fantasizing that mother and child might die and composing a poem to a Spanish dancer; how, also, when his wife announced her second pregnancy, he registered it as a personal aggression: "She was not unaware of the displeasure she was causing me and seemed to enjoy these pregnancies" (*U*, p. 349).

In a sense, the death of Vasconcelos' mother brought about not only the end of a family romance but its total dismantling. If it consolidates a pure and luminous union that harks back to those first, unforgettable recollections of the mother holding the child and the book on her lap, it also seems to trigger the autobiographer's desire to thwart, even at times to destroy, any positive family tie – or, for that matter, any positive tie to a woman – in the future. The two important relationships that Vasconcelos will narrate in later volumes – the one with Elena Arizmendi Mejía (the "Adriana" of *La tormenta*) and the one with Antonieta Rivas Mercado (the "Valeria" of *El proconsulado*) – both end in failure, tragedy, and finally in remarkable indifference on Vasconcelos' part. Disenchantment (and physical revulsion at the end of his life, as expressed in his *Letanías del atardecer*) will progressively taint his erotic as well as his emotional capacity, but will never quite make him abandon his promiscuous if increasingly vacuous quest.

Vasconcelos' double image – the defender of Polis, the disciple of Eros – was greeted by contradictory reviews and in general did not go down well. The candor, the audacity even, with which sexuality was referred to, coupled with the heroic national self-image, made, in the eyes of most readers, for an unstable combination. The autobiography had, above all, a *succès de scandale*. Perhaps because of those mixed reactions and doubtless because of the sharp turn to the right in his personal politics, Vasconcelos (like Sarmiento before him) undertook a new self-representation. He did not, however, as had his precursor, write a second autobiography. In a gesture reminiscent of his mother, who, in a memorable scene, had her very young son build a fire in the yard to burn, in "a pyre of printed words," all the books her disbelieving brother had left behind (*U*, p. 28), he resorted instead to scissors and paste. In 1958, at the peak of his ultramontane pamphleteering, Vasconcelos, with the help of two unnamed friends, expurgated his book. Adopting a stance quite exceptional in the autobiographical tradition, the "I" of this new *Ulises criollo* recomposes himself through erasure, imposes a new outlook – a new recollective pattern, that is, retrospectively, a new memory – on the material that had formerly constituted the very substance of his past. In so doing, he courts an entirely new readership. Explicitly disclaiming the foreword to the first edition ("this book needs no prologue"), the expurgated version resorts to a prologue not only to state its *raison d'être* but to provide a new, spurious perspective for the previous version:

Abiding by the words of that Penitential Psalm, "For I will declare mine iniquity; I will be sorry for my sin," I set out to write the volumes of my Memoirs as they stand in earlier editions, ever observant of the truth of my story.

Years have gone by and not a few of the events and scenes I had to relate then arouse a strong repulsion in me now. However, since it is no longer possible to destroy what was, at least the possibility remains to *erase what is unworthy of recollection*. [my emphasis][32]

In the name of the new image of himself and of the new readers he wishes to reach, Vasconcelos corrects the past. Replacing the original impulse of his self-writing – the exalted mythical quest – by contrition, he proposes, retroactively, the image of autobiographer as penitent and proceeds to savage his life story with a censor's zeal not unlike that of his mother. The *auto-da-fe* is as thorough as the one practiced on his uncle's books under maternal surveillance. Its consequences are, however, more decisive: today, the expurgated version of *Ulises criollo*, published by the archconservative Editorial

Jus, has more readers than the original. Unlike the other, unexpurgated version of Vasconcelos' *Ulises*, usually grouped in a
volume with his other autobiographical works, this one may be
purchased independently; in addition, it may be purchased at a
relatively low price.[33]

The substance of the deletions is easily imagined. Specific references to sexual encounters are suppressed, the more salient aspects
of Vasconcelos' boastful promiscuity are done away with, whole
chapters, whole sequences – such as the tempestuous relationship
with a demi-mondaine called María, a detailed analysis of the
effects on the self of a first passion – are excised from the text. As
with many censoring jobs arising more from impassioned prejudice
than systematic ideological strictures, this one is often arbitrary, not
to mention careless, both in substance and in narrative form. The
reader is not presented, *pace* Vasconcelos, with a new "I," nor is the
"possibility to erase what is unworthy of recollection" a viable one
here. The expurgated text is not simply a "new" story; it is the same
old story, crisscrossed with badly healed scars. At times, clumsy
deletions even arouse the very prurient curiosity Vasconcelos seeks
to blunt: the beginning of a sexual episode may inadvertently be left
in, while its conclusion (erased by the censor) is left to the reader's
imagination. However, what strikes today's reader as the most
daring revelation of *Ulises criollo*, the obsessive passion for the
mother, remains intact. The mother's intolerance may prompt the
censor's scissors but she herself remains untouched by their threat.

The death of the mother, in *Ulises criollo*, marks a break in
Vasconcelos' self-writing. Not only does it dismantle the family
romance, opening the door to a promiscuity that Vasconcelos will
later (and in name of the mother's very own prejudices) seek to
eradicate from this story, if not from his life: it also signals an
assumption of the mother's values, a total acceptance of a legacy
that will, from that moment on, tinge Vasconcelos' outlook. The
mother's death is a watershed between what one could loosely term
the lyric "I" in Vasconcelos, the story of the child hero basking in
his mother's love, and his epic "I," the story of the man who will
devote his action to saving Mexico. The difference between the two
makes itself felt in the structure, even in the tone of the narrative
after the mother's death. At the juncture of those two figurations of
self, in a passage that brings to mind both the culmination of Juan
Preciado's pilgrimage at his mother's urging, in *Pedro Páramo*, and

the historical revelation recorded in Neruda's "Alturas de Macchu Picchu," Vasconcelos takes stock of himself and, through his mother's memory, "becomes" Mexico. For the first time he returns to Oaxaca, the birthplace virtually unknown to him, the city of his maternal ancestors, a place which, throughout his childhood, had been an object of longing in family conversations. He returns alone or, the more aptly to underscore his isolation, with an unimaginative American businessman, the perfect foil for the passionate pilgrim:

Names learnt in my childhood rush to my mind. The neighborhoods of Carmen Alto and La Soledad; the Mirus and the Fandiños, families I used to hear spoken of and of whom I will not hear again. Here were the landscapes in which my mother took pleasure in her youth. My throat choked uncontrollably as I saw myself alone, the shelter of family love destroyed ... From my seat in the coach I looked over the houses, the doors, the intersections, seeking traces of my father's stories, thinking back to the photographs that used to be the family treasure. Everything I saw belonged in part to me. A particular one-storey, whitewashed house, with a long iron balcony and a peep-hole on the front door, startled me with a thought: her eyes must have seen this very same thing many times ... What she perhaps evoked in her last moments, what she thought she would never again see, she now contemplates in my mind. It was she, more than I, who was seeing her birthplace once again. Those images were something like a supplement. By incorporating them into my consciousness, like nourishment from a native environment, my personality would be richer, more coherent. Slowly, I was becoming more myself ... I had no relatives left there, of course; no one knew, nor would have cared to know, that I was coming, and this only increased my unease, as if entering my own house as a stranger ... It was the return not of the prodigal son but of his descendant, come to witness the ruin of his own lineage. Houses, mines, ranches were gradually being bought up by foreigners, such as the man who travelled with me. (pp. 287–288)

The evocation continues, growing in passion and poignancy as the old city, with its rich Colonial heritage, nestled in the mountains, is pictured in detail. The ritualistic aspects of the experience, its necromantic overtones as well as its inspirational force, become patent: "Estamos en el corazón pétreo del mundo" – "We are in the stone heart of the world" (p. 289). So does the bonding, a bonding with forebears, through the memory of the mother, that becomes national in scope: as the self becomes the repository of all his lineage – "from the past my attention drew sensations felt by my parents, by my grandparents, by all those whose blood I share" – so Oaxaca becomes the repository of an essential national tradition. The initial image of the child in his mother's arms, at one with her, is supplemented by a new figure that sustains Vasconcelos' self-conception and gives coherence to the remaining volumes of his autobiography, the figure of the hero at one with a country he and his mother have dreamed.[34]

Notes

The translation of all texts is my own, unless otherwise specified.

Introduction

1 Paul de Man, "Autobiography as De-facement," *Modern Language Notes*, 94 (1979), pp. 919–930.
2 For discussion of a similar evolutionary view of nineteenth-century North American literature prompting "pangs of cultural inadequacy," see William C. Spengemann in his *A Mirror for Americanists* (Hanover and London: University Press of New England, 1989), pp. 7–27.
3 Fredric Jameson, "Third-World Literature in the Era of Multinational Capitalism," *Social Text*, 15 (1986), pp. 65–88. For an effective critique of Jameson's position, see Aijaz Ahmad, "Jameson's Rhetoric of Otherness and the 'National Allegory'," *Social Text*, 17 (1987), pp. 3–25.
4 Antonio Porchia, *Voces* (Buenos Aires, 1943; rpt. Hachette, 1975), p. 80.
5 Clifford Geertz, *The Interpretation of Cultures* (New York: Basic Books, 1973). I quote: "Cultural forms can be treated as texts, as imaginative works built out of social materials … [they] are not merely reflections of a pre-existing sensibility analogically represented; they are positive agents in the creation and maintenance of such a sensibility" (pp. 449–451).

1 The reader with the book in his hand

1 Jorge Luis Borges, "The Gospel According to Mark," trans. N. T. di Giovanni in *Borges: A Reader*, ed. Emir Rodríguez Monegal and Alastair Reid (New York: E. P. Dutton, 1981), pp. 308–311. Subsequent citations appear in the text.
2 For a discussion of readerly distortion in García Márquez, see Roberto González Echevarría, "The Novel as Myth and Archive," *Modern Language Notes*, 99, 2 (1984), pp. 358–380. González Echevarría points out the emblematic reader in the library, a Melquíades in whom it is

easy to discover the trace of Borges. One might add that *One Hundred Years of Solitude* also plays havoc with the unwritten yet very real text made up of European stereotypes. As Jules Supervielle before him in *Débarcadères* and *L'Homme de la Pampa*, García Márquez uses hyperbole to mock the conventional, "tropical" view of Spanish America and its literature held by non-Spanish American readers.

3 I disagree with James Olney's assertion that "there are no rules or formal requirements binding the prospective autobiographer – no restraints, no necessary models, no obligatory observances gradually shaped out of a long developing tradition ..." ("Autobiography and the Cultural Moment" in *Autobiography: Essays Theoretical and Critical*, ed. James Olney [Princeton University Press, 1980], p. 3). On the contrary, it is my belief that there are such models, in autobiographical writing as in all writing; they are often successfully disguised, though, by the autobiographer's claim to originality, a claim that is in itself a model and a well-exploited gambit. On the subject of models, see Avrom Fleishman, *Figures of Autobiography. The Language of Self-Writing in Victorian and Modern England* (Berkeley–Los Angeles–London: University of California Press, 1983).

4 See Paul de Man, "Autobiography as De-facement," *Modern Language Notes*, 94 (1979), pp. 919–930.

5 Julio Jiménez Rueda, *Historia de la literatura mexicana* (Mexico: Ediciones Botas, 1953), p. 158, cited in Raymundo Ramos, *Memorias y autobiografías de escritores mexicanos* (Mexico: UNAM, 1967), p. xxiv.

6 Victoria Ocampo, *Autobiografía*. Vol. I: *El archipiélago* (Buenos Aires: Ediciones Revista Sur, 1979), p. 81. Subsequent references appear in the text.

7 See Silvia Meloni Trkulja, "L'autoportrait classé," *Corps écrit*, 5 (1983), pp. 127–133.

8 Domingo Faustino Sarmiento, *Recuerdos de provincia* in *Obras completas*, III, revised edition (Buenos Aires: Imprenta y Litografía Mariano Moreno, 1896), pp. 172–173. Subsequent references to *Recuerdos* appear in the text.

9 That a book devised to instruct a Dauphin of France should awaken such enthusiasm in the nurseries of Spanish American republics is not without irony. For further references to Fénelon in autobiographies, see Lucio V. Mansilla, *Mis memorias* (Buenos Aires: Hachette, 1955), p. 161, and Mariano Picón Salas, *Viaje al amanecer*, 1943; rpt. in *Obras selectas* (Madrid–Caracas: Edime, 1962), p. 76.

10 Enrique González Martínez, *El hombre del búho* in *Obras completas* (Mexico: El Colegio Nacional, 1971), p. 597. Subsequent references appear in the text. The title of this first volume of González Martínez's autobiography is, of course, a literary reference presupposing a power-

ful male precursor. It alludes to González Martínez's famous sonnet "Tuércele el cuello al cisne" ("Wring the Neck of the Swan"), his parricide text against Rubén Darío.

11 Sarmiento's mother had learned to read and write as a child but had lost her literacy for lack of practice. Not without pride, the son relates how she would sit and spin while he gave his sisters their nightly grammar lesson. Listening in, she would instantly solve many of the difficulties that baffled her daughters (p. 138).

Even in more recent autobiographies, mothers are not always considered worthy of the scene of reading. The Puerto Rican Nilita Vientós Gaston, in *El mundo de la infancia* (Río Piedras: Editorial Cultural, 1984), recalls her mother's reading with unmitigated scorn: "She loved to read romances in installments which I considered trash. Were she alive today, she would watch soap operas on television" (p. 21). It is to her father, instead, that Vientós Gaston feels indebted for "real" reading: "I was lucky that Papa liked reading and, against Mama's judgment, allowed me to read everything he had in his library, where Victor Hugo was king" (p. 44).

12 Jean-Jacques Rousseau, *Les Confessions* (Paris: Gallimard, La Pléiade, 1951), p. 8.

13 Elena Poniatowska, *Hasta no verte Jesús mío* (Mexico: Ediciones Era, 1969; rpt. 1985), pp. 114—115.

14 Manuel Rojas, *Imágenes de infancia* in *Obras escogidas* (Santiago de Chile: Ercilla, 1961), p. 358.

15 "Oda al libro," (1), *Odas elementales* in Pablo Neruda, *Obras completas*, 1 (Buenos Aires: Losada, 1957; rpt. 1967), p. 1097.

16 A good discussion of the way Neruda's poetry reflects his conflictive attachment to books may be found in Enrico Mario Santí, *Pablo Neruda. The Poetics of Prophecy* (Ithaca and London: Cornell University Press, 1982), especially chapters 3 and 4.

17 *Memorias*, vol. 1, p. 34.

18 For a penetrating analysis of the relations between Colonialism and the book, see Homi K. Bhabha, "Signs Taken for Wonders: Questions of Ambivalence and Authority under a Tree Outside Delhi, May 1816" in *"Race," Writing, and Difference*, ed. Henry Louis Gates, Jr. (The University of Chicago Press, 1986), pp. 163—184. Bhabha shrewdly observes that "colonial hybridity is not a *problem* of genealogy or identity between two *different* cultures which can then be resolved as an issue of cultural relativism. Hybridity is a *problematic* of colonial representation and individuation that reverses the effects of the colonialist disavowal, so that other 'denied' knowledges enter upon the dominant discourse and estrange the basis of its authority – its rules of recognition ... Hybridity reverses the *formal* process of disavowal so that the violent

dislocation, the *Enstellung* of the act of colonization, becomes the *conditionality* of colonial discourse" (p. 175).

19 Cited in Ricardo Sáenz Hayes, "Alberdi y Sarmiento" in *La polémica de Alberdi con Sarmiento y otras páginas* (Buenos Aires: M. Gleizer, 1926), p. 33.

20 *Mi defensa*, in *Obras*, III, p. 7. Subsequent references to *Mi defensa* appear in the text preceded by a *D*.

21 "In achieving the ability to 'read very well,' Sarmiento also gains access to culture without the mediation of the typical *letrados* of a traditional society, that is, of priests. Ability to read, the acquisition of cultural instruments and intellectual emancipation are fused in Sarmiento's personal experience" (Carlos Altamirano and Beatriz Sarlo, "Una vida ejemplar: la estrategia de *Recuerdos de provincia*" in *Literatura/ Sociedad* [Buenos Aires: Hachette, 1983], p. 175).

22 Sarmiento's critics rarely pass up an occasion to denounce his faulty erudition. Manuel Gálvez, one of his most intolerant biographers, points out that "he has devoured everything in a disorderly fashion, without teachers. There are many things he cannot have understood, but he retained them since he certainly was not lacking in memory. This deplorable intellectual training, devoid of the slightest discipline, marks Sarmiento's spirit for the rest of his life ... In these things, when one begins badly, one continues badly" (Manuel Gálvez, *Vida de Sarmiento. El hombre de autoridad* [Buenos Aires: Emecé, 1945], p. 42).

Sarmiento's own stance on this issue was ambivalent: he claimed total intellectual independence yet, as most autodidacts, was particularly sensitive to any accusation of cultural incompetence (see Sáenz Hayes, p. 33).

23 Andrés Bello, cited in Gálvez, *Vida de Sarmiento*, p. 115.

24 "Primera polémica literaria," *Obras completas*, I, p. 223.

25 "Las obras de Larra," *Obras completas*, I, p. 113.

26 "Cartas con Mitre," *Obras completas*, XLIX, p. 245.

27 Benjamin Franklin, one of Sarmiento's avowed models, gives a very similar defense of plagiarism: "I rather approv'd his giving us good sermons compos'd by others, than bad ones of his own manufacture" (*The Autobiography of Benjamin Franklin* [New York: Macmillan, 1967], p. 106).

28 "Even on those remote shores [Sarmiento refers to Chile] Raynal and Mably ruled supreme and *The Social Contract* still held considerable authority. The most advanced readers had already reached Benjamin Constant.

We would carry, or rather I would carry, in my pocket, Lerminier, Pierre Leroux, Tocqueville, Guizot, and on occasion would consult the *Dictionary of Conversation* and many other handbooks" ("Reminiscencias de la vida literaria" in *Obras completas*, I, p. 335).

29 See Paul Verdevoye, *Domingo Faustino Sarmiento. Educateur et publiciste (entre 1839 et 1852)* (Paris: Institut des Hautes Etudes de l'Amérique Latine, 1963), pp. 55–59. Alberto Palcos suggests that the pieces in *El Zonda* containing unacknowledged quotations from Leroux were probably written by Ignacio de Quiroga Rosas, another collaborator who had initiated Sarmiento in the study of French Socialist thought (Verdevoye, p. 57). Sarmiento, however, credits himself with the writing of most of the articles and most of his critics believe him.

30 Verdevoye, p. 114.

31 Adolfo Prieto, in the excellent pages devoted to Sarmiento in his *La literatura autobiográfica argentina* (1966; rpt. Buenos Aires: Centro Editor de América Latina, 1982), sees him as fitting Karl Mannheim's category of the *gesticulating adult* to perfection (p. 53).

32 *Facundo, Obras completas*, VII, p. 7. This farcical episode will find its parallel exactly one hundred years later when another governmental commission attempts to answer a new question: not *what does it mean* but, as it were, *where* does it mean. Neglecting the fact that Sarmiento himself has often indicated that it was written on a wall *inside* a building, the commission of 1940, opting for monumentality, decided it must have been written on a rock and accordingly placed a plaque on that rock. See Allison Williams Bunkley, *The Life of Sarmiento* (Princeton University Press, 1952), p. 136.

33 More recently, the characters in Ricardo Piglia's novel, *Respiración artificial* (1980), are to be found still discussing Sarmiento's problematic quotation. They know it is not from Fortoul, believe it to be from Volney, but, in the final analysis, this is of no concern to them: what really interests them is the basic irony of the situation, the fact that a book like *Facundo*, hailed by many as the founding text of Argentine literature, be heralded by a quotation that, firstly, is foreign, and, secondly, is false. An added irony to this, of course, is that Piglia's novel itself, due to a typographical error, gets caught up in Sarmiento's mistake. While its characters delight in Sarmiento's erroneous quotation, the novel in a way perpetuates it by twice spelling *Fourtol* instead of *Fortoul* (Ricardo Piglia, *Respiración artificial* [Buenos Aires: Pomaire, 1980], pp. 161–162).

34 Cited in Verdevoye, p. 76.

35 For additional insights into Sarmiento's problematic relationship with and manipulation of European culture, see Ricardo Piglia, "Notas sobre *Facundo*" in *Punto de Vista*, 3, 8 (1980), p. 17 and Julio Ramos, "Escritura y oralidad en el *Facundo*," *Revista Iberoamericana*, 143 (1988), pp. 551–572.

36 "La organización nacional," *Obras completas*, XLIX, p. 169. Ricardo Piglia discusses Sarmiento's penchant for analogy: "If Sarmiento's somewhat wild passion for culture seems excessive, it is because, for

him, to know is to compare. Everything takes on meaning once one
establishes analogies between what one wishes to explain and something else that has already been judged and set down in writing"
("Notas sobre *Facundo*," p. 17).

37 See Luisa López Grigera, "Lectura retórica de *Facundo*," *Letras* (Buenos
Aires), VI–VII (1982–1983), pp. 119–128, for a discussion of Sarmiento's
debt to Classical rhetoric in the composition of *Facundo*.

38 John E. Englekirk, in his exhaustive "Franklin en el mundo hispánico,"
Revista Iberoamericana, 41–42 (1956), pp. 319–372, singles out Sarmiento
as the only Spanish American autobiographer influenced by Franklin.

39 For a general discussion on the exemplary function of Franklin's
Autobiography, see William C. Spengemann, *The Forms of Autobiography*
(New Haven and London: Yale University Press, 1980). It is clear that
Sarmiento too conceives of biographies and autobiographies as *exempla*.
He wished to put Franklin's *Autobiography* on school curricula, so that
every student, on reading it, would wish to "ser un Franklincito" – to be
a little Franklin – and obviously desired the same inspirational qualities
for his *Recuerdos*. Indeed, *Recuerdos* may be described in the very terms
used by Spengemann to speak of Franklin: "The aim of the *Autobiography* . . . is not so much to explain how his life is justified by some
universal principle as to justify his life by persuading others to make its
conclusions universal" (p. 54). More discussion of Franklin's exemplary self-writing within the North American tradition may be found in
Robert F. Sayre, "Autobiography and the Making of America" in
Autobiography. Essays Theoretical and Critical. ed. James Olney (Princeton
University Press, 1980), pp. 146–168.

40 See Louis Marin, "Variations sur un portrait absent: les autoportraits
de Poussin," *Corps écrit*, 5 (1983), pp. 87–108, for the relation between
self-portraiture and death, or autobiography as "autobiothanatogra-
phy." For a reflection on autobiography, epitaphs and prosopopeia, see
Paul de Man, "Autobiography as De-facement," pp. 919–930.

41 When speaking of Funes, Sarmiento twice indicates that the Dean was
the sole possessor of the books he quoted from (and probably plagia-
rized). As for himself, he proudly tells how he and his friends in San
Juan were the only ones to own books by Hugo, Thiers, Tocqueville,
Guizot, Chateaubriand, and other French writers (*D*, pp. 9–10). In
another vein, Lucio V. Mansilla speaks of the impression books made
on him as an adolescent: "Books were very rare at the time and . . . the
impression I felt at the sight of the few dusty libraries in this noble city,
partly hidden from view by barred windows, was, I must confess, one of
fear" (*Entre-Nos. Causeries del jueves* [Buenos Aires: Hachette, 1963],
pp. 54–55).

42 For related comments on the scene of reading in two Brazilian

autobiographies, see Daniel Balderston, "As primeiras letras de Graciliano Ramos e José Lins do Rego," *Travessia*, 8–9 (Florianópolis, 1984), pp. 107–114.

2 From serf to self: the autobiography of Juan Francisco Manzano

1 Juan Francisco Manzano, *Autobiografía, cartas y versos de Juan Fco. Manzano*, with a preliminary study by José L. Franco (Havana: Municipio de La Habana, 1937), p. 33. Subsequent references appear in the text. This edition, unlike others, retains the idiosyncratic syntax and uncertain spelling of Manzano's original manuscript of 1835. I quote from it, translating Manzano's *tone* as best I can, respecting the run-on construction of his sentences, his peculiar punctuation and the belabored nature of his syntax, but I do not attempt to reproduce his misspellings. Translating in this manner seems to me preferable (and surely fairer to Manzano) than quoting from the much altered, cleaned up and ideologically conditioned English translation of 1840 published in *Poems by a Slave in the Island of Cuba, Recently Liberated; Translated from the Spanish by R. R. Madden, M. D. with the History of the Early Life of the Negro Poet, Written by Himself, to Which Are Prefixed Two Pieces Descriptive of Cuban Slavery and the Slave-Traffic, By R. R. M.* (London: Thomas Ward and Co., 1840). I find it equally inadvisable to translate from Ivan Schulman's modernized edition (Juan Francisco Manzano, *Autobiografía de un esclavo*, ed. Ivan A. Schulman [Madrid: Guadarrama, 1975]). I shall discuss these and other manicured versions of Manzano later on.

2 Letter of 25 June 1835, in *Autobiografía*, p. 84.

3 For a concise and informative account of the tumultuous relations between England and Spain (and hence Cuba) on the issue of slavery, see Franklin W. Knight, *Slave Society in Cuba during the Nineteenth Century* (Madison, Milwaukee and London: University of Wisconsin Press, 1970), especially chapter 3: "The Cuban Slave Trade, 1838–1865." For an overall vision of slavery in Cuba, reference to Manuel Moreno Fraginals, *The Sugarmill. The Socioeconomic Complex of Sugar in Cuba. 1760–1860* (New York and London: Monthly Review Press, 1976), is indispensable.

4 Francisco Calcagno, *Poetas de color*. 4th. edn (Havana: Imprenta Mercantil de los Herederos de Santiago Spencer, 1887), p. 64, note 1.

5 See John W. Blassingame's introduction to *Slave Testimony. Two Centuries of Letters, Speeches, Interviews, and Autobiographies* (Baton Rouge: Louisiana University Press, 1977).

6 Blassingame, p. xxviii.

7 Letter of 16 October 1834, in Juan Francisco Manzano, *Autobiografía*, p. 79.

8 Letter of 11 December 1834, *Autobiografía*, p. 80.
9 "He realizes that his poetry, whatever its value, must pass through del Monte's hands if it is to reach Europe. He suspects that his freedom, if he is ever to attain it, will also come, in one way or another, from those hands" (Roberto Friol, *Suite para Juan Francisco Manzano* [Havana: Editorial Arte y Literatura, 1977], p. 60).

Manzano may have exaggerated his devotion to del Monte, yet his loyalty was nonetheless real. This was made evident in his testimony in favor of del Monte during the cruel investigation following the Black rebellion known as the "Conspiración de la Escalera" in 1843.

10 Letter of 11 December 1834, *Autobiografía*, p. 81. In another letter, dated 25 February 1835, Manzano informs del Monte of his wedding (to a free woman) and brings up, once more, the subject of his freedom: "Let not Your Grace forget that J. F. will not be happy if he is not F. and now more than ever," *Autobiografía*, p. 83.

11 No text is more eloquent, in this respect, than del Monte's open letter defending himself from those who would implicate him in the thwarted Escalera conspiracy. The letter, published in *Le Globe* in August 1844 during del Monte's exile in Paris, is a remarkable mixture of realistic thinking, ideological straight-jacketing and irrational fear. Del Monte reasserts his wish to abolish slavery but then extends his wish to include the banishment of Blacks from the island, so that Cuba may become "the most brilliant beacon of civilization of the Caucasian race in the Spanish American world." The way in which del Monte refers to the conspirators' plans is revealing:

Suffice it to recall what, according to depositions made by the Blacks themselves, was the plan of the conspiracy. In the final analysis, it amounted to the destruction, by fire, of sugar mills and other country estates, and to the destruction, by knife and poison, of all white men, in order to take pleasure in their daughters and their wives with impunity and later establish a Black republic on the island, like the one in Haiti, under England's protectorate.
(Domingo del Monte, *Escritos*. 1. Ed. José A. Fernández de Castro [Havana: Colección de Libros Cubanos, Editorial Cultural, S. A., 1929], pp. 189–202)

At the beginning of this letter, del Monte had denied his involvement in the conspiracy, arguing that the depositions implicating him were extracted from the Black conspirators under duress. Ironically, in the paragraph quoted above, he resorts to those same depositions as truthful sources of information without making the same allowances.

12 "The standard imposed by the del Monte group, which was more reformist than abolitionist, called for 'moderation and restraint' in the depiction of the black slave ... Since del Monte knew he had a showpiece Black with a good image and intellectual capacity, why not display him?" (Richard L. Jackson, "Slavery, Racism and Auto-

biography in Two Early Black Writers: Juan Francisco Manzano and
Martín Morúa Delgado" in *Voices from Under. Black Narrative in Latin
American and the Caribbean*, ed. William Luis [Westport, CT: Greenwood
Press, 1984], pp. 56–57). For other examples of the typification of slaves
for abolitionist purposes, see Larry Gara, "The Professional Fugitive in
the Abolitionist Movement," *Wisconsin Magazine of History*, 48 (1965),
pp. 196–204.

   Ivan Schulman observes, for his part, that the ideal of the del Monte
group was the *negro racional* or the *criada de razón*, a reasonable,
non-rebellious "victim of society, unlikely to alienate the conservative
elements of the sacarocracy that staunchly defended the principle of the
slave's tyrannization – *tiranizar o correr el riesgo de ser tiranizado* – and the
continuation of the illegal slave trade. The resultant pathetic being
would, it was hoped, not only win converts to the *criollo*'s humanitarian
cause, but also court the mercy and justice of foreign readers, especially
the English, who, in turn, might bring pressure to bear on the Spanish
crown to enforce the slave treaties" (Ivan A. Schulman, "The Portrait
of the Slave: Ideology and Aesthetics in the Cuban Antislavery Novel"
in *Comparative Perspectives on Slavery in New World Plantation Societies*, eds.
Vera Rubin and Arthur Tuden [New York: New York Academy of
Sciences, 1977], p. 359).

13 José Z. González del Valle, *La vida literaria en Cuba*, cited in César
   Leante, "Dos obras antiesclavistas cubanas," *Cuadernos americanos*, 207
   (July–August 1976), p. 175.

14 Jackson, p. 56. Jackson's conjectures do not stop here. Concluding,
   from the end of Part one of the *Autobiografía* (the only one that remains),
   that Manzano was in the process of shedding his submissive image,
   Jackson speculates on why Part two went astray: "[W]e can assume
   that part 2 could well have been franker than part 1. Perhaps Manzano
   in part 2 forgot the original guidelines and expressed some views that,
   for all concerned including Manzano, were better left unsaid. Perhaps
   Manzano had tired of being circumspect and wanted to go faster and
   farther than his liberal white friends were prepared to go" (p. 58).

15 *Autobiografía*, pp. 83–84. The person alluded to at the end of the letter
   was the Marquesa de Prado Ameno, who died in 1853, a year before
   Manzano (Friol, p. 51).

16 See, for example, the English translation of this same letter in Juan
   Francisco Manzano, *The Life and Poems of a Cuban Slave*, ed. Edward J.
   Mullen (Hamden, CT: Archon Book, 1981) pp. 14–15. Much like
   Madden, the editor chooses to render Manzano's letters into "correct"
   English. I disagree with his choice and shall elaborate later on my
   disagreement.

17 *Autobiografía*, pp. 84–85.

18 Mythical overtones have been attributed to this purported "silence" of Manzano. Suárez y Romero speciously argues that "it was as a slave that he learned to read and write, as a slave that he composed his first poems, as a slave that he sketched the disturbing account of his troubled life, as a slave that he struck up friendships with the intellectuals who redeemed him ... [A]s if pain were his only inspiration, Juan Francisco Manzano became silent when the night of serfdom gave way to the dawn of freedom" (quoted in Antonio López Prieto, *Parnaso cubano. Colección de poesías selectas de autores cubanos*, 1 [Havana: Editorial Miguel de Villa, 1881], p. 253). By tracking down poems by Manzano published in periodicals after his manumission, Friol successfully challenges this myth and restores this "silence" to its true proportions (Friol, pp. 215–216).

19 Mullen in Juan Francisco Manzano, *The Life and Poems of a Cuban Slave*, p. 22. My emphasis. Several pages earlier, Mullen's critical assessment seemed to point in the opposite way: "Another plausible explanation [for the difference between Madden's text and Manzano's] would be that Madden's translation is in reality a reconstruction of the Spanish original designed to reflect abolitionist views, which would explain why the text highlights in particular the degradations of slavery" (p. 13).

20 "He was about thirty-eight years of age when he obtained his liberty. The price paid for it was 800 dollars. He obtained employment as a tailor for some time after he got his freedom, subsequently, he went out to service – then tried the business of a house-painter, and was not successful – was advised to set up as a confectioner, and lost all his money in that line, and eventually, settled down as a 'chef de cuisine' in occasional service" (Madden, in Manzano, *The Life and Poems of a Cuban Slave*, p. 39).

21 Friol, p. 34. For non-Cuban readers, identification seems to have been less easy: "Since Madden did not publish Manzano's full name in his translation, a number of American writers, among them Amelia E. Barr and William Wells Brown, confused Manzano with the better-known mulatto poet, Plácido (Gabriel de la Concepción Valdés, 1809–44), producing curious hybrid biographical sketches of the writers" (Mullen, in Manzano, *The Life and Poems of a Cuban Slave*, p. 12).

22 Madden, in Manzano, *The Life and Poems of a Cuban Slave*, p. 39.

23 A similar manipulation of the text, from the individual to the general, may be seen in Schulman's retitling of Manzano's autobiography, *Autobiografía de un esclavo* (an echo, perhaps, of Miguel Barnet's *Biografía de un cimarrón*, published to considerable acclaim a few years earlier). Indeed, Schulman's preliminary words, the *non sequitur* of the second sentence notwithstanding, confirm this shift towards the general:

[W]e decided not to reproduce the text of Franco's edition, which duplicates the original manuscript with all the orthographic and syntactic deficiencies that make it so hard to read. We believe that the contemporary reader, more than ever interested in matters of Black literature, slavery, underdevelopment and cultural dependence, requires a text both reliable and modern.

(Juan Francisco Manzano, *Autobiografía de un esclavo*, p. 10)

24 This representativeness can be used strategically, if not always by the authors themselves, by their enthusiastic critics. Thus Selwyn R. Cudjoe, when considering the autobiography of Maya Angelou, writes that Afro-American autobiography is "a form that tends to be bereft of any *excessive subjectivism* and *mindless* egotism ... the autobiographical subject emerging as an almost random member of the group, selected to tell his/her tale." Afro-American autobiography is therefore seen as "a *public* rather than a *private* gesture, *me-ism* gives way to *our-ism* and superficial concerns about *individual subject* usually give way to the *collective subjection* of the group" (cited in Elizabeth Fox-Genovese, "To Write Myself: The Autobiographies of Afro-American Women" in *Feminist Issues in Literary Scholarship* [Bloomington and Indianapolis: Indiana University Press, 1987], p. 165). The fact that Manzano was not an "almost random member" of his group but, in fact, a very exceptional one of course complicates this assessment.

25 William Luis, *Literary Bondage: Slavery in Cuban Narrative* (Austin: University of Texas Press, 1990), pp. 93–100.

26 On a larger scale, isolation was a well-known means of ensuring the good functioning of the slave system. Newly arrived Africans were routinely mixed up ethnically so that no slave group consisted of Africans of one ethnic origin. Communication was much impeded if not rendered impossible: "Plantation owners, in fact, had a vested interest in not permitting slaves to interact freely, for with social cohesion might come a sense of solidarity" (Manuel Moreno Fraginals, "Cultural Contributions and Deculturation" in *Africa in Latin America: Essays on History, Culture and Socialization*, ed. Manuel Moreno Fraginals, trans. Leonor Blum [New York: Holmes and Meier, 1984], p. 7).

27 "Boys and girls wore a one-piece shirt with one lateral seam.... Footwear was never handed out. There was even an eighteenth-century French decree forbidding giving shoes to Blacks because 'shoes tortured their feet'," Moreno Fraginals, "Cultural Contributions," p. 16.

28 A statement Madden incredibly mistranslates as "[M]y only comfort at that moment was the solitude of my room" (Manzano, *The Life and Poems*, p. 105).

29 With the exception of Antonio Vera León's perceptive analysis of Manzano in "Testimonios, reescrituras: la narrativa de Miguel Barnet," unpublished PhD dissertation, Princeton, 1987.

30 Friol, p. 48.
31 López Prieto, *Parnaso cubano*, p. 252.
32 For the way in which Blacks were denied education, see Ramón Guirao, "Poetas negros y mestizos en la época esclavista," *Bohemia*, 26 August 1934, pp. 43–44, 123–124.
33 "When, for reasons beyond their control, the slave-owners had no productive work for the slaves to do, they devised unproductive work for the slaves such as moving objects from one place to another and then returning them to their place of origin. A slave without work was an element of dissolution for the whole system, a factor of possible rebellion" (Moreno Fraginals, "Africa in Cuba: A Quantitative Analysis of the African Population in the Island of Cuba" in Vera Rubin and Arthur Tuden, eds., *Comparative Perspectives*, p. 200). Examples of this invented work to avoid empty time (or pastimes) may be found in Manzano: "It was my task every half hour to clean the furniture, whether it was dusty or not" (p. 48); and: "I was sent to polish the mahogany so that I would not spend my time weeping or sleeping" (p. 56).

   A study of time, of the different notations of time in Manzano's *Autobiografía* would be of definite interest. Critics have pointed to the apparent contradiction between Manzano's exceptional memory for literature and his poor memory concerning facts. Chronology and time notations are indeed blurry, imprecision alternating with very precise deictics ("a little before eleven," etc.). The following remarks on perception of time by slaves help clarify the controversy on time in Manzano's text: "After some time this accumulated fatigue became irreversible. The unnatural rhythm must have brought about a deepseated dissociation between human time and the time required for production, a total lack of synchronization between biological capabilities and the task that had to be performed" (Moreno Fraginals, "Cultural Contributions," p. 18).
34 Calcagno, *Poetas de color*, p. 50.
35 Antonio Olliz Boyd, "The Concept of Black Awareness as a Thematic Approach in Latin American Literature" in *Blacks in Hispanic Literature*, ed. Miriam de Costa (Port Washington, NY – London: Kennikat Press, 1977), p. 69.
36 Miriam de Costa, "Social Lyricism and the Caribbean Poet/Rebel" in *Blacks in Hispanic Literature*, pp. 115–116. For a somewhat more balanced judgment on the phenomenon of imitation, see Samuel Feijóo, "African Influence in Latin America: Oral and Written Language" in *Africa in America*, p. 148.
37 Letter of 11 December 1834 to Domingo del Monte, Manzano, *Autobiografía*, p. 82.
38 *Poetas de color*, p. 51.

39 "In Manzano, with his exaggerated rhetoric, his excessive decorum, his exalted sentimentalism, we see how the impossibility of breaking out of a literary code forces the black writer to master it through exhaustion and excess" (Roberto González Echevarría, "Nota crítica sobre Pedro Barreda, *The Black Protagonist in the Cuban Novel*" in *Isla a su vuelo fugitiva* [Madrid: Porrúa Turanzas, 1983], p. 245).

40 See the Suárez y Romero letter describing his editing task in Friol, p. 231.

41 Max Henríquez Ureña, *Panorama histórico de la literatura cubana* (Puerto Rico: Ediciones Mirador, 1963), p. 184.

3 The theatrics of reading: body and book in Victoria Ocampo

1 The autobiographical nature of the entire works of Victoria Ocampo is patent. My study will focus on the posthumously published *Autobiografía* comprising six volumes: I. *El archipiélago* (Buenos Aires: Ediciones Revista Sur, 1979); II. *El imperio insular* (Buenos Aires: Ediciones Revista Sur, 1980); III. *La rama de Salzburgo* (Buenos Aires: Ediciones Revista Sur, 1981); IV. *Viraje* (Buenos Aires: Ediciones Revista Sur, 1982); V. *Figuras simbólicas. Medida de Francia* (Buenos Aires: Ediciones Revista Sur, 1983); VI. *Sur y Cía.* (Buenos Aires: Ediciones Revista Sur, 1984). Subsequent references to these editions appear in the text. I shall also discuss a good number of Ocampo's first-person chronicles and essays collected in ten volumes under the general title of *Testimonios*.

2 Another version of this first scene of reading may be found in "De la cartilla al libro" in *Testimonios*, 6a serie (Buenos Aires: Sur, 1963): "Before learning [the alphabet], I so loved stories, and books because they had stories in them, that, according to my mother, I would settle down to read, with an open book in my hands, repeating a story that I knew by heart and turning the pages at the right moment" (p. 137).

3 "[I] pretended to read. My eyes followed the black signs without skipping a single one, and I told myself a story out loud, being careful to utter all the syllables" (Jean-Paul Sartre, *The Words*. Trans. Bernard Frechtman [New York: George Braziller, 1964], p. 48).

4 Sartre, p. 44.

5 The second volume of the autobiography, *El imperio insular*, presents an incisive critique of the education of Argentine women in the late nineteenth century. To back it, Ocampo includes the letters she wrote to her friend Delfina Bunge in adolescence: "I wanted to stress how much I suffered, how much I was mentally tortured, early on in my adolescence, by the situation of women. That suffering was not without

cause. I was wasting my time, I was hopelessly wasting my time. And those lost years are impossible to recover later on (I mean in discipline, in seriousness towards study)" (II, p. 143).

6 "Malandanzas de una autodidacta" in *Testimonios*, 5a serie (Buenos Aires: Sur, 1957).

7 In addition to her autobiography, specific references to childhood reading may be found in "Ordenar el caos," a review article on Graham Greene's autobiography (*Testimonios*, 9a serie [Buenos Aires: 1975], pp. 58–67), and in "La influencia de la lectura sobre nuestra infancia" in the same volume of *Testimonios*.

8 *Testimonios*, 6a serie, p. 143.

9 "Palabras francesas," in *Testimonios* (Madrid: Revista de Occidente, 1935), p. 35.

10 "Emily Brontë, terra incognita" in *Testimonios*, 2a serie (Buenos Aires: Sur, 1941), pp. 115–116.

11 Victoria Ocampo, "El aguilucho" in *Testimonios*, 8a serie (Buenos Aires: Sur, 1971), p. 100. Subsequent references to this piece appear in the text.

12 For an almost identical version of this discovery, see II, pp. 62–63.

13 Letter to Delfina Bunge, 3 August 1908, quoted in Doris Meyer, *Victoria Ocampo. Against the Wind and the Tide* (New York: George Braziller, 1979), p. 31.

14 In these performances, Ocampo notes rapturously, "I expressed myself fully, entirely. I *communicated*," *Autobiografía*, IV, p. 103. Of her concession to the wishes of her parents, she writes to Ortega y Gasset: "I have sacrificed to my parents convictions I should have sacrificed to no one. Given my character, the sacrifice should have been not to sacrifice myself but to sacrifice them. That is, to sacrifice the false view they had of things (in MY opinion) even if it made them suffer. But I was a coward out of love. It's a fault I still have and I don't know that I'll ever be rid of it" (Letter to Ortega, cited in II, p. 175).

15 "In those years, the attitude of Argentine 'society' towards a woman writer was not particularly indulgent ... [Writing] was considered scandalous, as much as driving a car in the streets of Buenos Aires. For the latter I was showered with insults. And what passers-by shouted at me when they saw me go by at the wheel of my car, others thought when they read my articles" (III, p. 105).

16 *Virginia Woolf en su diario* (Buenos Aires: Sur, 1944), pp. 44–45.

17 A detailed, personal account of the political struggle for women's rights in that period may be found in the second volume of María Rosa Oliver's autobiography, *La vida cotidiana* (Buenos Aires: Sudamericana, 1969), pp. 350–355.

18 Sandra M. Gilbert and Susan Gubar, "Infection in the Sentence: The

Woman Writer and the Anxiety of Authorship" in *The Madwoman in the Attic* (New Haven and London: Yale University Press, 1979), pp. 45–92.

19 *Testimonios*, 8a serie, p. 195. Ocampo quotes from Valéry's "De la diction des vers" in *Pièces sur l'art, Oeuvres*, II (Paris: Gallimard, La Pléiade, 1966), p. 1255.

20 Thus for example Doris Meyer writes: "... Victoria had identified her adolescent heroes. Not surprisingly, they were all characters in her favorite books, and all of them were men ... [F]emale roles were singularly uninspiring at the turn of the century. Both in life and literature, the Victorian age fostered the notion that a woman should be chaste and long-suffering ..." (Meyer, p. 27). The statement implies a view of identification that is strictly mimetic and coeval: it does not allow for the possibility of anachronism in the process of *literary* identification.

21 Meyer does not mention Madame de Staël in her biography of Ocampo. Yet Ocampo writes to Delfina Bunge in 1906: "Mme Necker de Saussure was right to observe in a footnote: '*In writing, she wished to express what she carried within her far more than to achieve a work of art.*' More than ever have I had the familiar feeling of living what I was reading. I was *Corinne*. Her fate was mine" (II, p. 166). Later in the same volume, Ocampo again resorts to Madame de Staël "because I find her so useful to determine my own position" (II, p. 179).

   Drieu la Rochelle, a friend and sometime lover of Ocampo, compares her in his journals to Madame de Staël. The comparison, in fact, is far from flattering: "Victoria will have been my Madame de Staël. But she was less substantial; in a few months, I was practically free from her grip" (Pierre Drieu la Rochelle, *Sur les écrivains*, ed. F. Grover [Paris: Gallimard, 1964], p. 208). Ocampo defends herself gallantly (II, p. 167). For further reference to Madame de Staël and politics, see IV, p. 14.

22 *De Francesca a Beatrice*. Epilogue by José Ortega y Gasset. 2nd edn (Madrid: Revista de Occidente, 1928), p. 27.

23 Delfina Bunge, nine years Ocampo's senior, wrote poetry in French at the time these letters were exchanged. The friendship would soon die out due to Bunge's growing religious prejudice and the protofascist ideology she shared with her husband, the writer Manuel Gálvez. Besides poetry and essays on religion, Bunge published a childhood memoir in Spanish, *Viaje alrededor de mi infancia* (Buenos Aires: Imprenta Guadalupe, 1941).

24 Years later Ocampo tells an interviewer: "In my childhood, in my adolescence and in my first plunge into young adulthood, I lived in books what I could not live in life, because life was full of absurd taboos

for a girl or a young woman when I was at either stage. After that, I lived in life what I had lived before in literature and literature paled. It was used to relate, more or less indirectly or directly, what was lived [*lo vivido*]" (interview with Fryda Schultz de Mantovani in *Testimonios*, 8a serie [Buenos Aires: Ed. Sur, 1971], p. 297).

25 Nora Domínguez and Adriana Rodríguez Persico, in a generally thoughtful article, suggest Racine as Ocampo's intertext in this third volume, with the character of Hermione as her emblem. Their notion that Ocampo "performs" her text is convincing. However, since Racine's text is never summoned in *La rama de Salzburgo* in any constructive way, the suggestion seems rather hasty ("Autobiografía de Victoria Ocampo. La pasión del modelo," *Lecturas críticas*, 2 [Buenos Aires, 1984], pp. 22–33).

26 As a point of curiosity, I quote from a footnote in an Argentine translation of the *Commedia*, a translation sponsored by the Fondo Nacional de las Artes on whose board of directors Ocampo served: "A similar role [that of go-between] is played by an inanimate object, the book, in the relationship between wife and brother-in-law. The episode constitutes an early but unquestionable example of the harmful influence of certain readings," Dante Alighieri, *La Divina Comedia*, translation, prologue and notes by Angel Battistessa (Buenos Aires: Ediciones Carlos Lohlé, 1972) p. 313, n. 137. The narrowness of the translator and critic ironically echoes the parental and societal repression Ocampo fought all her life.

27 Marcelle Thiébaux argues that women's reading is intolerable to patriarchal discourse and that it is constantly interrupted, redirected and incorporated into the (patriarchal) text. "Dante records Francesca's own story of how reading about adultery stirred her and her lover's passion. The fateful kiss interrupts the reading: 'That day we read no further.' Now she is a text in hell" ("Foucault's Fantasia for Feminists: The Woman Reading" in *Theory and Practice of Feminist Literary Criticism*, eds. Gabriela Mora and Karen S. Van Hooft [Ypsilanti, Michigan: Bilingual Press/Editorial Bilingüe, 1982], p. 53). I take issue with some points of this particular interpretation while not disagreeing with its general argument. Francesca's and Paolo's reading is less an act of voyeuristic titillation than a moment of knowledge (indeed, Dante uses the verb *conoscere* twice): reading does more than arouse the two lovers, it allows them to recognize and to name. Thus "the fateful kiss" does not interrupt the reading but in a sense continues it. Janet Beth Greenberg ("The Divided Self: Forms of Autobiography in the Writings of Victoria Ocampo," unpublished PhD dissertation, University of California, Berkeley, 1986) concurs with Thiébaux's interpretation of the Francesca episode and, extending it to Ocampo,

speaks of a voyeuristic dimension in Ocampo's reading of Dante (p. 150), a view I do not share.

28 The additional fact that she enters the literary scene with a text in French prompts Beatriz Sarlo to comment shrewdly: "Foreign language was the language of feminine consumption not of production. Victoria Ocampo subverts it, making it productive – to read, to receive, is also to quote, to give back ... She gives back what her family had given her in childhood but changes its sign: what her social milieu considered an ornament, Victoria Ocampo turns into an instrument" (*Una modernidad periférica: Buenos Aires 1920–1930* [Buenos Aires: Nueva Visión, 1988], p. 91).

29 The predicament of male critics when confronted with women's texts is not infrequent, nor are the contradictory statements they issue on the texts themselves. For a similar situation, see Gilbert and Gubar on the conflictive reception of Emily Dickinson, *The Madwoman in the Attic*, pp. 541–543.

30 For a lucid critique of some versions of this position, see Ann Rosalind Jones, "Writing the Body: Toward an Understanding of *L'Ecriture féminine*," in *Feminist Criticism. Essays on Women, Literature and Theory*, ed. Elaine Showalter (New York: Pantheon Books, 1985), pp. 361–377.

31 Of her misunderstanding with one of those men, Ocampo writes: "Maybe he ignored (as do most men) up to what point I was capable of feeling passion (dissociated from amorous passion) for a book, an idea, for a man who would incarnate that book, that idea, without having that passion invade other regions of my being. Those regions seemed to have their own laws, their requirements, their rights to veto in accordance with their nature. If the man-book-idea was not accepted by that other part of myself ... distance became definitive and frontiers were set up. This is what happened to me with Ortega" (III, p. 110). On her particularly irksome misunderstanding with Keyserling she wrote *El viajero y una de sus sombras* (Buenos Aires: Sudamericana, 1951), and also devoted a good portion of the fourth volume of her autobiography to the subject.

32 "Carta a Virginia Woolf" in *Testimonios*, p. 9.

33 On Ocampo's *Testimonios* as subjective and ahistorical constructs, see Marta Gallo, "Las crónicas de Victoria Ocampo," *Revista Iberoamericana*, 132–133 (1985), pp. 679–686.

34 Thus Cortázar comments on the immediacy of Ocampo's *testimonios* as verbal performances: "All I know of her are her books, her voice and *Sur*." He adds: "This book [*Soledad sonora*] forces us to accept the role of direct interlocutors ... Each chapter bites into its subject matter with an impulse that is both confidential and defiant ..." (Julio Cortázar, "Soledad sonora," *Sur*, 192–3–4 [1950], p. 294).

35 "Palabras francesas" in *Testimonios*, p. 34. In this same piece, an interesting example of linguistic soul-searching, she adds:

> Add to this that our society was somewhat indifferent to matters of the mind, even quite ignorant. Many of us, unconsciously, had ended up believing monstrosities. For example, that the Spanish language was incapable of expressing what lay beyond the purely material, practical aspects of life; a language in which it was a bit ridiculous to strive for precision, that is, nuance ... Many of us used Spanish like those travelers who learn a few words in the language of the country they are visiting because those words are useful in getting them out of trouble in their hotels, at the station, in shops. But that is as far as they go.   (p. 36)

36 It is interesting that the other Ocampo sister to become a writer, Silvina, went through a similar struggle, torn between an inadequate command of written Spanish and the ease with which she wrote in the other language – English, in her particular case. See Noemí Ulla, *Encuentros con Silvina Ocampo* (Buenos Aires: Editorial de Belgrano, 1982), p. 16.

37 A way of "speaking the written" that Ocampo admired in her favorite performers, Marguerite Moreno (whose acting she preferred to the declamatory style of a Sarah Bernhardt) and Laurence Olivier. ("*Hamlet* y Laurence Olivier" in *Soledad sonora* [Buenos Aires: Sudamericana, 1950], pp. 194–195).

38 Michel Foucault, "L'écriture de soi," *Corps écrit*, 5 (Paris: Presses Universitaires de France, 1983), pp. 8, 12.

39 On *Sur* as a form of "personal writing," see María Luisa Bastos, "Escrituras ajenas, expresión propia: *Sur* y los *Testimonios* de Victoria Ocampo," *Revista Iberoamericana*, 110–111 (1980), pp. 123–137; and "Dos líneas testimoniales: *Sur*, los escritos de Victoria Ocampo," *Sur*, 348 (1981), pp. 9–23.

40 Beatriz Sarlo, *Una modernidad periférica*, p. 89.

41 The most complete evaluation of *Sur*'s merits and shortcomings is that of John King, *Sur. A Study of the Argentine Literary Journal and Its Role in the Development of a Culture. 1931–1970* (Cambridge University Press, 1986). See also María Luisa Bastos; Eduardo Paz Leston, *El proyecto de la revista Sur, Capítulo*, 106 (Buenos Aires: Centro Editor de América Latina, 1981); Beatriz Sarlo *et al.* "Dossier: La revista Sur," *Punto de vista*, 17 (1983), pp. 7–14; Nicolás Rosa, "*Sur*, o el espíritu y la letra," *Los libros*, 15–16 (1971), pp. 4–6; Blas Matamoro, "*Sur*: la torre inclinada" in *Genio y figura de Victoria Ocampo* (Buenos Aires: Eudeba, 1986), pp. 201–308.

42 "Virginia Woolf en mi recuerdo" in *Testimonios*, 2a serie (Buenos Aires:

Sur, 1941), pp. 415–428. English version in Doris Meyer, *Victoria Ocampo. Against the Wind and the Tide*, pp. 235–240.

43 For competing self-representations in autobiographies written by women, see Sidonie Smith, *A Poetics of Women's Autobiography. Marginality and the Fictions of Self-Representation* (Bloomington and Indianapolis: Indiana University Press, 1987), especially chapter 3: "Woman's Story and the Engendering of Self-Representation."

44 *Testimonios*, p. 12.

45 This attitude, one should add, is not exclusive to Ocampo. See Sandra M. Gilbert and Susan Gubar, "'Forward into the Past': The Female Affiliation Complex" in *No Man's Land. The Place of the Woman Writer in the Twentieth Century*, vol. I: *The War on Words* (New Haven and London: Yale University Press, 1987), pp. 165–224. On Ocampo's attitude in particular, see Matamoro, p. 80.

46 Mary Jacobus, *Reading Woman. Essays in Feminist Criticism* (New York: Columbia University Press, 1986), p. 132.

47 *Ibid.* p. 286.

4 Childhood and exile: the Cuban paradise of the Countess of Merlin

1 See for example Roy Pascal, "The Autobiography of Childhood" in *Design and Truth in Autobiography* (Cambridge, MA: Harvard University Press, 1960); Peter Coveney, *The Image of Childhood* (Baltimore: Penguin Books, 1967); Luann Walthur, "The Invention of Childhood in Victorian Autobiography" in *Approaches to Victorian Autobiography*, ed. George P. Landow (Athens: Ohio University Press, 1979); Richard Coe, *When the Grass Was Taller: Autobiography and the Experience of Childhood* (New Haven: Yale University Press, 1984); Susannah Egan, *Patterns of Experience in Autobiography* (Chapel Hill and London: University of North Carolina Press, 1984); Michael Long, *Marvell, Nabokov. Childhood and Arcadia* (Oxford: Clarendon Press, 1984); Brian Finney, *The Inner I: British Literary Autobiography of the Twentieth Century* (London and Boston: Faber and Faber, 1985).

2 As Frederick Luciani persuasively argues, not a few of those details from Sor Juana's early years, considered by most critics as "precious bits of real life incrusted in the letter's dense rhetorical matrix," are themselves literary constructs, "grounded as much in other texts as in life." ("Octavio Paz on Sor Juana Inés de la Cruz: The Metaphor Incarnate," *Latin American Literary Review*, 15, 30 [1987], pp. 11–12).

3 Jean Starobinski, "The Style of Autobiography" in *Autobiography: Essays Theoretical and Critical*, ed. James Olney (Princeton University Press, 1980), p. 82.

4 The legal connotations of these terms – *notes* instead of *chapters*, *files* instead of *books* – forcibly remind the reader of the division of *Lazarillo de Tormes* into *tratados*, treatises. It also confirms the thesis expounded by Roberto González Echevarría ("The Life and Adventures of Cipión and Berganza: Cervantes and the Picaresque," *Diacritics* 10:3 [1980] pp. 15–26) and Antonio Gómez-Moriana ("Autobiographie et discours rituel. La confession autobiographique au tribunal de l'Inquisition," *Poétique*, 56 [1983], pp. 444–460) as to the legalistic foundation of both picaresque and first-person narrative in Hispanic literatures.

5 José Miguel Guridi y Alcocer, *Apuntes de la vida de D. José Miguel Guridi y Alcocer* (Mexico: Moderna Librería Religiosa de José L. Vallejo, 1906), p. 13.

6 "Rousseau states 'Plutarch is my man.' In the same way we could say, 'Rousseau is ours.' We knew *The Profession of Faith of the Savoyard vicar*, lengthy though it is, by heart," José Zapiola y Cortés, *Recuerdos de treinta años (1810–1840)*, 5th edn [Santiago: Guillermo Miranda, 1902], p. 36). Hernán Díaz Arrieta sees Zapiola as "a product of his time, saturated by the prevailing spirit of the *Encyclopédie*, rapidly succumbing to the spell of Rousseau who had also been poor and rejected, and was, like him, a musician" (*Memorialistas chilenos* [Santiago: Zig-Zag, 1960], p. 29).

7 Juan Bautista Alberdi, *Autobiografía* (Buenos Aires: El Ateneo, 1927), p. 45. Alberdi's passion for Rousseau is of a most intense, personal nature. In a letter to a friend he describes his emotions on seeing Rousseau's portrait by Fantin-Latour in Geneva: "I have rarely seen a more beautiful face in my life ... I confess that, had I been born a woman, I would have found it hard to deny that man my sympathy. Now I fully understand Mme. de Warens' infatuation" (cited in Ricardo Sáenz Hayes, "Alberdi en el país de Rousseau" in *La polémica de Alberdi con Sarmiento y otras páginas* [Buenos Aires: M. Gleizer, 1926], p. 57).

8 Childish pastimes, for example, are presented less for themselves than for their ideological import: "From my mother I took to colonial crafts and from my father I absorbed the ideas and prejudices of the revolutionary period. Following these contradictory impulses, I spent my free time in happy contemplation of my clay saints, painted in proper colors, but was prepared to abandon them, in their quiet niches at a moment's notice in order to join in a great battle across the street between the two armies which my neighbor and I had prepared a month before, using up great supplies of bullets to thin out the ranks of our gaudy, crudely fashioned soldiers" (*Recuerdos de provincia* in *Obras completas*, III [Buenos Aires: Imprenta y Litografía Mariano Moreno, 1896], p. 167).

9 Luis Montt, Introd. to Vicente Pérez Rosales, *Recuerdos del pasado (1814–1860)* (Santiago: Biblioteca de Escritores de Chile, 1910), p. viii.

10 An early and enthusiastic reader of *The Social Contract*, Mansilla distances his own autobiographical venture from that of Rousseau: "My idea ... is not to ignore the restraints of propriety, nor to forsake scruples, in the style of J. J. Rousseau. So much of what he writes is sheer cynicism!" (*Mis memorias* [Buenos Aires: Hachette, 1955], p. 63).

11 Regarding Rousseau's mark on Spanish American autobiography, I disagree with Tulio Halperín Donghi who writes: "Rousseau dared propose what, from its very title, echoed the message inherited from early Christianity; his *Confessions* were also, in their way, the history of a soul whose course was less linear and more tormented than the one offered by his great precursor. This is a dimension that will appear more and more in autobiographies written in the nineteenth century. That dimension affects, no doubt, the (now so frequent) inclusion of childhood in the autobiographical account. If childhood does not contribute to the public man, it does contribute to the total being." ("Intelectuales, sociedad y vida pública en Hispanoamérica a través de la literatura autobiográfica" in *El espejo de la historia. Problemas argentinos y perspectivas latinoamericanas* [Buenos Aires: Editorial Sudamericana, 1987], p. 54. My contention is, precisely, the opposite: (1) that this "dimension" introduced by Rousseau touches few nineteenth-century autobiographies and then only towards the end of the century; and (2) that the childhood story, when incorporated into nineteenth-century autobiography, is used less to express "total man" than to foreshadow the achievements of the adult. In that sense, it does indeed, proleptically, "contribute to the public man."

12 One explanation that I would definitely *not* consider is that of Richard Coe in an otherwise valuable book. Addressing the lack of childhood autobiographies in general "among the Mediterranean-Latin peoples," Coe suggests "that the close-knit patterns of family relationships in these Catholic Latin countries, persisting as they do right through adult life, make it difficult, perhaps impossible, for the writer to consider his child-self as something markedly distinct from his adult-self" (*When the Grass Was Taller: Autobiography and the Experience of Childhood* [New Haven: Yale University Press, 1984], p. 277). The usual reduction of the unknown Other to infantilism reappears here with a nasty twist.

13 Georges Gusdorf, "Conditions and Limits of Autobiography" in *Autobiography. Essays Theoretical and Critical*, ed. James Olney (Princeton University Press, 1980), p. 36.

14 What Richard Coe observes of Montaigne might in fact be applied to the early Spanish American autobiographer: his "virtually total"

neglect of childhood, in addition to reflecting the attitude of his period towards that stage in life, stems from the fact that he is "concerned primarily with *adult* responsibilities" (p. 20).

15 The posture has, of course, European Romantic antecedents, of which Victor Hugo's "Ce siècle avait deux ans," with its melding of personal and national history, is a good example. James Fernández, in an insightful dissertation, "Strategies of Self-Defense: Episodes in Nine-teenth-Century Spanish Autobiography" (unpublished PhD disser-tation, Princeton University, 1988), discusses a similar tendency in Spain. Compared to its European counterparts, the Spanish American variant of the posture places greater emphasis on the genetic link and the messianic calling that turn the individual and his country into one, indissoluble, *corpus gloriosus*.

16 Domingo Faustino Sarmiento, *Cartas de Sarmiento a la Señora María Mann* (Buenos Aires: Publicación de la Academia Argentina de Letras, 1936), p. 160.

17 Vicente Fidel López, 1854 prologue to his *La novia del hereje o La Inquisición en Lima*, cited in Emilio Carilla, *El romanticismo en la América Hispánica* (Madrid: Gredos, 1967), vol. II, p. 67, n. 13.

18 Significantly, Alberdi allows himself here to cite Rousseau and thinks longingly back to childhood using *La Nouvelle Héloïse* as *aide-mémoire*: "This novel [Alberdi writes in a letter] ... is linked in my memory to the recollections of the first years of my life. Its harmony and its beauty bring back to my soul memories of the first feelings experienced in my youth, as do the choruses of *The Barber of Seville* and the strains of the music that accompanied our happy and bustling childhood reunions. All of those sweet moments, so happy and so far beyond our reach, the hopeful dreams of our first years, our days full of generous enthusiasm and faith in the future, the joyful outings to San Pedro and to San Isidro, our common friends, some of them wandering around the world, others dead on the battlefield, the past fortunes of our country, all this comes to my mind when I read this book full of such charming recollections." And he adds, in a process of total identification with Rousseau's character: "If Julie, as Rousseau describes her, had really existed and were to return today to life to read her letters, she would not relive her memories of those bygone days of her first youth more poignantly than I do as I reread them myself ... " (cited in Sáenz Hayes, *La polémica de Alberdi con Sarmiento y otras páginas*, pp. 53–54).

19 Benjamin speaks of "an emphatic striving for dissociation with the outmoded – which means, however, with the most recent past. These tendencies direct the visual imagination which has been activated by the new, back to the primeval past. In the dream in which, before the eyes of each epoch, that which is to follow appears in images, the latter

appear wedded to elements from prehistory, that is, of a classless society". (Walter Benjamin, "Paris, Capital of the Nineteenth Century," *Reflections*, ed. Peter Demetz [New York and London: Harcourt Brace Jovanovich, 1978], p. 148).

Olmedo's dubious blend of nineteenth-century heroism and pre-Columbian mythology – the last Inca, Huayna Capac, appears to Bolívar on the battlefield of Junín – may be seen from this perspective. The subsequent popularity of *indianismo* could also be viewed as an effort to elude the immediate past in favor of a primeval, autochtonous one opening onto a utopian future.

20 Carilla gives an exhaustive list of nineteenth-century political exiles whose poetry is devoted to the recreation of the native land (*El romanticismo*, pp. 28–29). Unfortunately, as is the case throughout his book, he does not move beyond his catalogue of authors into a worthwhile discussion of the texts themselves.

21 In an unexpected turn, her name is cited as a possible model for the marquise de San-Réal in Balzac's *La Fille aux yeux d'or*. See Rose Fortassier's preface to Honoré de Balzac, *La Duchesse de Langeais. La Fille aux yeux d'or* (Paris: Gallimard, "Folio," 1976), pp. 26–27.

22 Adriana Méndez Rodenas, "Voyage to *La Havane*: La Condesa de Merlin's Pre-View of National Identity," *Cuban Studies/Estudios Cubanos*, 16 (1986), p. 75.

23 Mercedes Santa Cruz y Montalvo, Condesa de Merlin, *Mis doce primeros años e Historia de Sor Inés* (Havana: Imprenta El Siglo XX, 1922), p. 21. Subsequent references appear in the text.

24 Forbidden to read Rousseau as an adolescent, the Condesa looks forward to marriage to free her from the prohibition: "The praises and even the criticism I had heard about [Rousseau] stirred my desire to read his works and when I thought of the day I got married, one of the greatest pleasures I foresaw in that future was the possibility of reading *La Nouvelle Héloïse* and the *Confessions*" (pp. 111–112).

25 Alberdi's autobiography, subtitled *Mi vida privada*, begins with a promise of intimacy that the narrative itself never really keeps: "My life, told *en famille*, told to my own family, is a private text of little interest to the public. The family into which I was born, even limited to my most direct relatives, is so large that printing this piece is the most economical means of reproducing it. Nevertheless, it will remain private and confidential. I shall use the form best suited to intimate conversation, that of correspondence" (*Autobiografía*, p. 39). Franklin himself had written: "By my rambling digressions I perceive myself to be grown old. I us'd to write more methodically. But one does not dress for private company as for a publick hall" (*The Autobiography of Benjamin Franklin* [New York: Macmillan, 1967], p. 11).

26 See Victoria Ocampo, "Malandanzas de una autodidacta" in *Testimonios*, 5a serie (Buenos Aires: Sur, 1957). Self-deprecation, however, is not an attitude peculiar to the female autobiographer, nor does the opening of autobiography onto the *petite histoire* pertain exclusively to her domain. Well after the Condesa, the Argentine Eduardo Wilde in his *Aguas abajo* (1914) and the Chilean Benjamín Subercaseaux in his *Niño de lluvia* (1938) – writers, it might be argued, who in some way perceive themselves as marginal to the literary scenes of their respective periods – would also indulge in this particularly intimate form of recreating the past through the childhood story.

27 *Histoire de la Soeur Inès*, Paris, 1832. Subsequently, this text would always be published with the childhood memoirs, as a second part of the volume.

28 See Richard A. Butler, *The Difficult Art of Autobiography* (Oxford: Clarendon Press, 1968), p. 19.

29 See Méndez Rodenas, pp. 86–91.

30 The French version was published in 1844. A much abridged Spanish version, titled *Viaje a La Habana* and prefaced by Gertrudis Gómez de Avellaneda, came out in Madrid that same year. For a modern edition, see *Viaje a La Habana*, introduction by Salvador Bueno (Havana: Editorial de Arte y Literatura, 1974).

31 Salvador Bueno documents the Condesa's requests for help from Domingo del Monte and José Antonio Saco (pp. 32–33) and her borrowings from Cirilo Villaverde, Ramón de Palma and others (*Viaje a La Habana*, pp. 46–49). Similar information may be found in Domingo Figarola Caneda's very valuable though untidy *La Condesa de Merlin* (Paris: Editions Excelsior, 1928).

32 Del Monte's review is quoted *in extenso* in Figarola Caneda, p. 134.

33 *Ibid.* p. 136.

34 For a lengthier discussion of *María* along these lines, see my "Paraíso perdido y economía terrenal en *María*," *Sin Nombre*, 14, 3 (1984), pp. 36–55. Also Doris Sommer's shrewd reading, "El mal de *María*: (Con)fusión en un romance nacional," *MLN*, 104, 2 (1989), pp. 439–474.

35 The muted sexuality of the protagonist's contact with his mother does not escape Alfonso Reyes in his "Algunas notas sobre la *María* de Jorge Isaacs," *Obras completas*, VIII (Mexico: Fondo de Cultura Económica, 1958), pp. 271–273.

36 Coe, p. 218.

37 Mikhail Bakhtin, "Forms of Time and of the Chronotope in the Novel," *The Dialogic Imagination* (Austin: University of Texas Press, 1981), pp. 127–128.

5 A school for life: Miguet Cané's "Juvenilia"

1 The bibliography on the Generation of 1880 is too vast to enumerate here. The reader may refer with profit to a collective volume, *La Argentina del Ochenta al Centenario*, eds. Gustavo Ferrari and Ezequiel Gallo (Buenos Aires: Sudamericana, 1980), also to Noé Jitrik, *El 80 y su mundo* (Buenos Aires: Jorge Alvarez, 1968), and David Viñas, *Literatura argentina y realidad política* (Buenos Aires: Jorge Alvarez, 1964).

2 It was also a text that would be much imitated. For a list of similar school-boy sagas, see Antonio Pagés Larraya, "*Juvenilia*. Un título y una actitud en nuestra literatura," *La Nación*, Buenos Aires, 21 January 1960. See also Adolfo Prieto, *La literatura autobiográfica argentina* (1966; rpt. Buenos Aires: Centro Editor de América Latina, 1982), p. 173.

3 Rudyard Kipling, *Stalky and Co.* (London: Macmillan and Co., 1927), p. viii.

4 Cané himself notifies his reader of that difference, which he attributes less to his own benevolence than to differences in national temperament. Describing his first days as a new boy, constantly under the scrutiny of the others, he writes: "I thought I felt a thousand conspiracies brewing around me, those conspiracies that in our midst, because of our gentle national spirit, only turn into more or less heavy practical jokes but that in Oxford and Cambridge lead to unheard-of brutality, offense, servitude and torment" (Miguel Cané, *Juvenilia* [Buenos Aires: Talleres Gráficos Argentinos, 1927], p. 40). Subsequent references appear in the text.

5 Before *Juvenilia*, Cané had collected articles written previously in periodicals under the title *Ensayos* (1877), a step he would later regret, as he confided to a disciple, Martín García Mérou. See the latter's introduction to Miguel Cané, *Prosa ligera* (Buenos Aires: Casa Vaccaro, 1919), pp. 14–15.

6 Maurice Halbwachs argues that the tendency of the old to dwell on childhood recollections is not so much explained by biological factors as it is by the place given them by society – a place of relative inactivity where they are encouraged to remember and indeed where their memory is prized as an asset (*Les Cadres sociaux de la mémoire* [1925; rpt. Paris–The Hague: Mouton, 1975], p. 105). One should add that this inclination to reminisce, too often dismissed as dotage when excessive – "every social function tends towards its own exaggeration," writes Halbwachs – is at the same time exalted for its didactic value, as a lesson in beginnings. Cané benefits, as later will Picón Salas, from the latter attitude: while not old, he courts that form of respect that turns his childhood story into a wise man's lesson.

7 In this thoughtful evaluation of the Argentine generation of 1837, Rodó

devotes several interesting pages to Miguel Cané senior, valuing him more for his literary promise than for his achievements as a critic (José Enrique Rodó, "Juan María Gutiérrez y su época," *La tradición intelectual argentina* [Buenos Aires: Eudeba, 1968], pp. 30–41). For another good piece on Cané's father, see Manuel Mujica Láinez, *Miguel Cané (Padre). Un romántico porteño* (Buenos Aires: Ediciones C.E.P.A., 1942).

8 Martín García Mérou, Cané's secretary when he was ambassador to Venezuela, recalls watching Cané write *Juvenilia* in "little notebooks I made for him myself." "Mi padre" precedes *Juvenilia* in one of these notebooks and was first published in a newspaper many years after Cané's death. Since then publishers often include it as a prologue to *Juvenilia.*

9 "Mi padre" in Miguel Cané, *Ensayos* (Buenos Aires: Editorial Sopena, 1939), p. 163. Subsequent references appear in the text.

10 Prieto, pp. 111–157.

11 Carlos Guido y Spano, best remembered as a poet, was the son of General Tomás Guido, one of the most distinguished figures in the wars of independence. His autobiography, entitled *Carta confidencial a un amigo que comete la indiscreción de publicarla*, was published in 1879. Lucio V. Mansilla, who published the first (and what would be the only) volume of *Mis memorias* in 1904, was the nephew of Juan Manuel de Rosas.

12 Prieto, pp. 175–176.

13 Martín García Mérou in Miguel Cané, *Prosa ligera*, p. 9.

14 The reader-identification courted by *Juvenilia* manifested itself promptly. Eduardo Wilde, another member of the generation of 1880, responds with an enthusiastic letter: "I reach for your *Juvenilia* and read ten pages. That is enough. I am no longer myself, I am the one whose impressions you describe in your book. ... Your book will be read in schools with affection and delight, and outside schools, with the sweet melancholy of memory" (Eduardo Wilde, "Carta sobre *Juvenilia*" in *Páginas escogidas* [Buenos Aires: Editorial Estrada, 1955], pp. 224–232).

15 Cané refers only once to his mother's visits with a mixture of pathos and irony. Returning to the Colegio as an adult he recognizes "the bench where my mother used to sit, clutching my hands, patting me, her eyes full of tears, holding me close till night fell and we had to part. She left me her heart in a kiss and ... ten *pesos* that I would rush to exchange for cigarettes" (p. 152). Women are notoriously absent from *Juvenilia*. As objects of desire – the peasant girls students go dancing with – they are anonymous and socially inferior. Cané's juvenile erotica is to be found elsewhere, for example in his partially autobiographical short story "Si jeunesse savait!"

6 The search for Utopia: Picón Salas looks forward to the past

1 José Santos Chocano, *Memorias: Las mil y una aventuras* (Santiago: Editorial Nascimento, 1940), p. 36.

2 If the autobiographer does dwell on his childhood, it is likely that he will take pains to justify the fact for reasons other than nostalgia. Such is the case of Ramón Subercaseaux who pointedly writes: "If, in the first chapters especially, I deal mostly with events of my childhood and early youth, let it be understood that I do this to make known what the education and the customs corresponding to my social sphere in the second half of the past century were like," *Memorias de cincuenta años* (Santiago: Imprenta y Litografía Barcelona, 1908), p. vi.

3 Richard Coe mentions "the pressures exerted by intellectual fashion on the one hand and by ideology on the other" that lead the adult author to observe "a kind of retrospective conformism that seems too good to be true." Goethe's childhood interest in things medieval, as evoked in *Dichtung und Wahrheit*, might have been influenced retrospectively, argues Coe, by the Romantic discovery of the Medieval and the Gothic (Coe, p. 36). In the same way, and retrospectively perhaps, Oliver and Neruda stress their very early awareness of social injustice and their desire to correct it. The "truth" or "falseness" of these assertions is irrelevant; what matters is that they establish an ideological pattern which is basic to these authors' self-images.

4 Gusdorf, generally so aware of the influence of the present on the retrieval of the past, seems oddly naive on the subject of childhood: "Now an infant is not yet an historical figure; the significance of his small existence remains strictly private. The writer who recalls his earliest years is thus exploring an enchanted realm that belongs to him alone" ("Conditions and Limits of Autobiography" in *Autobiography. Essays Theoretical and Critical*, ed. James Olney (Princeton University Press, 1980, p 37). The infant's being or not being a historical figure is a moot point here. What matters is the stance adopted by the adult when recalling that childhood.

5 Ernest Renan, *Souvenirs d'enfance et de jeunesse*, ed. J. Pommier (Paris: Libr. Armand Colin, 1959), p. 1.

6 Likening him to Alfonso Reyes in a somewhat generous comparison, Guillermo Sucre applies to Picón Salas the phrase Picón himself used to describe the Mexican writer: he was "an elucidator, an interpreter, an organizer" (Mariano Picón Salas, *Viejos y nuevos mundos*, ed. Guillermo Sucre [Caracas: Biblioteca Ayacucho, 1983], p. xli).

7 Mariano Picón Salas, "Pequeña confesión en sordina," *Obras selectas* (Madrid–Caracas: Ediciones Edime, 1962), p. ix.

8 Ester Azzario writes that the memories set down in *Viaje* "are fixed

236 NOTES TO PAGES 110–120

once and for all and [the author] will not refer to them again as he himself declares in the prologue to his *Obras selectas*" (*La prosa autobiográfica de Mariano Picón Salas* [Caracas: Ediciones de la Universidad Simón Bolívar, 1980], p. 38). While this is true in a very narrow sense – Picón will not *retell* his story in detail – there is a constant harking back to those first memories throughout his work.

9 *Obras selectas*, p. ix.
10 Mariano Picón Salas, *Las nieves de antaño (Pequeña añoranza de Mérida)* (Maracaibo: Ediciones de la Universidad del Zulia, 1958), p. 16.
11 *Viaje al amanecer* in *Obras selectas*, p. 6. The same declaration is repeated in *Las nieves de antaño*, p. 17.
12 Emile Benveniste, "Structure des relations de personne dans le verbe," *Problèmes de linguistique générale* (Paris: Gallimard, 1966), p. 235.
13 Mariano Picón Salas, *Mundo imaginario* (Santiago: Editorial Nascimento, 1927), p. 8.
14 *Buscando el camino, Odisea de Tierra Firme, Un viaje y seis retratos, Viaje al amanecer* and *Regreso de tres mundos* are but a few examples of those titles. The first two were written in Chile, where Picón sought exile between 1923 and 1936, during the dictatorship of Juan Vicente Gómez in Venezuela. *Viaje al amanecer* was written in the United States where Picón lived in 1942 and 1943. For more complete information on Picón Salas' *errancias*, see the detailed biographical account given by Azzario.
15 *Mundo imaginario*, p. 7.
16 Mariano Picón Salas, *Odisea de Tierra Firme. Relatos de Venezuela* (Santiago: Editorial Zig-Zag, 2nd. edn. 1940), p. 15.
17 See Gabriela Mora, "Mariano Picón-Salas autobiógrafo: Una contribución al estudio del género autobiográfico en Hispanoamérica" (unpublished PhD dissertation, Smith College, 1971), pp. 119–120. Mora's study, which has the considerable merit of having been the first to attempt an overall view of autobiographical writing in Spanish America, refers to this resemblance very briefly but does not elaborate on it.
18 *Obras selectas*, p. xiv.
19 *Mundo imaginario*, p. 7.
20 *Obras selectas*, pp. 3–4. Subsequent references to *Viaje al amanecer* appear in the text.
21 M. Bakhtin, *The Dialogic Imagination*, p. 235.
22 *Buscando el camino*, p. 41.
23 *Buscando el camino*, p. 44.
24 The connection with Isaacs hinted at in this last paragraph will be confirmed in the opening page of Picón's *Regreso de tres mundos*. The shy *señorito* has now fully bloomed into a provincial dandy. He has also become a less than attractive student of paternalism:

Perhaps I still miss being that adolescent provincially dressed in linen, riding
his white horse along the fields of Andean Venezuela ... I would tie up my
horse ... lie down on the grass full of fantasies, and, smoking a cigarette, would
compose naive lines (in the simple meter of popular poetry) that spoke,
contradictorily, of the joys of life and the anxiety of living ... Physical love could
be found under a bush, be picked like coffee branches off the colorful skirt or the
muddy frock of a peasant girl. A little struggle – no more – with her and you feel,
in anticipation, the gasp of pleasure, and you bend her, like a coffee-tree branch
laden with red and humid berries tasting of saliva, to the leaf-covered ground.
You spend the night in a peasant cottage and pay the peons who have worked
for you all week, you listen to the complaints and grievances they voice in an
archaic language, partake of the hot spicy soup and even try out your gun (it is
best that they respect you) on the turtle-doves that fly across the cloudy sky.
(Mariano Picón Salas, *Regreso de tres mundos. Un hombre en su generación*
[Mexico: Fondo de Cultura Económica, 1959], p. 19)

25 *Ibid.* pp. 12–13.
26 For an excellent analysis of the magisterial tradition stemming from
Rodó, see Roberto González Echevarría's "The Case of the Speaking
Statue: *Ariel* and the Magisterial Rhetoric of the Latin American
Essay" in his *The Voice of the Masters. Writing and Authority in Modern
Spanish American Literature* (Austin: University of Texas Press, 1985),
pp. 8–32.
27 "Caracas" in *Páginas de Venezuela, Obras selectas*, p. 234. Subsequent
references to this essay appear in the text.
28 Picón is not alone in this salvaging of things Spanish to offset the
invasion of North American imperialism. A similar defence of trivial
symbols of *hispanidad* may be found, for example, in José Vasconcelos'
Ulises criollo:

In those days Spanish dance was the filter for a Dionysian reconciliation with
our Hispanic past. In the midst of a wave of invasive Yankee customs and after
nearly a century of resentful distance, we avidly drank the waters of a common
lineage. What diplomacy could not achieve, what philosophers did not even
try, was accomplished in an instant by *Flamenco* dancing ... In one stroke, the
much maligned castanet-clacking Spain united nations of common descent in a
way that had proved impossible to politicians and intellectuals.
Ulises criollo in *Memorias*, I (Mexico: Fondo de Cultura Económica,
1982], p. 305.

29 For useful comments on autobiography and *costumbrismo* see Francisco
Sánchez-Blanco, "La concepción del 'yo' en las autobiografías españolas del siglo XIX: De las 'vidas' a las 'memorias' y 'recuerdos', " *Boletín de
la Asociación de profesores de español*, 15, 29 (1983), pp. 29–36. Sánchez-
Blanco accurately notes that, in *costumbrista*-type autobiographies,
"impressions of the world replace self-absorption and personal
anecdote. The hero of the autobiography gradually abandons an active

perspective, forsakes his own actions in order to narrate the past as a pure observer and witness. The 'I' identifies with his collected impressions" (p. 32). However, adds the author, describing a process that could well be applied to Picón Salas, "when that 'I' tries to introduce himself, he ends up seeing himself not as an individual but as one more 'type' within the social picture"(p. 33).

30 Georges Gusdorf, *Mémoire et personne* (Paris: Presses Universitaires de France, 1951), I, p. 250.

31 Enrique Larreta's autobiography, *Tiempos iluminados* (Buenos Aires–Mexico: Espasa Calpe Argentina, 1939), furnishes another, class-tinged example of this ideological restoration. The author of *La gloria de don Ramiro* evokes the Spanish housemaids of his childhood, lauds not only those "forgotten shadows but also ... all of popular Spain, the Spain that is eternal" (p. 18). Never once does Larreta reflect on the situation of "popular Spain" at the moment he writes – 1939.

32 For illuminating comments on old cities as repositories of communal memory and as agents of ideological bonding, see Maurice Halbwachs, *La Mémoire collective* (Paris: Presses Universitaires de France, rpt. 1968), pp. 125–137. Halbwachs speaks of European cities, in which a core of *fixité* always remains, whatever the changes. The malleable character of the newer Latin American city makes this concept more relative. It is perhaps to compensate for this that the urge to fabricate a core appears in writers such as Picón Salas.

33 *Regreso de tres mundos*, p. 22.

7 A game of cutouts: Norah Lange's "Cuadernos de infancia"

1 Of these forgotten figures – Blacks and Chinese immigrants who fought for Cuba's independence – Méndez Capote writes: "I believe that the history of Cuba remains to be written: the sediment on which the Republic was founded has yet to be gone over ... An impartial historian is needed, one with patience and without prejudice, who, besides being very well informed, will not be afraid of offending so that justice may be done" (*Memorias de una cubanita que nació con el siglo* [Barcelona: Argos Vergara, 1984], p. 10).

2 Beatriz de Nóbile, *Palabras con Norah Lange* (Buenos Aires: Carlos Pérez Editor, 1968), p. 18.

3 Lange's speeches were later collected in a volume, *Estimados congéneres* (Buenos Aires: Losada, 1968).

4 Norah Lange, *Cuadernos de infancia*, 3rd edn (Buenos Aires: Losada, 1942), p. 141. Subsequent references appear in the text.

5 Lange is well aware that *Cuadernos de infancia* strays from the more conventional approaches to childhood. To a question about her treatment of those early years she answers: "There are writers who

write of their childhood looking for magical aspects, revealing certain fantasies that would only pertain to children. I went about it in a different way" (Nóbile, p. 9).

6 Thus, for example, *Ir*ma becomes *Ir*ene, Chich*ina* becomes Georg*ina*, a biblical *Ruth* becomes a no less biblical *Susana*, and so on.

7 Lange herself, in her interview with Beatriz de Nóbile, admiringly mentions conversations with Felisberto Hernández in Paris in 1948, at a time when the Uruguayan writer was barely known in his own country, let alone Argentina (Nóbile, p. 22).

8 See Estelle C. Jelinek, Introduction, *Women's Autobiographies. Essays in Criticism* (Bloomington: Indiana University Press, 1980), p. 17.

9 The bilingual mixture of words appears in the original.

10 Jorge Luis Borges, "Estudio epílogo" in Eduardo Wilde, *Páginas muertas* (Buenos Aires: Editorial Minerva, n.d.) p. 242.

11 After *Cuadernos*, Lange would go on to write *Antes que mueran* (Buenos Aires: Losada, 1944), a more abstract exercise in recollection and fragmented imagery not devoid, however, of autobiographical markers. Then she will clearly enter the domain of fiction with *Personas en la sala* (Buenos Aires: Losada, 1950) and *Los dos retratos* (Buenos Aires: Losada, 1956). When asked to describe *Personas en la sala*, Lange replies: "It is sheer spying. I have already said that people and objects are the only things that interest me in life. Related to that preference is my favorite activity, spying. It gives me enormous pleasure. I would be in heaven if I could spy on people when they think no one is looking. It interests me psychologically because people let go when they are alone" (Nóbile, p. 23).

12 For an overview of this negative criticism, some of it quite vitriolic, see Adriana Rosman Askot, "Aspectos de la literatura femenina argentina: la ficción de Norah Lange" (unpublished PhD dissertation, Princeton, 1987).

13 "To justify an unorthodox life by writing about it is to *reinscribe* the original violation, to reviolate masculine turf" (Nancy K. Miller, cited in Carolyn G. Heilbrun, *Writing a Woman's Life* [New York and London: W. W. Norton, 1988], p. 11).

8 Autobiography as history: a statue for posterity

1 William Matthews' remarks on British autobiographers are quite applicable here:

[F]ew autobiographers put into their books very much of that private, intimate knowledge of themselves that only they can have. Oftener than not, they shun their own inner peculiarities and fit themselves into patterns of behavior or character suggested by ideas and ideals of their periods and by the fashions in autobiography with which they associate themselves. The laws of literature and the human reluctance to stand individually naked combine to cheat the expectations of the readers who hope to find in autobiographies many revelations of men's true selves.

(*British Autobiographies: An Annotated Bibliography* [Berkeley: University of California Press, 1955], p. viii)

2 José María Guridi y Alcocer, *Apuntes de la vida de D. José Miguel Guridi y Alcocer* (Mexico: Moderna Librería Religiosa de José L. Vallejo, 1906), p. 9.

3 *Ibid.* p. 7.

4 Domingo Faustino Sarmiento, *Obras completas*, III, pp. 224–225. Subsequent references to *Recuerdos de provincia* appear in the text. References to *Mi defensa*, also included in this volume of *Obras completas*, appear in the text preceded by a *D*.

5 Cited in A. O. J. Cockshut, *Truth to Life. The Art of Biography in the Nineteenth Century* (New York and London: Harcourt Brace Jovanovich, 1974), p. 9.

6 The full quotation, taken from Villemain's *Cours de littérature* and used as an epigraph to the first edition of *Facundo*, reads as follows: "I ask from the historian love of humanity and of freedom: his impartial justice must not be impassive. On the contrary, he must feel inspired, hopeful, pained or elated by what he writes", *Obras completas*, VII, p. 7. Subsequent references to *Facundo* appear in the text.

7 A celebrated letter to his friend and reader Valentín Alsina, published in the second edition of *Facundo* in 1851, shows Sarmiento cautious on the subject of revisions and well aware of the effect to be gained by leaving the book in its original, "ungainly" form: "I have used your precious notes with moderation, saving the most substantial ones for more auspicious times and better planned projects, fearful that in touching up such a shapeless work it would lose its primitive appearance and the robust and eager boldness of its undisciplined conception" (Domingo Faustino Sarmiento, *Facundo* [Buenos Aires: Ediciones Culturales Argentinas, 1961], p. 21).

8 Cited by Lionel Gossman in his illuminating "History as Decipherment: Romantic Historiography and the Discovery of the Other," *New Literary History*, 18, 1 (1986), p. 26.

9 Alberdi harshly criticizes both Sarmiento and Bartolomé Mitre for their highly personal, poorly documented attempts at historiography: "There are two ways of writing history: either following tradition and popular legend, which usually results in a history which is the product of vanity, a sort of *political mythology* with a historical base; or following documents, which is writing real history, something few dare do for fear of hurting the country's vanity with the truth" (Juan Bautista Alberdi, *Grandes y pequeños hombres del Plata* [Buenos Aires: Fernández Blanco, 1962], pp. 15–16).

10 Charges of self-centeredness were, however, levied against Sarmiento. "Neither you nor I, as persons, are subjects substantial enough to attract public attention," admonished Alberdi (in Ricardo Sáenz Hayes, *La polémica de Alberdi con Sarmiento y otras páginas* [Buenos Aires: Gleizer, 1926], p. 39). Alberdi's reaction to *Recuerdos de provincia*, as the third of his *Cartas quillotanas* shows, was particularly strong. In 1849, a defensive Sarmiento writes to Vicente Fidel López who presumably was trying to dissuade him from writing *Recuerdos*: "Have you noticed something remarkable – that in Chile I have conquered the right to speak of myself, of my own matters, with the same openness that Rosas does, in *La Gaceta*? They know that that is my defect, and they tolerate it" (Alberto Palcos, *Sarmiento. La vida. La obra. Las ideas. El genio* [Buenos Aires: Emecé, 1962], p. 103). Others besides López, most notably Mitre and Félix Frías, tried to discourage Sarmiento (Palcos, p. 102). Mitre "kept telling him that the book was a mistake" (Augusto Belín Sarmiento, *Sarmiento anecdótico (Ensayo biográfico)* [Saint Cloud: Imp. P. Belin, 1929], p. 45).

11 On Sarmiento's biographical approach to history, Ezequiel Martínez Estrada writes: "[A]ll his biographies, be their subject Argentine or American, condense ... fundamental forms of his conception of history or, in the eloquent motto he himself coined, of that dialectical antithesis, Civilization and Barbarism. Thus considered, biography ... takes on the value of a symbol, or to put it more precisely, of a metaphor, as a way of making the abstract ... more comprehensible" (*Sarmiento* [Buenos Aires: 1946; rpt. Sudamericana, 1966], pp. 117–118).

12 Samper writes in his prologue: "The number of eminent men that my country can count on, in every party, is quite considerable. If I ventured to write biographies of all of them, beginning with the immortal Nariño, I would have to write a library, undertaking a task far superior to my capabilities and resources. It was not my intention to write *biographies* but simple biographical *sketches*. If, given the quality of the artist's work, the Gallery they form is modest, it is great and luminous on account of the moral stature and the brilliance of the originals" (*Galería nacional de hombres ilustres o notables, o sea colección de bocetos biográficos* [Bogotá: Imprenta de Zalamea, 1879], p. vi). Like Sarmiento, the biographer Samper also wrote his autobiography, *Historia de una alma [sic]. Memorias íntimas y de historia contemporánea* (Bogotá: Imprenta de Zalamea Hermanos, 1881).

13 On this subject, I am indebted to Nicolas Shumway's "Bartolomé Mitre and the Gallery of Argentine Celebrities" in his *The Invention of Argentina* (Berkeley: University of California Press, forthcoming). Shumway perceptively analyzes this historiographical venture, authored by many (amongst them Juan María Gutiérrez, Tomás

Guido, Sarmiento himself) but unquestionably masterminded by Bartolomé Mitre, as an exercise in "officialist" historiography. In addition to paving a way to the future, the *Galería* strived to "legitimize both his [Mitre's] aspirations as a national leader and Buenos Aires' grip on the country."

14 Eduardo Wilde, "Recuerdos, recuerdos" in *Obras completas*, v (Buenos Aires: Lajouane, 1938), p. 134.

15 For the role of the Romantic historian as interpreter of a mute past, see Gossman, pp. 23–57. For Sarmiento's views on French historiography, see his "Los estudios históricos en Francia," *Obras*, II (Buenos Aires: Imprenta y Litografía Mariano Moreno, 1896), p. 199.

16 A. O. J. Cockshut comments on the little space afforded childhood in nineteenth-century English *biographies*, remarkable at a time when, as he puts it, "Wordsworth was the idol of the intellectuals and Dickens of the crowd." He concludes that "the absence of childhood from the biographies is a fortuitous consequence of the fashionable method of composition," meaning by that an excessive reliance on documents. Documents, needless to say, do not usually record childhood events (*Truth to Life*, pp. 17–18).

17 Pierre Janet, *L'Evolution de la mémoire et de la notion du temps* (Paris: Editions Chahine, 1928), p. 461.

18 E. Pichon, "Essai d'étude convergente des problèmes du temps," cited in Georges Gusdorf, *Mémoire et personne* (Paris: Presses Universitaires de France, 1951), I, p. 51.

19 The following is an apt example of how lyrical evocation consciously corrects "objective" description in *Recuerdos de provincia*: "My mother's house, the fruit of her industry, whose adobes and fences could be computed in yards of cloth, woven by her hands to pay for the construction, has suffered some additions in these past years that make it merge with the other, average houses. However, its original form is the one that clings to the poetry of the heart, the indelible image that stubbornly comes to my mind ... " (p. 147).

20 "When the autobiographer has gained that firm vantage point from which the full retrospective view on life can be had, he imposes on the past the order of the present. The fact once in the making can now be seen together with the fact in its result. By this superimposition of the completed fact, the fact in the making acquires a meaning it did not possess before. The meaning of the past is intelligible and meaningful in terms of the present understanding; it is thus with all historical understanding" (Karl J. Weintraub, "Autobiography and Historical Consciousness," *Critical Inquiry*, I, 4 [1975], p. 826). Georges Gusdorf, in his "Conditions and Limits of Autobiography" (1956; rpt. in *Auto-biography. Essays Theoretical and Critical*, ed. James Olney [Princeton

University Press, 1980], pp. 28–48), had already explored this retrospective assignation of meaning, on the part of the autobiographer, to past events.

21 For useful comments on group pressure on an individual's retrieval of the past, see Charles Blondel, *Introduction à la psychologie collective* (Paris: Armand Colin, 1928), from where I extract the following quote: "It is evident that our recollections vary, become more precise, change or disappear according to the groups to which we successively belong. While we live within one group, our passions, our interests demand that we keep in mind facts belonging to the life of that group, to that of its members, to ours ... As soon as we leave that group, we begin to discard the assorted memories that had gathered in our minds for the use of that group, and the rapidity with which we do this is inversely proportionate to the time we have spent as members of the group" (p. 135).

22 André Gide, *Journal 1889–1939* (Paris: Gallimard, "Pléiade", 1955), p. 29. Gide adds: "One might say the following, which I see as a sort of inverted sincerity (in the artist): He must tell his life not in the way he has lived it but must live it in the way he will tell it. In other words: so that the portrait of himself that is his life is identical to the ideal portrait he desires. More simply: that he be the way he wants himself to be."

23 Sarmiento cleverly summons two sets of readers amongst those compatriots, readers to a point exclusive of each other; or, perhaps more accurately, he envisages two successive, quite different readings of his text. One set of readers is composed of those *compatriots* to whom he dedicates the book; as his contemporaries, they will understand his precise references and sympathize with him. The others are the compatriots who will read in the future; they will not really understand the references but will be touched by the exemplum, the "statue for posterity." These readers, I have argued, are foreseen by the two, divergent epigraphs to *Recuerdos* (Sylvia Molloy, "Inscripciones del yo en *Recuerdos de provincia*", *Sur*, 350–351 [1982], pp. 131–140). For a discussion of the different kinds of readers a text can summon, see, on Montaigne's *Essais*, Claude Blum, "La peinture du moi et l'écriture inachevée," *Poétique*, 53 (1983), pp. 60–71.

24 Always eager to see through Sarmiento's alleged goals, Alberdi sees *Recuerdos* not as the fulfillment of public duty but as a self-serving venture:

The telling of your story has not taught you anything that you did not know. Your work has been of no service to the Argentine Republic and I doubt that it has been of any service to you. In our country, so rich already in noteworthy men, this is the first example of a citizen who publishes two hundred pages and a genealogical tree to relate his life, that of all the members of his extended

NOTES TO PAGES 152–155

family and even that of his servants. San Martín did not allow his portrait to be painted. Rivadavia, Monteagudo, Passo, Alvear and a hundred Argentine heroes are without biographies and the Republic itself, all glory and heroism, is without history ... But your own biography is not just an exercise in vacuity, it is, in politics, a well-known, frequently used means of establishing one's name as a candidate to a high position – a legitimate desire that turns you, however, into a tireless agitator.

>   (*Cartas quillotanas*. Preceded by an explanatory letter by D. F. Sarmiento [Buenos Aires: Ed. La Cultura Argentina, 1916], pp. 133–134)

For an excellent analysis of the change in attitude from *Mi defensa* to *Recuerdos de provincia*, see Tulio Halperín Donghi, "Sarmiento: su lugar en la sociedad argentina posrevolucionaria," *Sur*, 341 (1977), pp. 121–135. For additional, very insightful comments on *Recuerdos* as presentation of a political candidate, see Carlos Altamirano and Beatriz Sarlo, "Una vida ejemplar: la estrategia de *Recuerdos de provincia*" in their *Literatura/Sociedad* (Buenos Aires: Hachette, 1983), pp. 163–208.

25 In a letter to the historian Vicente Fidel López, he smugly declares: "I am preparing a fat book entitled *Recuerdos de provincia*, or something like that, in which, with the same candor as Lamartine, I compose my own panegyric. I assure you, my friend, that ridicule will shatter itself against so many good things, so worthy of being told, and that, willingly or by force, they will have to forgive this audacity" (Palcos, p. 103).

26 Martínez Estrada, p. 18.

27 *Rasgos de la vida de Domingo F. Sarmiento por su hermana Bienvenida*, introduction by Antonio P. Castro (Buenos Aires: Museo Histórico Sarmiento, 1946), p. 30.

28 In his *English Autobiography. Its Emergence, Materials, and Form* (Berkeley and Los Angeles: University of California Press, 1954), Wayne Shumaker mentions the not uncommon exclusion of siblings, children, spouses and (less often) parents in English autobiography (pp. 42–43), in particular, in the *Autobiography* of John Stuart Mill (pp. 145–146). Shumaker's comments, too broad in scope, do not elaborate on these exclusions.

29 Palcos generally speaks of Sarmiento as an only male child (p. 20) but does briefly mention the brother: "Another child, Honorio, died when he was eleven, leaving a strong impression on the mind of Domingo Faustino who asserted, no less, that this brother was more intelligent than he was" (p. 17). Gálvez refers to him incorrectly as Horacio. (*Vida de Sarmiento. El hombre de autoridad* [Buenos Aires: Emecé, 1945], p. 18).

I add a personal anecdote to illustrate my point. In 1982, when doing research in the Museo Nacional Sarmiento in Buenos Aires, I asked the secretary for information on the elusive Honorio and was told emphatically that all of Sarmiento's male siblings had died at birth or very soon thereafter. Firm in my purpose, I asked to see the famous *libreta* where Sarmiento's mother kept her record of family births and deaths. In the shabby little notebook, written in crude script, I was gratified to find (and the secretary disquieted to see) the dates that confirmed Honorio's short life.

30 Paul de Man, "Autobiography as De-facement," *Modern Language Notes*, 94 (1979), pp. 919–930.

31 In a letter sent from Chile in 1848 to José Ignacio Flores, a dear friend from childhood, Sarmiento alludes to his brother. While not naming him, he makes clear, by comparison, the importance Honorio had in his life: "For me you are a friend different from the rest, you are the inseparable childhood companion, the neighbor, the brother I once had. Now that so many impressions crowd my memory, I often return to childhood recollections, always so sweet, always so simple, and you are always a natural part of them" (Julia Ottolenghi, *Sarmiento a través de un epistolario* [Buenos Aires: Jesús Méndez, 1939], p. 41).

32 Georges Gusdorf, "Conditions and Limits of Autobiography," p. 36.

33 For a thoughtful analysis of Sarmiento's interpretation of Madame de Lamartine, see Tulio Halperín Donghi, "Lamartine en Sarmiento: *Les Confidences* y *Recuerdos de provincia*," *Filología* (Buenos Aires), 20, 2 (1985), pp. 177–190.

34 Benjamin Franklin, *The Autobiography of Benjamin Franklin* (New York: Macmillan, Literary Heritage, 1967), p. 73.

35 Sarmiento had known Benita Martínez Pastoriza, a native of San Juan married to a much older Chilean business man, for years. They married in 1848, a few months after the death of Benita's husband, and "Doña Benita's only son, Domingo Fidel, who had been born in the Chilean capital on 25 April 1845, took on the name of Sarmiento, who was his real father" (Palcos, p. 92).

36 Domingo Faustino Sarmiento, *Memorias* in *Obras completas*, XLIX (Buenos Aires: Imprenta y Litografía Mariano Moreno, 1900), p. 293. A book on Sarmiento's women did in fact appear much later: César Guerrero, *Mujeres de Sarmiento* (Buenos Aires: 1960).

37 Another autobiography that should be read in the same spirit, as a winning gesture within the rhetoric of the *discours amoureux*, is Gertrudis Gómez de Avellaneda's autobiography, written in the form of a letter to the man she loves. See *Autobiografía y cartas*, 2nd edn (Madrid: Imprenta Helénica, 1914).

9 Shrines and labyrinths: a place to remember

1 José Lezama Lima, *Paradiso*. Trans. Gregory Rabassa (New York: Farrar Straus and Giroux, 1974), p. 160.

2 Jorge Luis Borges, *Evaristo Carriego* (Buenos Aires: Emecé, 1955), p. 33.

In a similar spirit, Gusdorf quotes a phrase from Geneviève Fauconnier: "The memories of others are a book without image" (*Mémoire et personne*, 1, 104).

3 Borges, *Evaristo Carriego*, p. 20.

4 Ocampo, *Autobiografía*, 1, pp. 10–11. Subsequent references appear in the text.

5 For a useful reflection on the relation between family and history in the perception of time, see Tamara K. Hareven, "Family Time and Historical Time," *Daedalus*, 106 (1977), pp. 57–70.

6 Victoria Ocampo, *Testimonios*, 5a serie (Buenos Aires: Sur, 1957), p. 28.

7 Genealogy (on which this conception of history is based) serves as a powerful agent of discrimination especially in times when these self-proclaimed "first families" feel threatened. Tamara Hareven points to the popularity and increasing elitism in the United States at the turn of the century of movements like the Daughters of the American Revolution in reaction to massive foreign immigration. Hareven discusses the more recent preoccupation with genealogy found in minority groups: "The emphasis on individual identification with genealogy has ... shifted from the search for legitimization of exclusive status to a concern with emergent identity" (Tamara K. Hareven, "The Search for Generational Memory: Tribal Rites in Industrial Society," *Daedalus*, 107, 4 [1978], pp. 137–149). This attitude, reflected in the preoccupation with roots, repressed traditions and communal identity so often encountered in oral chronicles, is particularly interesting to analyze in the context of Spanish American oral autobiographies or *testimonios*.

8 María Rosa Oliver, *Mundo, mi casa* (Buenos Aires: Sudamericana, 2nd edn 1970), p. 57. Oliver's autobiography finally rejects the conflation between national history and family chronicle. If the metaphor of the family home is maintained in the title, it is applied to the world, not to the family, the country, or an élite.

9 Walter Benjamin, "Theses on the Philosophy of History" in *Illuminations* (New York: Schocken Books, 1978), p. 255.

10 Enrique Larreta, *Tiempos iluminados* (Buenos Aires–Mexico: Espasa Calpe, Argentina, 1939), pp. 14–16.

11 Gregorio Aráoz de Lamadrid, *Memorias* (Buenos Aires: Establecimiento de Impresiones de Guillermo Kraft, 1895); José María Paz, *Memorias póstumas del Brigadier General D. José María Paz, con variedad de otros documentos inéditos de alta importancia* (Buenos Aires: Imprenta de la revista, 1855).

12 Fear of change was a common enough feeling in the Argentine bourgeoisie, ever since the generation of 1880 voiced its discomfort around the turn of the century. So was xenophobia, manifest in

autobiography and blatantly present in the fiction of Miguel Cané, Eugenio Cambaceres, Julián Martel. For more explicit examples of xenophobia in Larreta, see his *Las dos fundaciones de Buenos Aires* (Buenos Aires: Espasa Calpe, 1944). For more documentation on the issue, see Gladys Onega's very thorough *La inmigración en la literatura argentina (1880–1910)* (Rosario: Facultad de Filosofía y Letras, Cuadernos del Instituto de Letras, 1965).

13 For useful remarks on mnemonic strategies and commemoration, see Eugene Vance, "Roland and the Poetics of Memory" in *Textual Strategies. Perspectives in Post-Structuralist Criticism*, Josué V. Harari (Ithaca–New York: Cornell University Press, 1979), pp. 374–403.

14 Walter Benjamin, "Zentralpark. Fragments sur Baudelaire," *Charles Baudelaire. Un poète lyrique à l'apogée du capitalisme* (Paris: Petite Bibliothèque Payot, 1982), pp. 239–240.

15 *Ibid.* p. 239. Note also: "Where there is experience in the strict sense of the word, certain contents of the individual past combine with material of the collective past. The rituals with their ceremonies, their festivals ... [keep] producing the amalgamation of these two elements of memory again and again" (Benjamin, "On Some Motifs in Baudelaire" in *Illuminations*, p. 159).

16 In his insightful *La Mémoire collective* (1950; rpt. Paris: P.U.F. 1968), Maurice Halbwachs also calls attention to two types of memory:

> One could say there is individual memory and, in a manner of speaking, collective memory. In other words, an individual would resort to two types of memory. However, according to whether he resorts to one or the other, he will adopt two very different, even contrasting, attitudes. On the one hand, his recollections will position themselves within the frame of his personality or his personal life; from recollections held in common with others he will only retain the aspects allowing him to distinguish himself from those others. On the other hand, he will be capable at times of acting merely as a member of a group, evoking and keeping alive impersonal recollections, in the measure that they are of interest to a group. (p. 35)

17 The same recollection, appearing in different texts by the same author (say, in an autobiography, in a piece of fiction and in an essay), will function according to the rules of each of those texts and may serve very different purposes. For a fine discussion of this point, see Elizabeth Bruss' introduction to her *Autobiographical Acts: The Changing Situation of a Literary Genre* (Baltimore and London: Johns Hopkins University Press, 1976), pp. 1–18. Examples of this may be found elsewhere in Ocampo; compare, for instance, her memories of the black servants in the autobiography (I, 93–95) with the more aestheticized description of those same servants in "Cartones de Figari," *Testimonios*, 6a serie (Buenos Aires: Sur, 1963), pp. 11–17.

18 For another reading of the variations on this first recollection in
Ocampo, see Luis Gusmán, "Tres escenas de Victoria Ocampo," *Sitio*,
2 (Buenos Aires, 1983), pp. 64–66. For a good analysis of memory in
Ocampo, see Agnes Lugo-Ortiz, "Memoria infantil y perspectiva
histórica en *El archipiélago* de Victoria Ocampo," *Revista Iberoamericana*,
140 (1987), pp. 651–661.

19 Patricia Drechsel Tobin, *Time and the Novel. The Genealogical Imperative*
(Princeton University Press, 1978).

20 An eloquent example of such an integration is the one proposed by
Ricardo Güiraldes' *Don Segundo Sombra*, a text only tangentially autobiographical but clearly counting on a communal recognition of the
past. As Noé Jitrik pertinently observes, Güiraldes' evocation of the
gaucho was chosen by many as a filter to a past they had never known
but into which they were anxious to fit. Significantly, the first translation of *Don Segundo Sombra* was into Yiddish. See Noé Jitrik, *"Don
Segundo Sombra"* in *Escritores argentinos. Dependencia y libertad* (Buenos
Aires: Ediciones El Candil, 1967). On a more general level, the creation
of such communities has been studied by Benedict Anderson in
Imagined Communities. Reflections on the Origin and Spread of Nationalism
(London: Verso/New Left Books, 1983).

21 Enrique Gómez Carrillo, *Treinta años de mi vida*, 1 (Buenos Aires: Casa
Vaccaro, 1918), p. 19.

22 Rubén Darío, *Autobiografía* in *Obras completas*, 1 (Madrid: Afrodisio
Aguado, 1950), p. 102. Enough has been written about the Spanish
American writer's passion for Paris for me not to go into it here. See
Baldomero Sanín Cano's autobiography, *De mis vidas y otras vidas*
(Bogotá: Editorial ABC, 1949), pp. 27–30, for a telling contrast
between this popular cosmopolitan travel to Paris and the hardships of
travelling, at the turn of the century, inside a geographically inhospita-
ble Colombia.

23 *Treinta años de mi vida*, 3 vols. (Madrid: Mundo Latino, 1919). For a
good commentary of Gómez Carrillo's views on travel and travellers, as
exposed in "La psicología del viajero," see Aníbal González, *La crónica
modernista hispanoamericana* (Madrid: José Porrúa Turanzas, 1983). For
other discussions of the "life as journey" theme, see William C.
Spengemann, "Eternal Maps and Temporal Voyages," *Exploration*, 2
(1974), pp. 1–7, and Jean-Claude Berchet, "Un voyage vers soi,"
Poétique, 53 (1983), pp. 91–108.

24 For an excellent analysis of the ties between journalism and literature
and the role of the foreign correspondent at the turn of the century,
see Julio Ramos, "Contradicciones de la modernización literaria en
América Latina: José Martí y la crónica modernista" (unpublished
PhD dissertation, Princeton, 1986, in particular chapter 3).

25 "*Habla el algarrobo* is a key text ... in which patrimony tells the story of its proprietor. Property is its protagonist; family history is narrated by the family summer property. The image of the individual ephemeral mortals who own it expands as time passes, aspires to eternity in the archetype of The Proprietor, fortified and protected by inheritance laws" (Blas Matamoro, *Oligarquía y literatura* [Buenos Aires: Ediciones del Sol, 1975], p. 229).

26 Enrique López Albújar, *De mi casona. Un poco de historia piurana a través de la biografía del autor* (Lima: Imprenta Lux, 1924), p. 10. Subsequent references appear in the text.

27 Two years before its publication, López Albújar himself gave the book an ideological slant by declaring it part of the project he had begun with *Cuentos andinos* of "writing literature that is clearly Peruvian" (Enrique López Albújar, *Memorias*. Preface by Ciro Alegría [Lima: Talleres Gráficos Villanueva, 1963], p. 15). The *Cuentos* were indeed acclaimed for the way in which they strived to reflect a Peruvian, more specifically Indian, mentality (see José Carlos Mariátegui, *Siete ensayos de interpretación de la realidad peruana* [Santiago de Chile: Editorial Universitaria, 1955], pp. 253–255).

28 Benjamin, "Theses on the Philosophy of History," p. 255.

29 For an insightful analysis of the effects this exclusion had on Mansilla, see Adolfo Prieto, *La literatura autobiográfica argentina*, p. 147.

30 *Ibid.* p. 127.

31 "La desabrochada e intolerable parlería de un Mansilla," Paul Groussac, *Los que pasaban* (Buenos Aires: Jesús Menéndez, 1919), p. 80.

32 Lucio V. Mansilla, *Entre-Nos. Causeries del jueves*. Introduction by Juan Carlos Ghiano (Buenos Aires: Hachette, 1963), p. 628. This edition gathers all of the *causeries* from the four-volume 1889–1890 edition. Subsequent references appear in the text preceded by *EN*.

33 See, for example, *Entre-Nos*, pp. 166, 331, and 628.

34 Lucio V. Mansilla, *Mis memorias* (Buenos Aires: Hachette, 1955), p. 61. Subsequent references appear in the text.

35 Lucio V. Mansilla, *Charlas inéditas* (Buenos Aires: Eudeba, 1966), p. 49.

36 For the problematics of memory (memory as obstacle to presence) as experienced in the second half of the nineteenth century, see Eugenio Donato, "The Ruins of Memory: Archaeological Fragments and Textual Artifacts," *Modern Language Notes*, 93, 4 (1978), pp. 575–596.

37 Mansilla cannot completely let go of the issue of lineage and legitimacy. Between those he calls "los Mansilla finos – sin mezcla conocida" (the elegant Mansillas, of unmixed blood, as far as anyone knew), and his own "impure" family, contact is scarce and superficially civil, a fact he resents (pp. 101–104). In addition, despite his mockery of genealogical

pretentiousness, Mansilla claims to have found proof in the Bibliothèque Nationale to sustain his grandmother's claim that the Mansillas
are remotely related "to the Dukes of Normandy and the House of
Austria" (p. 102).

38 Prieto, pp. 137–138.

39 *Ibid.*, pp. 141–142.

40 This recourse to scientific vocabulary to neutralize the aggression is
perceptively analyzed by Marina Kaplan in "Gauchos e indios: la
frontera y la producción del sujeto en obras argentinas del siglo
diecinueve" (unpublished PhD dissertation, Tulane University, 1987),
pp. 180–196. Kaplan also construes this scene as a decisive break in
Mansilla's life and persuasively argues that it is the matrix for the many
episodes of *Una excursión a los indios ranqueles* where Mansilla, through
intermediary gaucho narrators, tells stories of displacement and
punishment.

41 For a shrewd analysis of the relation between travel and self-
representation in Mansilla, see Julio Ramos, "Entre otros: *Una excursión
a los indios ranqueles* de Lucio V. Mansilla," *Filología*, 21, 1 (Buenos
Aires, 1986), pp. 143–171.

42 For a thoughtful discussion of spatial practices within the city in
relation to rhetoric and memory, see Michel de Certeau, "Walking in
the City" in *The Practice of Everyday Life* (Berkeley and Los Angeles:
University of California Press, 1984), pp. 91–114.

43 Foreign travelers were often disagreeably surprised by the lack of
privacy of Buenos Aires homes, with their railroad lay-out of interconnecting rooms and patios, reminiscent of Roman and Arab dwellings.
Benjamín Subercaseaux, in his childhood memoir, describes similar
old houses in Santiago de Chile (*Niño de lluvia* [Santiago: Ercilla, 1962],
p. 29). So does Enrique Larreta in his partly autobiographical *Las dos
fundaciones de Buenos Aires* (Buenos Aires: Espasa Calpe, 1944, p. 160).
Art historian Damián Bayón makes good use of Mansilla's descriptions
in his "La casa colonial porteña vista por viajeros y memorialistas"
(*Actes du XLIIe Congrès International des Américanistes*, proceedings of
Conference, Paris, 2–9 September 1976, [Paris: Fondation Singer-
Polignac, 1976], pp. 159–170) and comments on one such reaction:
"What the otherwise intelligent English observer deemed an unforgiva-
ble error in the lay-out of houses proved nonetheless the most 'func-
tional' solution within a family system based on paternalism and
hierarchy. The fact that one had to go through bedrooms, one's own
and those of other family-members, allowed for a sort of permanent
surveillance (especially at night) of the comings and goings of the
inhabitants of the house" (p. 169).

44 It is a mistake to consider *Mis memorias*, as does Juan Carlos Ghiano in

his preliminary study to the Hachette edition, in the same category as
Cané's *Juvenilia* and Wilde's *Aguas abajo*, as a childhood story of the
1880s. The child's story is *one* of Mansilla's goals but he does not focus
on it exclusively.

The reason why Mansilla did not continue his text is not known. One
can only conjecture as to the spaces he would have chosen for his "I"
later on. But by the time he tackled volume one of *Mis memorias*,
Mansilla had, in a way, already written its continuation: *Una excursión a
los indios ranqueles* is the autobiographical account of the adult projected
into another *different* space, that of the Indian other. It is another
version of the exploration, another charting venture of the "I."

45 For an informative and entertaining account of the architectural
renewal of Buenos Aires and the modernization of its street system (the
Avenida de Mayo, in the style of Haussman's boulevards, was opened
in 1895), see Francis Korn, *Buenos Aires 1895. Una ciudad moderna*
(Buenos Aires: Editorial del Instituto, 1981).

46 Prieto, p. 156.

47 An heir to the generation of 1880, Enrique Larreta would elaborate
further on the threat posed by immigration to a harmonious urban
development: "Today it would be absurd to deplore that Buenos Aires
has not kept the appearance it had in the past. Nevertheless, one could
well imagine a city that would have been a grandiose development of
the village of yesteryear. Then the invasion of 'all the men in the world'
took place. It was impossible for the immigrant, when he got rich, to
renounce the architecture of his own country. Bad taste in itself, if
uniformly sustained and firm in its style, might have been of some
aesthetic interest. But heterogeneity is ugliness at its worst" (Larreta,
Las dos fundaciones, p. 161).

48 For an earlier approach to the subject, see Sylvia Molloy, "Imagen de
Mansilla" in *La Argentina del Ochenta al Centenario*, ed. G. Ferrari and
E. Gallo (Buenos Aires: Sudamericana, 1980), pp. 745–759.

49 Mansilla remembers an outing with his little sister in the course of
which he saw dead bodies surrounded by a flock of crows. The
coachman, when asked by the children if the men were asleep, casually
answered, "They've been beheaded [*degollados*]," referring to the secret
police's favored mode of doing away with political enemies, and adds,
"Just some savages ..." – *salvajes* being the usual name for Rosas'
adversaries (pp. 226–227).

50 See chapter 2, page 123.

51 For an excellent study of conversation as "genre," and the tactical
approaches to which it gives rise, see Alan Pauls, "Sobre las causeries
de Mansilla: una causa perdida," *Lecturas críticas* (Buenos Aires), 2
(1984), pp. 4–15.

10 First memories, first myths: Vasconcelos' "Ulises criollo"

1 Prieto, p. 53.

2 Vito Alessio Robles, *Mis andanzas con nuestro Ulises* (Mexico: Botas, 1938), p. 34.

3 José Joaquín Blanco, *Se llamaba Vasconcelos. Una evocación crítica* (Mexico: Fondo de Cultura Económica, 1977), p. 22.

4 Lord Lyon, "Ulises criollo, académico: por mi raza hablará Cantinflas," *Todo*, 7, 386 (1941). "Through My Race, Cantinflas Will Speak": a take-off on the motto of the University, the phrase is also a broad allusion to *La raza cósmica*, the book that had brought Vasconcelos considerable notoriety.

5 Blanco, p. 9.

6 *El proconsulado* in *Memorias*, II (Mexico: Fondo de Cultura Económica, 1982), p. 1141. I shall quote from this edition in two volumes of Vasconcelos' autobiography containing *Ulises criollo* and *La tormenta* in the first volume and *El desastre* and *El proconsulado* in the second volume. Subsequent references appear in the text, preceded by *U*, *T*, *DS*, or *PR*, to indicate which book I quote from.

7 Blanco, p. 66.

8 Or as Carlos Monsiváis notes, speaking of Vasconcelos' efforts to explore the different manifestations of cultural nationalism: "What is important is to produce symbols and myths, to imagine a heroic past and to people it, in a Wagnerian manner, with twilight gods like Cuauhtémoc," " Notas sobre la cultura mexicana en el siglo XX" in *Historia general de México*, IV (Mexico: El Colegio de México, 1977), p. 349.

9 On the composition of self for symbolic purposes, so patent in Vasconcelos and Sarmiento, one may usefully consult Daniel Arasse, "*La prudence* de Titien ou l'autoportrait glissé à la rive de la figure," *Corps écrit*, 5 (1983), pp. 109–115, in which, following Panofsky, the author studies self-depiction as an "allegorical support."

For the specific nationalistic twist given the symbolic composition of self, see Robert F. Sayre, "Autobiography and the Making of America" in *Autobiography. Essays Theoretical and Critical*, ed. James Olney (Princeton University Press, 1980). Sayre sees national intent as a distinctive trait of American autobiography – "the very identification of autobiography *in* America *with* America" (p. 147). He adds: "American autobiographers have generally connected their own lives to the national life or to national ideas ... From the times of Columbus, Cortez [*sic*], and John Smith, America has been an idea, or many ideas" (pp. 149–150). Despite the allusion to the Spanish conquest, Sayre's observations are limited to autobiography in the United States. This annoying parochialism notwithstanding, his remarks are useful to approach a certain type of Spanish American autobiography.

10 Monsiváis, p. 355.

11 "The flexibility of memory may obey a kind of mythology. Memory will then function like an enclosed space where the individual is able to win, without much effort, the battles he has lost in reality.

Memory thus runs the risk of being made to serve legend, a legend that reconstitutes an event in order to make it more satisfactory, more faithful to what it was. Memory takes ideal for its norm, an ideal that may be personal or social" (Gusdorf, *Mémoire et personne*, 1, 269).

12 Referring to other notorious Oedipal ties in Mexican literature, mainly in the work of poets, Enrique Krause perceptively writes: "Vasconcelos' prose Oedipus has gone by unnoticed, when it is doubtless more profound, more significant and more complex [than the others]. He devotes a third of *Ulises criollo* to evoking it. The first love story [Vasconcelos] tells in his memoirs is not the passion for Adriana but the passion for his mother, Carmen Calderón. All of Vasconcelos' lives issue from and lead back to this bond," Enrique Krauze, "Pasión y contemplación en Vasconcelos," *Vuelta*, 78 (1978), p. 12.

13 On the subject of autobiographies that use the subject's birth for an opening, see Louis Marin, "The Autobiographical Interruption: About Stendhal's *Life of Henry Brulard*," *Modern Language Notes*, 93 (1978), p. 597–617.

14 Macedonio Fernández, "Autobiografía" in *Papeles de Recienvenido* (Buenos Aires: Losada, 1944), p. 109.

15 See Victoria Ocampo, *Autobiografía*, 1, p. 51. For a useful discussion on narrative sequence in autobiography, see Bruno Vercier, "Le Mythe du premier souvenir: Pierre Loti, Michel Leiris," *Revue d'Histoire Littéraire de la France*, 6 (1975), especially pp. 1033–1036.

16 "If one considers that autobiography is primarily a going back to origins, one understands that the *first* recollection will play a very special role and that, as such, it is endowed with mythical value ... The individual, and above all the autobiographer, *is* memory. Assimilation occurs very rapidly between that particular faculty and the whole being, so that the first recollection marks the real birth of the individual" (Bruno Vercier, "Le Mythe du premier souvenir," p. 1032). For an analysis of the ideological underpinnings of the "first recollection," see Renée Balibar, "*Pierre, commencement d'une vie bourgeoise*" in *Les Français fictifs* (Paris: Hachette, 1974), pp. 169–182.

17 Richard Coe writes that "the choice of the recollection is by no means arbitrary, but has been carefully selected by the subconscious mind from among innumerable other possibilities as being specifically relevant to the shaping of subsequent identity: a fully meaningful event

which relates so intimately to a whole personality that it comes to be felt as the symbolic starting point of consciousness (*When the Grass Was Taller* [New Haven: Yale University Press, 1984], p. 97).

18 Paul Jay, *Being in the Text* (Ithaca and London: Cornell University Press, 1984).

19 Enrique González Martínez, *El hombre del búho. Misterio de una vocación* in *Obras completas* (Mexico: El Colegio Nacional, 1971), p. 576.

20 As a critic writes of Hugo's first memory: "I would think that the meaning of that recollection, if not its very existence, is revealed by contiguity ... [T]he author yields to a polyphonic interpretation, and we cannot disassociate one recollection from the others. It is the concurrence of all these elements that makes for the first recollection ..." (R. Bourgeois, "Signification du premier souvenir" in *Stendhal et les problèmes de l'autobiographie*, ed. Victor Del Litto [Grenoble: Presses Universitaires de Grenoble, 1976], p. 88).

21 "The memory appears in granular form, abruptly condensed around an image which is itself bathed in an affective atmosphere. The certitude with which this image formulates itself is not enough proof of its veracity. We face our first recollections as we face those dreams we are never quite sure of not having invented retrospectively. Besides, a kind of contamination has taken place between what we ourselves remember and what outside witnesses may have told us," Gusdorf, *Mémoire et personne*, II, p. 375. To Gusdorf's last sentence should be added a third contaminating agent – what we ourselves wish to do with that first recollection.

22 The similarities between Vasconcelos' text and the novel published by Rulfo in 1955 are quite striking but, to my knowledge, have not been studied. Beyond this first, remarkable similarity, there are other points of contact – the mythical overtones of the quest, the quester as victim, the culmination of the search, the identification with the mother – that I shall comment on further. I do not know to what extent Vasconcelos may have influenced Rulfo.

23 As José Joaquín Blanco writes: "He made Imperialism his best card in the same way that politicians made Revolution theirs. For Vasconcelos, all of Mexico's ills came from the United States and its Protestantism" (p. 208).

24 Jean Starobinski, "Jean-Jacques Rousseau et le péril de la réflexion" in *L'Oeil vivant* (Paris: Gallimard, 1961), p. 137.

25 André Green, "Atome de parenté et relations oedipiennes" in *L'Identité*, ed. Claude Lévi-Strauss [Paris: Grasset, 1977], p. 90).

26 More than the Telemachus who searches for his father, one thinks of the Telemachus coveting his mother: "[T]elemachus prepares to string the bow – which would have given him Penelope as his wife – but

Odysseus frowns at him and he desists; it is a detail surviving from the Ulysses story, uncritically retained in the *Odyssey*" (Robert Graves, *The Greek Myths*, 2 [London: Penguin Books, 1969], p. 376).

27 Juan Carlos Ghiano, "Autobiografía y recato," *Ficción*, 14 (Buenos Aires, 1958), cited in Adolfo Prieto, pp. 18–19.

28 Monsiváis, p. 355. Less generous critics have attributed this confessional zeal to Vasconcelos' passion for scandal and desire for popularity. Thus Vito Alessio Robles, feeling his own political activity to be misrepresented in *Ulises criollo* and writing to set the record straight, states maliciously:

Without a doubt, the two most popular men in Mexico are, first, Agustín Lara and, second, Pepe Vasconcelos. The slummy songs of the first are hummed by everyone and his music is a big favorite with all. The books written by the second are avidly devoured with morbid delight. No writer has achieved in Mexico the success achieved by Vasconcelos, not exactly as a philosopher or a historian, but as the author of more or less murky and entirely false stories
(*Mis andanzas con nuestro Ulises*, pp. 7–8)

29 Blanco, p. 51.

30 Krauze speaks of a maternal "legacy" the "mark of an intensely erotic, mystical harmony that Vasconcelos would fiercely try to recover throughout his life" (p. 13).

31 On the subject, see Blanco, pp. 195–196.

32 José Vasconcelos, *Ulises criollo*, 2nd expurgated edn (Mexico: Editorial Jus, 1964), p. 5.

33 Unexpurgated versions of *Ulises criollo* may also be read in the hard to get edition by Editorial Botas, the book's original publisher; in the 1957 edition of the *Obras completas* by Libreros Mexicanos Unidos; and in the already mentioned 1982 four-volume edition of the *Memorias* by the Fondo Nacional de Cultura Económica. The last two are fairly expensive editions.

34 For very perceptive comments on the "maternal sites of memory" that are particularly applicable to Vasconcelos, see Michel Beaujour, *Miroirs d'encre* (Paris: Seuil, 1980), p. 22.

Bibliography

1 Spanish American autobiographies

Abreu Gómez, Ermilo. *La del alba sería*. Prologue by Ricardo Latcham. Mexico: Botas, 1954.

Alberdi, Juan Bautista. *Autobiografía*. Prologue by Jean Jaurès. Buenos Aires: El Ateneo, 1927.

Bunge, Delfina. *Viaje alrededor de mi infancia*. Buenos Aires: Imprenta Guadalupe, 1941.

Cané, Miguel. *Juvenilia*. Vienna, 1882; rpt. Buenos Aires: Talleres Gráficos Argentinos, 1927.

Castelnuovo, Elías. *Memorias*. Buenos Aires: Ediciones Culturales Argentinas, 1974.

Chocano, José Santos. *Memorias: Las mil y una aventuras*. Santiago: Nascimento, 1940.

Darío, Rubén. *La vida de Rubén Darío escrita por él mismo*. Barcelona: Casa Editorial Maucci, n/d [1915]; rpt. in *Obras completas*, I. Madrid: Afrodisio Aguado, 1950.

D'Halmar, Augusto [Augusto Thomson]. *Recuerdos olvidados*. Santiago: Nascimento, 1975.

Elizondo, Salvador. *Salvador Elizondo*. Mexico: Empresa Editorial, 1968.

Fernández, Macedonio. *A fotografiarse*. In *Papeles de Recienvenido y Continuación de la Nada*. Buenos Aires: Losada, 1944.

Fernández Moreno, Baldomero. *Vida, memorias de Fernández Moreno*. (Contains *La patria desconocida* and *Vida y desaparición de un médico*.) Introduction by Fernández Moreno. Buenos Aires: Guillermo Kraft, 1957.

Gálvez, Manuel. *Amigos y maestros de mi juventud. Recuerdos de la vida literaria*, I. Buenos Aires, 1944; rpt. Buenos Aires: Hachette, 1966.

Gómez Carrillo, Enrique. *Treinta años de mi vida*. Libro 1°: *El despertar de un alma*. Buenos Aires: Casa Vaccaro, 1918; also vol. x, *Obras completas*. Madrid: Mundo Latino, n/d [1918].

Treinta años de mi vida. Libro 2°: *En plena bohemia*, vol. xvi, *Obras completas*. Madrid: Mundo Latino, n/d [1919].

256

Treinta años de mi vida. Libro 3° y último: *La miseria de Madrid.* Buenos Aires: Casa Vaccaro, 1921.

Gómez de Avellaneda, Gertrudis. *Autobiografía y cartas (hasta ahora inéditas) de la ilustre poetisa Gertrudis Gómez de Avellaneda, con un prólogo y una necrología por Don Lorenzo Cruz de Fuentes.* 2nd revised edn. Madrid: Imprenta Helénica, 1914.

González Martínez, Enrique. *El hombre del búho. Misterio de una vocación.* Mexico: Cuadernos Americanos, 1944; rpt. *Obras completas.* Mexico: El Colegio Nacional, 1971.

La apacible locura. Segunda parte del hombre del búho. Mexico: Cuadernos Americanos, 1951; rpt. *Obras completas.* Mexico: El Colegio Nacional, 1971.

González Vera, José Santos. *Cuando era muchacho.* Santiago: Nascimento, 1951.

Guido y Spano, Carlos. *Autobiografía.* Buenos Aires: El Ateneo, 1929.

Guridi y Alcocer, José Miguel. *Apuntes de la vida de D. José Miguel Guridi y Alcocer.* Mexico: Moderna Librería Religiosa de José L. Vallejo, 1906.

Iduarte, Andrés. *Un niño en la revolución mexicana.* Mexico: Ed. Obregón, 1954.

Lange, Norah. *Cuadernos de infancia.* Buenos Aires: Losada, 1937.

Antes que mueran. Buenos Aires: Editorial Losada, 1944.

Larreta, Enrique. *Tiempos iluminados.* Buenos Aires–Mexico: Espasa Calpe Argentina, 1939.

López Albújar, Enrique. *De mi casona. Un poco de historia piurana a través de la biografía del autor.* Lima: Imprenta Lux, 1924.

Memorias. Preface by Ciro Alegría. Lima: Talleres Gráficos Villanueva, 1963.

Mansilla, Lucio V. *Mis memorias.* Paris, 1904; rpt. Introduction by Juan Carlos Ghiano. Buenos Aires: Hachette, 1955.

Entre-Nos. Causeries del jueves. Paris, 1889–1890; rpt. Introduction by Juan Carlos Ghiano. Buenos Aires: Hachette, 1963.

Manzano, Juan Francisco. *Autobiografía.* Introduction by José L. Franco. Havana: Municipio de La Habana, 1937.

Mastronardi, Carlos. *Memorias de un provinciano.* Buenos Aires: Ediciones Culturales Argentinas, 1967.

Méndez Capote, Renée. *Memorias de una cubanita que nació con el siglo.* 1964; rpt. Barcelona: Argos Vergara, 1984.

Hace muchos años una joven viajera. Havana: Editorial Letras Cubanas, 1983.

Neruda, Pablo. *Confieso que he vivido. Memorias.* Buenos Aires: Losada, 1974.

Para nacer he nacido. Barcelona: Seix Barral, 1978.

Ocampo, Victoria. *El archipiélago. Autobiografía,* 1. Buenos Aires: Ediciones Revista Sur, 1979.

El imperio insular. Autobiografía, ii. Buenos Aires: Ediciones Revista Sur, 1980.

La rama de Salzburgo. Autobiografía, iii. Buenos Aires: Ediciones Revista Sur, 1981.

Viraje. Autobiografía, iv. Buenos Aires: Ediciones Revista Sur, 1982.

Figuras simbólicas. Medida de Francia. Autobiografía, v. Buenos Aires: Ediciones Revista Sur, 1983.

Sur y Cia. Autobiografía, vi. Buenos Aires: Ediciones Revista Sur, 1984.

Testimonios. Madrid: Revista de Occidente, 1935.

Testimonios. 2a. serie. Buenos Aires: Sur, 1941.

Testimonios. 3a. serie. Buenos Aires: Sudamericana, 1946.

Soledad sonora (Testimonios. 4a. serie). Buenos Aires: Sudamericana, 1950.

Testimonios. 5a. serie. Buenos Aires: Sur, 1957.

Testimonios. 6a. serie. Buenos Aires: Sur, 1963.

Testimonios. 7a. serie. Buenos Aires: Sur, 1967.

Testimonios. 8a. serie. Buenos Aires: Sur, 1971.

Testimonios. 9a. serie. Buenos Aires: Sur, 1975.

Testimonios. 10a. serie. Buenos Aires: Sur, 1977.

Oliver, María Rosa. *Mundo, mi casa.* Buenos Aires: Sudamericana, 1970.

La vida cotidiana. Buenos Aires: Sudamericana, 1969.

Mi fe en el hombre. Buenos Aires: Carlos Lohlé, 1981.

Orrego Luco, Luis. *Memorias del tiempo viejo.* Introduction by Héctor Fuenzalida Villegas. Santiago: Ediciones de la Universidad de Chile, 1984.

Oyarzún, Luis. *La infancia.* Santiago: Ediciones "Revista Nueva," 1949.

Pérez Rosales, Vicente. *Recuerdos del pasado (1814–1860).* 1882; rpt. Santiago: Biblioteca de Escritores de Chile, 1910.

Picón Salas, Mariano. *Mundo imaginario.* Santiago: Nascimento, 1927.

Viaje al amanecer. Mexico: Ediciones Mensaje, 1943.

Las nieves de antaño. (Pequeña añoranza de Mérida). Maracaibo: Ed. de la Universidad del Zulia, 1958.

Regreso de tres mundos. Un hombre en su generación. Mexico: Fondo de Cultura Económica, 1959.

Pitol, Sergio. *Sergio Pitol.* Mexico: Empresa Editorial, 1967.

Prieto, Guillermo. *Memorias de mis tiempos.* Mexico: Librería de la Vda. de Bouret, 1906.

Rojas, Manuel. *Imágenes de infancia.* Santiago: Babel, 1955; rpt. in *Obras escogidas*, i. Santiago: Ercilla, 1961.

Samper, José María. *Historia de una alma [sic]. Memorias íntimas y de historia contemporánea.* Bogotá: Imprenta de Zalamea Hermanos, 1881.

Sanín Cano, Baldomero. *De mis vidas y otras vidas.* Bogotá: Editorial ABC, 1949.

Santa Cruz y Montalvo, Mercedes, Condesa de Merlin. *Mis doce primeros años e Historia de Sor Inés.* 1831; rpt. Havana: Imprenta "El Siglo XX," 1922.

Santiván, Fernando [Fernando Santibañez]. *Memorias de un tolstoyano.* Santiago: Zig-Zag, 1955; rpt. in *Obras completas,* II. Zig-Zag, 1965.

Confesiones de Santiván. Santiago: Zig-Zag, 1958; rpt. in *Obras completas,* II. Santiago: Zig-Zag, 1965.

Sarmiento, Domingo Faustino. *Mi defensa.* 1843; rpt. in *Obras,* III. Buenos Aires: Imprenta y Litografía Mariano Moreno, 1896.

Recuerdos de provincia. 1850; rpt. in *Obras,* III. Buenos Aires: Imprenta y Litografía Mariano Moreno, 1896.

Memorias. In *Obras,* XLIX. Buenos Aires: Imprenta y Litografía Mariano Moreno, 1900.

Subercaseaux, Benjamín. *Niño de lluvia y otros relatos.* Santiago: Ercilla, 1962.

Subercaseaux, Ramón. *Memorias de cincuenta años.* Santiago: Imprenta y Litografía Barcelona, 1908.

Tapia y Rivera, Alejandro. *Mis memorias, o Puerto Rico como lo encontré y como lo dejo.* New York: De Laisne & Rossboro, 1928; rpt. Río Piedras: Editorial Edil, 1979.

Torres Bodet, Jaime. *Tiempo de arena.* Mexico: Fondo de Cultura Económica, 1965.

Vasconcelos, José. *Ulises criollo. La vida del autor escrita por él mismo.* I: *Ulises criollo;* II: *La tormenta;* III: *El desastre;* IV: *El proconsulado.* Mexico: Botas, 1935–1939; rpt. as *Memorias,* I–II. Mexico: Fondo de Cultura Económica, 1982.

Vega, Bernardo. *Memorias de Bernardo Vega.* Ed. César Andreu Iglesias. 1977; rpt. Río Piedras: Eds. Huracán, 1984.

Vientós Gaston, Nilita. *El mundo de la infancia.* Mexico: Editorial Cultural, 1984.

Wilde, Eduardo. *Aguas abajo.* In *Obras completas,* II. Buenos Aires: Peuser, 1917–1923.

Yáñez, María Flora. *Visiones de infancia.* Santiago: Zig-Zag, 1947.

Historia de mi vida. Santiago: Nascimento, 1980.

Zapiola y Cortés, José. *Recuerdos de treinta años (1810–1840).* Santiago: Guillermo Miranda, 1902.

II Selected critical bibliography

(A) On authors

Alberdi, Juan Bautista. *Grandes y pequeños hombres del Plata.* Buenos Aires: Fernández Blanco, 1962.

Altamirano, Carlos and Beatriz Sarlo. "Una vida ejemplar: la estrategia de *Recuerdos de provincia.*" In *Literatura/Sociedad.* Buenos Aires: Hachette, 1983.

Azzario, Ester. *La prosa autobiográfica de Mariano Picón Salas*. Caracas: Ediciones de la Universidad Simón Bolívar, 1980.

Bastos, María Luisa. "Escrituras ajenas, expresión propia: *Sur* y los *Testimonios* de Victoria Ocampo." *Revista Iberoamericana*, 110–111 (1980), pp. 123–137.

"Dos líneas testimoniales: *Sur*, los escritos de Victoria Ocampo." *Sur*, 348 (1981), pp. 9–23.

Belín Sarmiento, Augusto. *Sarmiento anecdótico (Ensayo biográfico)*. Saint Cloud: Imp. P. Belin, 1929.

Blanco, José Joaquín. *Se llamaba Vasconcelos*. Mexico: Fondo de Cultura Económica, 1977.

Bunkley, Allison Williams. *The Life of Sarmiento*. Princeton University Press, 1952.

Cortázar, Julio. "Soledad sonora." *Sur*, 192–3–4 (1950), p. 294.

Díaz Arrieta, Hernán. *Memorialistas chilenos*. Santiago: Zig-Zag, 1960.

Domínguez, Nora and Rodríguez Persico, Adriana. "Autobiografía de Victoria Ocampo: la pasión del modelo." *Lecturas críticas*, 2 (Buenos Aires, 1984), pp. 22–33.

Echagüe, Juan Pablo. "Orígenes psicológicos de *Recuerdos de provincia*." In *Paisajes y figuras de San Juan*. Buenos Aires: Editorial Tor, 1933.

Feal, Rosemary Geisdorfer. *Novel Lives: The Fictional Autobiographies of Guillermo Cabrera Infante and Mario Vargas Llosa*. Chapel Hill: North Carolina Studies in the Romance Languages and Literatures, 1986.

Fernández, James. "Strategies of Self-Defense: Episodes in Nineteenth-Century Spanish Autobiography." Unpublished PhD dissertation, Princeton University, 1988.

Figarola Caneda, Domingo. *La Condesa de Merlin*. Paris: Editions Excelsior, 1928.

Friol, Roberto. *Suite para Juan Francisco Manzano*. Havana: Editorial Arte y Literatura, 1977.

Gálvez, Manuel. *Vida de Sarmiento. El hombre de autoridad*. Buenos Aires: Emecé, 1945.

González Echevarría, Roberto. "The Case of the Speaking Statue: *Ariel* and the Magisterial Rhetoric of the Latin American Essay." In *The Voice of the Masters. Writing and Authority in Modern Latin American Literature*. Austin: University of Texas Press, 1985.

Greenberg, Janet Beth. "The Divided Self: Forms of Autobiography in the Writings of Victoria Ocampo." Unpublished PhD dissertation, University of California, Berkeley, 1986.

Guiñazú, Cristina. "La autobiografía de Victoria Ocampo: Memoria, seducción, collage." Unpublished PhD dissertation, Yale University, 1989.

Halperín Donghi, Tulio. "Sarmiento: su lugar en la sociedad argentina posrevolucionaria," *Sur*, 341 (1977), pp. 121–135.

"Lamartine en Sarmiento: *Les Confidences* y *Recuerdos de provincia*," *Filología*, 20, 2 (1985), pp. 177–190.

"Intelectuales, sociedad y vida pública en Hispanoamérica a través de la literatura autobiográfica." In *El espejo de la historia. Problemas argentinos y perspectivas latinoamericanas*. Buenos Aires: Sudamericana, 1987.

Jackson, Richard L. "Slavery, Racism and Autobiography in Two Early Black Writers: Juan Francisco Manzano and Martín Morúa Delgado." In *Voices from Under. Black Narrative in Latin America and the Caribbean* ed. William Luis. Westport, CT: Greenwood Press, 1984, pp. 55–64.

Kaplan, Marina. "Gauchos e indios: la frontera y la producción del sujeto en obras argentinas del siglo diecinueve." Unpublished PhD dissertation, Tulane University, 1987.

Krauze, Enrique. "Pasión y contemplación en Vasconcelos," *Vuelta*, 78 (1978), p. 12.

Lugo-Ortiz, Agnes. "Memoria infantil y perspectiva histórica en *El archipiélago* de Victoria Ocampo," *Revista Iberoamericana*, 140 (1987), pp. 651–661.

Madden, R. R. *Poems by a Slave in the Island of Cuba, Recently Liberated; Translated from the Spanish by R. R. Madden, M. D. with the History of the Early Life of the Negro Poet, Written by Himself, to Which are Prefixed Two Pieces Descriptive of Cuban Slavery and the Slave-Traffic*. London: Thomas Ward and Co., 1840.

Matamoro, Blas. *Genio y figura de Victoria Ocampo*. Buenos Aires: Eudeba, 1986.

Méndez Rodenas, Adriana. "Voyage to *La Havane*: La Condesa de Merlin's Pre-View of National Identity," *Cuban Studies/Estudios Cubanos*, 16 (1986).

Meyer, Doris. *Victoria Ocampo. Against the Wind and the Tide*. New York: George Braziller, 1979.

Molloy, Sylvia. "Imagen de Mansilla." In *La Argentina del Ochenta al Centenario*, ed. G. Ferrari and E. Gallo, Buenos Aires: Sudamericana, 1980, pp. 745–759.

"Inscripciones del yo en *Recuerdos de provincia*," *Sur*, 350–351 (1982), pp. 131–140.

"At Face Value: Autobiographical Writing in Spanish America," *Dispositio*, 9, 24–26 (1984), pp. 1–18.

"Dos proyectos de vida: *Cuadernos de infancia* de Norah Lange y *El archipiélago* de Victoria Ocampo," *Filología*, 20, 2 (1985), pp. 279–293. Also in *Femmes des Amériques*, Travaux de l'Université de Toulouse–Le Mirail, 1986, pp. 177–189.

"Madre patria y madrastra: figuración de España en la novela familiar de Sarmiento," *La Torre*, nueva época, 1 (1987), pp. 45–58.

"Sarmiento, lector de sí mismo en *Recuerdos de provincia*," *Revista Ibero-americana*, 143 (1988), pp. 407–418.

Mora, Gabriela. "Mariano Picón Salas autobiógrafo: Una contribución al estudio del género autobiográfico en Hispanoamérica." Unpublished PhD dissertation, Smith College, 1971.

Mullen, Edward J. Introduction to Juan Francisco Manzano, *The Life and Poems of a Cuban Slave*. Hamden, CT: Archon Book, 1981.

Nóbile, Beatriz de. *Palabras con Norah Lange*. Buenos Aires: Carlos Pérez Editor, 1968.

Nowak, William J. "La personificación en *Recuerdos de provincia*: la desper-sonalización de D. F. Sarmiento," *Revista Iberoamericana*, 143 (1988), pp. 585–602.

Ottolenghi, Julia. *Sarmiento a través de un epistolario*. Buenos Aires; Jesús Méndez, 1939.

Palcos, Alberto. *Sarmiento. La vida. La obra. Las ideas. El genio.* Buenos Aires: Emecé, 1062.

Pauls, Alan. "Sobre las causeries de Mansilla: una causa perdida," *Lecturas críticas*, 2 (Buenos Aires, 1984), pp. 4–15.

Piglia, Ricardo. "Notas sobre *Facundo*." In *Punto de vista*, 3, 8, 1980.

Prieto, Adolfo. *La literatura autobiográfica argentina*. 1966; rpt. Buenos Aires: Centro Editor de América Latina, 1982.

Ramos, Julio. "Entre otros: *Una excursión a los indios ranqueles* de Lucio V. Mansilla," *Filología*, 21, 1 (Buenos Aires, 1986), pp. 143–171.

"Escritura y oralidad en el *Facundo*," *Revista Iberoamericana*, 143 (1988), pp. 551–572.

Ramos, Raymundo. *Memorias y autobiografías de escritores mexicanos*. Mexico: UNAM, 1967.

Saénz Hayes, Ricardo. *La polémica de Alberdi con Sarmiento y otras páginas*. Buenos Aires: M. Gleizer, 1926.

Sarlo, Beatriz. "Decir y no decir. Erotismo y represión." In *Una modernidad periférica: Buenos Aires 1920–1930*. Buenos Aires: Nueva Visión, 1988.

Schulman, Iván. Prologue to Juan Francisco Manzano, *Autobiografía de un esclavo*. Madrid: Guadarrama, 1975.

Verdevoye, Paul. *Domingo Faustino Sarmiento. Educateur et publiciste (entre 1839 et 1852)*. Paris: Institut des Hautes Etudes de l'Amérique Latine, 1963.

Wilde, Eduardo. "Carta sobre *Juvenilia*." In *Páginas escogidas*. Buenos Aires: Editorial Estrada, 1955, pp. 224–232.

(B) Selected general readings

Anderson, Benedict. *Imagined Communities: Reflections on the Origin and Spread of Nationalism*. London: Verso/New Left Books, 1983.

Arasse, Daniel. "*La prudence* de Titien ou l'autoportrait glissé à la rive de la figure," *Corps écrit*, 5 (1983), pp. 109–115.

Bakhtin, Mikhail. "Forms of Time and of the Chronotope in the Novel." In *The Dialogic Imagination*. Austin: University of Texas Press, 1981.

Barthes, Roland. *Roland Barthes par Roland Barthes*. Paris: Seuil, 1975.

"L'ancienne rhétorique: aide-mémoire," *Communications*, 16 (1970), pp. 172–223.

Beaujour, Michel. *Miroirs d'encre*. Paris: Seuil, 1980.

Benjamin, Walter. "Theses on the Philosophy of History." In *Illuminations*. New York: Schocken Books, 1978.

Berchet, Jean-Claude. "Un voyage vers soi," *Poétique*, 53 (1983), pp. 91–108.

Bhabha, Homi K. "Signs Taken for Wonders: Questions of Ambivalence and Authority under a Tree Outside Delhi, May 1816." In *"Race," Writing, and Difference*, ed. Henry Louis Gates, Jr. University of Chicago Press, 1986, pp. 163–184.

Blassingame, John W. "Black Autobiographies as Histories and Literature," *Black Scholar*, 5 (1973–74), pp. 2–9.

Blondel, Charles. *Introduction à la psychologie collective*. Paris: Armand Colin, 1928.

Bourgeois, R. "Signification du premier souvenir." In *Stendhal et les problèmes de l'autobiographie*, ed. Victor Del Litto. Grenoble: Presses Universitaires de Grenoble, 1976, pp. 87–91.

Bromwich, David. "The Uses of Biography," *Yale Review* (Winter 1984), pp. 161–176.

Bruss, Elizabeth. *Autobiographical Acts. The Changing Situation of a Literary Genre*. Baltimore and London: Johns Hopkins University Press, 1976.

Butler, Richard A. *The Difficult Art of Autobiography*. Oxford: Clarendon Press, 1968.

Butler, Thomas (ed.) *Memory*. London: Basil Blackwell, 1989.

Certeau, Michel de. "Walking in the City." In *Practice of Everyday Life*, Berkeley and Los Angeles: University of California Press, 1984, pp. 91–114.

Cockshut, A. O.J. *Truth to Life. The Art of Biography in the Nineteenth Century*. New York and London: Harcourt Brace Jovanovich, 1974.

Coe, Richard. *When the Grass Was Taller: Autobiography and the Experience of Childhood*. New Haven: Yale University Press, 1984.

Cooley, Thomas. *Educated Lives: The Rise of Modern Autobiography in America*. Columbus: Ohio State University Press, 1976.

Cox, James M. "Autobiography and America," *Virginia Quarterly Review*, 47 (1971), pp. 252–277.

de Man, Paul. "Autobiography as De-facement," *Modern Language Notes*, 94 (1979), pp. 919–930.

Derrida, Jacques. *Mémoires for Paul de Man*. New York: Columbia University Press, 1986.

Donato, Eugenio. "The Ruins of Memory: Archeological Fragments and Textual Artifacts," *Modern Language Notes*, 93, 4 (1978), pp. 575–596.

"The Museum's Furnace: Notes toward a Contextual Reading of *Bouvard et Pécuchet*." In *Textual Strategies. Perspectives in Post-Structuralist Criticism*, ed. Josué V. Harari, Ithaca–New York: Cornell University Press, 1979, pp. 213–238.

Egan, Susannah. *Patterns of Experience in Autobiography*. Chapel Hill and London: University of North Carolina Press, 1984.

Englekirk, John E. "Franklin en el mundo hispánico," *Revista Iberoamericana*, 41–42 (1956), pp. 319–372.

Finney, Brian. *The Inner I: British Literary Autobiography of the Twentieth Century*. London and Boston: Faber and Faber, 1985.

Fleishman, Avrom. *Figures of Autobiography. The Language of Self-Writing in Victorian and Modern England*. Berkeley–Los Angeles–London: University of California Press, 1983.

Foucault, Michel. "L'écriture de soi," *Corps écrit*, 5 (1983), pp. 3–23.

Fox-Genovese, Elizabeth. "To Write Myself: The Autobiographies of Afro-American Women." In *Feminist Issues in Literary Scholarship*, ed. Shari Benstock. Bloomington and Indianapolis: Indiana University Press, 1987.

Gasché, Rodolphe. "Self-Engendering as a Verbal body," *Modern Language Notes*, 93 (1978), pp. 677–694.

Gilbert, Sandra M. and Gubar, Susan. "'Forward into the Past': The Female Affiliation Complex." In *No Man's Land. The Place of the Woman Writer in the Twentieth Century*, vol. 1: *The War on Words* (New Haven and London: Yale University Press, 1987), pp. 165–224.

Gómez-Moriana, Antonio. "Autobiographie et discours rituel. La confession autobiographique au tribunal de l'Inquisition," *Poétique*, 56 (1983), pp. 444–460.

Gossman, Lionel. "The Innocent Art of Confession and Reverie," *Daedalus*, 107 (Summer, 1978), pp. 59–77.

"History as Decipherment: Romantic Historiography and the Discovery of the Other," *New Literary History*, 18, 1 (1986).

Gusdorf, Georges. *Mémoire et personne*. I and II. Paris: Presses Universitaires de France, 1951.

"Conditions and Limits of Autobiography." In *Autobiography. Essays Theoretical and Critical*, ed. James Olney. Princeton University Press, 1980.

Halbwachs, Maurice. *Les Cadres sociaux de la mémoire*. 1925; rpt. Paris–The Hague: Mouton, 1975.

La Mémoire collective. 1950; rpt. Paris: Presses Universitaires de France, 1968.

Hareven, Tamara K. "Family Time and Historical Time," *Daedalus*, 106 (1977), pp. 57–70.

"The Search for Generational Memory: Tribal Rites in Industrial Society," *Daedalus*, 107, 4 (1978), pp. 137–149.

Heilbrun, Carolyn. *Writing a Woman's Life*. New York: W. W. Norton, 1988.

Holyoke, S. J. "Montaigne's Attitude toward Memory," *French Studies*, 25, 3 (1971), pp. 257–270.

Jacobus, Mary. *Reading Woman. Essays in Feminist Criticism*. New York: Columbia University Press, 1986.

Janet, Pierre. *L'Evolution de la mémoire et de la notion du temps*. Paris: Editions Chahine, 1928.

Jay, Paul. *Being in the Text*. Ithaca and London: Cornell University Press, 1984.

Jelinek, Estelle C. (ed.) *Women's Autobiographies. Essays in Criticism*. Bloomington: Indiana University Press, 1980.

Lejeune, Philippe. *Le Pacte autobiographique*. Paris: Seuil, 1975.

Marin, Louis. "The Autobiographical Interruption: About Stendhal's *Life of Henry Brulard*," *Modern Language Notes*, 93 (1978), pp. 597–617.

"Variations sur un portrait absent: les autoportraits de Poussin," *Corps écrit*, 5 (1983), pp. 87–108.

Martens, Lorna. "Saying 'I'," *Stanford Literature Review*, 2, 1 (1985), pp. 27–46.

Meloni Trkulja, Silvia. "L'autoportrait classé," *Corps écrit*, 5 (1983), pp. 127–133.

Neisser, Ulric (ed.) *Memory Observed. Remembering in Natural Contexts*. San Francisco: W. H. Freeman, 1982.

Olney, James. "Autobiography and the Cultural Moment." In *Autobiography: Essays Theoretical and Critical*, ed. James Olney. Princeton University Press, 1980.

Pascal, Roy. "The Autobiography of Childhood." In *Design and Truth in Autobiography*. Cambridge, MA: Harvard University Press, 1960.

Renza, Louis. "The Veto of the Imagination: A Theory of Autobiography." In *Autobiography. Essays Theoretical and Critical*, ed. James Olney, Princeton University Press, 1980, pp. 268–295.

Sánchez Blanco, Francisco. "La concepción del 'yo' en las autobiografías españolas del siglo XIX: De las 'vidas' a las 'memorias' y 'recuerdos'," *Boletín de la Asociación de los profesores de Español*, 15, 29 (1983), pp. 29–36.

Sayre, Robert F. "Autobiography and the Making of America." In *Autobiography. Essays Theoretical and Critical*, ed. James Olney, Princeton University Press, 1980, pp. 146–168.

Smith, Sidonie. *A Poetics of Women's Autobiography. Marginality and the Fictions of Self-Representation*. Bloomington and Indianapolis: Indiana University Press, 1987.

Spacks, Patricia Meyer. *Gossip*. University of Chicago Press, 1986.

Spengemann, William C. "Eternal Maps and Temporal Voyages," *Exploration*, 2 (1974), pp. 1–7.

The Forms of Autobiography. New Haven and London: Yale University Press, 1980.

Stanton, Domna C. "Autogynography: Is the Subject Different?" In *The Female Autograph*. New York: New York Literary Forum, 1984, pp. 5–22.

Starobinski, Jean. "Jean-Jacques Rousseau et le péril de la réflexion." In *L'Oeil vivant*, Paris: Gallimard, 1961.

"The Style of Autobiography." In *Autobiography. Essays Theoretical and Critical*, ed. James Olney. Princeton University Press, 1980, pp. 73–83.

Thiébaux, Marcelle. "Foucault's Fantasia for Feminists: The Woman Reading." In *Theory and Practice of Feminist Literary Criticism*, eds. Gabriela Mora and Karen S. Van Hooft, Ypsilanti, Michigan: Bilingual Press/Editorial Bilingüe, 1982, p. 53.

Vance, Eugene. "Roland and the Poetics of Memory." In *Textual Strategies. Perspectives in Post-Structuralist Criticism*, ed. Josué V. Harari, Ithaca–New York: Cornell University Press, 1979, pp. 374–403.

Vercier, Bruno. "Le Mythe du premier souvenir: Pierre Loti, Michel Leiris," *Revue d'Histoire Littéraire de la France*, 6 (1975), pp. 1029–1046.

Walthur, Luann. "The Invention of Childhood in Victorian Autobiography." In *Approaches to Victorian Autobiography*, ed. George P. Landow. Athens: Ohio University Press, 1979, pp. 64–83..

Weintraub, Karl J. "Autobiography and Historical Consciousness," *Critical Inquiry*, 1, 4 (1975).

The Value of the Individual. Self and Circumstance in Autobiography. University of Chicago Press, 1978.

White, Hayden. "The Historical Text as Literary Artifact." In *Tropics of Discourse*. Baltimore and London: Johns Hopkins University Press, 1978.

Index